WriteCME Roadmap

How to Thrive in CME with No Experience, No Network, and No Clue

Alexandra Howson, PhD

ALEXANDRA HOWSON, PHD

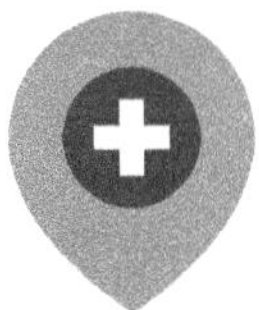

WRITECME ROADMAP

How to Thrive in Continuing
Medical Education with No Experience,
No Network, and No Clue

WriteCME Roadmap

ISBN: 979-8-9901810-0-7

Tilt Publishing
700 Park Offices Drive, Suite 250
Research Triangle, NC 27709

For Maureen Watt, who always believed.
Always and everything to Richard, Holly, and Jodie.

"The effort and expertise Alexandra Howson has invested in 'WriteCME Roadmap' are truly commendable. This pioneering book fills a 50-year gap, offering a detailed and accessible roadmap that will transform how new writers hone their craft to become CME/CE professionals."

— BRIAN MCGOWAN, PhD, Chief Learning Officer & Co-Founder, ArcheMedX, Inc.

" Alex Howson is the mentor I wish I'd had when starting out. Reading 'WriteCME Roadmap' feels like having coffee with a brilliant friend who's determined to see you succeed. Her deep expertise and unflinching encouragement make this an indispensable guide for CME writers at any stage."

— ANNE JACOBSON, MSPharm, Writer & Medical Education Specialist

" We've needed this book for so long! A true pioneer among CME/CE medical writers, Alex offers a thoroughly researched, comprehensive, and highly accessible resource that will benefit any medical writer interested in pursuing CME/CE as a focus.

By turns practical, instructive, and uplifting, this book will help elevate the craft of CME/CE medical writing and the field as a whole."

— EVE J WILSON, PhD, FACEHP, Medical Director, PlatformQ Health

"WriteCME Roadmap is much more than a comprehensive, insightful, and practical guide for aspiring freelance CME/CE medical writers. By providing a thorough discussion of the history and pillars of CME/CE, the book also serves as a modern foundational resource for new and experienced CME/CE content developers across various organizational structures. Whether you're beginning your freelance career, onboarding a new employee, or studying for the CHCP exam, WriteCME Roadmap is a valuable addition to the field."

— SARA FAGERLIE, PhD, CHCP, Founder, Cancer Communicator, LLC

"This is a must-read — not just for writers wanting to make a career in the CE world, but for everyone, new or old to the industry. I've been in the space for over 15 years and there were several nuggets of information I wasn't previously aware of. Kudos for a succinct look at the past, present, and future of continuing education."

— GREG SALINAS, PhD, President, CE Outcomes LLC

"WriteCME Roadmap fills a void at a critical time in our industry. While important conversations about ethical use of AI across health professions, including medical writing, take up more of the oxygen, it is refreshing to have a resource that supports the professional develoment of the community of individuals that keep our industry credible and thriving."

— GRESELDA BUTLER, Director, Medical Affairs and Healthcare Education Professional

"A must read for everyone in the CME/CPD/CE field!

In clear, concise language, Alex Howson has captured the key elements of the accreditation and medical education fields for medical writers, CE compliance, outcomes, and any involved in the CME/CPD/CE ecosystem."

— ALEXANDER MICELLI, PhD, Adjunct Instructor, Lindenwood University

"Alex Howson explains the complex components of continuing education for health professionals and medical writing in such an accessible way that a person at any level could comprehend the concepts and feel empowered. She has distilled all of this in one lovely book written in such a graceful, friendly style that I feel like I sat down and had tea after a yoga class with her and talked shop! Her relatable writing style reads as if she is telling a friend about her day at work. This book could and should be required reading for anyone in the CE/CME/CPD profession."

— ELIZABETH G. FRANKLIN, PhD, University of Mississippi Medical Center

"Brilliantly crafted and impeccably comprehensive, this book stands as the definitive guide for anyone aspiring to break into the field of Continuing Medical Education (CME) writing. With its rich practical examples and crucial watch-outs in a highly regulated industry, this book not only educates but also protects its readers. It's not just a book; it's a mentor—caring, kind, and brilliant, guiding you through every step towards success. Whether you're navigating potential pitfalls or seeking to enhance your well-being while thriving professionally, this guide covers it all. Consider this not just a must-read but a perennial reference—the gold standard in CME/CE writing."

— REGINA SIH-MEYNIER, Pharm.D. Oh Universe

"WriteCME Roadmap is like having a knowledgeable friend guide you through the CME industry. Alexandra's engaging style and comprehensive coverage of topics kept me hooked. The sections on adult learning principles and AI applications were particularly fascinating."

— NÚRIA NEGRÃO, PhD, Medical Writer & AI Consultant

If you have ever wondered what it would take to become an independent consultant or writer in the medical field, look no further! In this insightful book, Alexandra Howson has successfully pulled together the myriad of details and information needed for a career in medical writing. With warmth, honesty, and humor, Alex shares her journey, provides expert guidance and resources, and offers unique insights from colleagues in the field. Read this book and see where it takes you!

— DEBBIE PLATEK, MS, CHCP, President, CME Mentors Inc.

"Such a treasure vault of information, explained clearly and through practical examples, without ever sounding condescending. Your readers will be lucky to have this roadmap in their hands. Your style is crisp and no-nonsense, and the text is beautifully structured."

— PAULIINA RASI, Content Strategist & Copywriter for Small Businesses with Mighty Missions

"A must-read for anyone serious about a career in CME/CE writing! The WriteCME Roadmap offers comprehensive insights, practical advice, and actionable steps, making it an invaluable companion for excelling in the field. Alex's candid and motivating guidance ensures you have the tools needed to succeed."

— RHONA FRASER, BVMS

"CME writers are journalist-adjacent in their commitments to accuracy, curiosity, clarity, and the public interest. Borne of her expertise and experience, what Alex provides here is a comprehensive, craft-oriented, and career-enlightening help. Readers are sure to feel equipped and inspired."

— BEN RIGGS, Senior communications specialist, Kettering Health

"A book of this size and scope is an enormous undertaking, but then, the author is a giant in our field. Readers can expect to come away with a broad sense of CME writing as the specialized and highly skilled profession it is becoming, as well as practical tips on how to earn money tomorrow. WriteCME Roadmap covers all the bases. Alex has hit a home run, and she will help you score your first – or next – base hit."

— DON HARTING, MA, MS, ELS, CHCP,
President, Harting Communications LLC

"In WriteCME Roadmap, Alex has leveraged her extensive experience and network to curate diverse insights and expert guidance, creating a richly balanced resource. This comprehensive guide, which includes invaluable lessons and advice on starting and growing a business, goes beyond other resources focused solely on competencies. Readers will not only read it once but will revisit its bookmark-worthy sections for continuous reference."

— KAREN ROY, CEO and Cofounder, Infograph-ed LLC

"In this all-encompassing 'how-to' book, Alex Howson takes the reader on a journey that builds self-confidence, offers practical nuggets of advice, and examines the nuanced CME/CE writers niche. Alex's lifelong passion in healthcare and education will provide you with a rock solid foundation for building the sustainable and successful freelance writing business you crave. Read this book!"

— ANITA MISRA-PRESS, PhD

"WriteCME Roadmap is an invaluable resource for both newcomers and seasoned medical writing professionals. The book demystifies the complexities of the continuing medical education (CME) industry with clear, practical guidance and personal ancedotes, making it accessible to all levels of experience. Whether you're just starting out or looking to refine your skills, this comprehensive guide will help you navigate and excel in the CME industry."

— KRISTEN DASCOLI, Award-Winning Medical Writer, Editor, and Business Consultant

Acknowledgements

Despite appearances, it takes many people to write a sole-authored book. Thanks to clients, colleagues, and peers who schooled me over the years in CME skills and competencies. Particularly heartfelt thanks are due to Eve Wilson, PhD, FACEhp; Anne Jacobson, MSPharm, CHCP; Diana Durham, PhD; Christine Welniak; Anita Misra-Press, PhD; and Genevieve Walker, PhD, for generously sharing their knowledge and wisdom with me over the years. Thanks to Victoria Anderson for giving me my first official CME project many moons ago. And when my draft didn't hit the mark, she graciously walked me through the text and helped me course correct. We all need a Victoria!

I owe thanks to many readers at different stages of the book's development. Eve Wilson and Anne Jacobson kept the manuscript on track regarding compliance, CME competencies, and writing craft; Diana Durham contributed significantly to my understanding of accreditation history. Christine Welniak helped shape Chapter 10 with her extensive expertise on project and client management. Audrie Tornow, CHCP, FACEHP, provided insight into the various roles and responsibilities that people have in the CME ecosystem, while Angelique Vinther, CHCP, shared insights on outcomes measures and analysis.

I am exceptionally grateful to reviewers who provided detailed feedback on the pre-publication manuscript. Karen Roy, MSc, BCMAS, Greselda Butler, CHCP, CCEP, and Brian McGowan, PhD, CHCP, FACEhp, suggested helpful corrections in my discussion of Medical Affairs and its role in independent medical education. Don Harting, MA, MS, ELS, CHCP, Alexander Miceli, PhD, MBA, CHCP, Debbie Platek, MS, CHCP, Elizabeth Franklin, PhD, and Greg Salinas, PhD, helped me address inaccuracies concerning accreditation, compliance, and industry support. Sara Fagerlie, PhD, CHCP, and Núria Negrão, PhD, suggested additional content on the business of freelancing, and Kristen Dascoli made suggestions about readability. Special thanks to Ben Riggs for his wisdom on writing, and to Rhona Fraser, BVMS, for sharing insights on maintaining a beginner's mind. Regina Sih-Meynier, PharmD, has been a source of energy and inspiration during the book's accouchement (and thanks to Claire Bonneau for reminding me of the power of this word!).

Thanks to Write Medicine podcast guests who have generously shared their insights to listeners hungry for information about the ever-evolving field of CME. Thank you too, WriteCME Pro members, coaching clients, and students in my University of Chicago classes on medical writing and editing ethics. Your questions, energy, and enthusiasm keep me grounded and consistently ignite my curiosity.

WriteCME Roadmap would not exist without the team at Tilt Publishing. Kristen Moxley and Laura Kozak have been marvelous editors guiding me through the publishing process. Thanks to them, the Tilt design team, and to Joe Pulizzi, who has created an amazing publishing venture.

And last, but by no means least, I am deeply grateful to Bhaval Shah, PhD, President and Co-Founder of Infograph-Ed, for generously creating and providing beautiful illustrations for the book.

Contents

Contents

Introduction

"When I was a little girl, I wanted to grow up and be a CME professional." Said no one, ever. And yet, here we are.

Welcome to *WriteCME Roadmap*, a guide for aspiring writers and other professionals ready to create continuing medical education (CME) and continuing education (CE) for health professionals. I am excited to share my deep expertise in health care and education to help you break into this dynamic and rewarding field.

If you're reading this book, my guess is that you have a professional background of some sort (perhaps a health professional, academic, researcher, or journalist) and you are looking for a new challenge. Perhaps you're feeling frayed at the edges; a little frazzled with the work you are currently doing, and ready for work that can bring some autonomy and flexibility to your life. You are a lifelong learner, an information synthesizer, and are keen to support health professionals in their clinical work or improve patient outcomes.

You are not alone in your desire to create a working life that feeds your desire to learn and supports you and your family with sustainable income. But you are probably also feeling a little lost, unsure of where to start, what skills you will need, and how to break into the highly satisfying CME/CE writing field. You likely have questions and concerns, like:

1. What is CME/CE, and what are its prospects?
2. Is CME/CE writing a viable career option?
3. What competencies are necessary to excel in this field?
4. How do I get started?
5. How do I find clients and opportunities in the CME/CE field?

I have been in your shoes. I know how daunting it can feel to move out of one professional context and identity into exploring another. At some point, we have all been beginners with no prior experience in CME/CE. As you'll know if you listen to my podcast, Write Medicine, this field is filled with folks who refer to themselves as accidental CME/CE professionals who stumbled across continuing education. They had never heard of CME/CE, but somehow the occupational paths they took led them right into this field. And once they arrived, they didn't want to leave.

In other words, I know quite a lot of what you're probably feeling right now. I also know this: I have made every mistake under the CME sun, and I do not want you to make the same mistakes. So, this roadmap is designed to help you create an itinerary and get to your destination faster.

WriteCME Roadmap is designed to build your confidence and help you step into CME/CE as a writer with an expert by your side who has a compass and knows the specialist gear you'll need. Drawing on decades of my own experiences as a nurse, an academic, and a CME/CE writing professional, *WriteCME Roadmap* is a relatable and authoritative guide. I've honed a specialized set of skills that have allowed me to thrive in this field for almost twenty years, and I am here to pass those skills to you. You will find industry insights and resources to help you navigate the field and establish yourself as a CME/CE writer, as well as practical guidance on how to build a freelance writing business from the ground up.

With me as your guide, you will be poised to create engaging content that helps health professionals stay up to date with standards of care and emerging therapies, deliver high-quality care to patients, and, ultimately, improve health care quality and patient outcomes. My goal is to equip you with strategic knowledge, actionable steps, and hands-on tools so you can create stellar educational content, deliver value to your clients and employers, enhance the learning experience of health professionals, and confidently build a sustainable CME/CE writing niche.

But I didn't start with confidence! In fact, I had no experience in CME/CE, no professional network, and really, no clue.

Unease with Academia

Every established CME/CE professional gets asked the question, "How did you get started?" My flippant answer to that question is that no one would hire me, and I couldn't get a job.

Straight out of high school, I trained as a registered general nurse at the South Lothian College of Nurses and Midwifery at the Royal Infirmary of Edinburgh, Scotland. This was back in the old days (actually, 1981). Student nurses in the United Kingdom were considered students, but we worked in clinical settings only eight weeks after starting college. We were supposed to be supernumerary and not left on our own to undertake tasks and look after patients. But often, we were. This did not faze me. I enjoyed the challenge of clinical problem-solving, providing physical care, and learning when to call in reinforcements. (This meant other, more senior student nurses, maybe the staff nurse; never the ward sister, as charge nurses were then known. We were supposed to "get on with it.")

Following initial training, I was certified as an operating room nurse (OR) or theater nurse, as OR nurses are called in the United Kingdom, and worked as a trauma OR nurse for many years in a Level 1 trauma center.

But academia called. I studied for a master's degree in sociology, then worked for a doctorate and trained as a qualitative researcher. I was an academic for well over a decade at the universities of Edinburgh and Aberdeen, teaching undergraduate and postgraduate courses on gender, the body, and health; doing qualitative research; and publishing books and research papers. But academia became politically and financially challenging in the United Kingdom, and by 1999 I had two young children. I had gone part-time, which, in retrospect, was the kiss of death to my academic career. The seeds of dys-ease with academia had been sown, and I knew I needed to find a way to work outside the academy.

Yet I had no clue what that work might or even could be.

In 2004, my family moved from Scotland to the United States, and I spent a year as a visiting scholar at Berkeley ("finishing" a book that I had already written and was with the publisher). I did not network and connect with that community as much as I could have. In retrospect, it seems clear that I had neither the heart nor the energy to continue to invest in academia as a career path.

Instead, I spent an inordinate amount of time on the internet, looking for jobs outside academia. I lost count of the number of résumés I submitted to prospective employers, but because I was spending so much time on the internet, I noticed something else.

I was living in a free agent nation.

Free Agent Nation[1]

Daniel Pink published *Free Agent Nation: The Future of Working for Yourself* in 2002. I borrowed it from our local library (we had no discretionary money for things like books) and devoured its message, which predicted the rise of self-employment and the independent workforce in the United States. Pink argued that more and more people

> were choosing to work as freelancers, consultants, and entrepreneurs, rather than in traditional, full-time jobs, driven by technological advancements, the desire for greater autonomy and flexibility, and disillusionment with the constraints of conventional corporate life. This thesis is as prescient as ever and is what essentially everyone is talking about in 2024. Working for yourself is not a new thing. The difference between free agents now and 20 years ago is that in the noughties, free agents were "mompreneurs" and software consultants, whereas now free agents are content creators, writers, and others.

◇◇

You know who is also a free agent? Me, as a freelance CME/CE writer.

Are you next?

Here are the five steps that helped me break into CME/CE writing. They can help you too.

1. Embrace a Freelance Identity

As a result of reading *Free Agent Nation*, I began to explore job and gig sites like eLance (now Upwork) and Guru.com, rather than looking for employment. This mindset shift from job hunting to looking for freelance work was transformative. I edited book manuscripts for lawyers (like Areva Martin's *Journey to the Top*) and wrote white papers and reports for academics and entrepreneurs who did not like to write (or didn't know how to).

Picking up work on gig sites gave me the confidence to try other things:

- I signed on as an online academic editor with *ScienceDocs* and another business (whose name I cannot now remember) and substantively edited dozens of academic manuscripts.
- I connected with other former academics who were building businesses, working freelance, or working as independent writers

or editors, which led to connections with academics looking for substantive editors and coaches. So for a few months I coached academic writers (like Rebecca Altman, whose book *The Song of Styrene: An Intimate History of Plastics* is forthcoming from Scribner Books).

- Coaching academic writers alongside my teaching experience as a nurse ("see one, do one, teach one" was still the primary clinical teaching modality back in the 1980s), landed me a gig as an adjunct instructor at the University of California–Berkeley Extension, where I taught a 12-week course on substantive editing.
- I also did a lot of cold calling, looking through the Yellow Pages (does anyone use these anymore?) to find organizations that published research in reports or white papers. This tactic landed me a gig as a research consultant for Resource Development Associates, a public sector capacity-building company in the San Francisco Bay Area.

Between 2004 and 2006 I wrote or edited scores of publications in different formats and for assorted clients. This miscellany of work developed confidence, generated income, told me that I could make a living from editing and writing, and provoked a mindset shift.

I began to see myself as a freelance writer rather than a former academic. It took a while and some other steps to get me into medical writing and then CME/CE writing.

But the emergence of self-identity as a freelance writer was a turning point in my career trajectory.

Use Upwork Strategically

Many writers advise against using gig sites like Upwork as a way to find freelance medical writing work. There is not a lot of work for accredited CME/CE on these sites, and rates are low for nonaccredited CME/CE compared to what you can ask as a bona fide CME/CE writer. However, if you are moving out of a clinical or academic setting with absolutely no experience in freelance writing, it is worth doing a couple of low-stakes projects that are posted on these job platforms. They remove the need to cold call potential clients because the site includes prospects who are actively looking to hire someone.

Here is how nurse writer Claire Bonneau has used Upwork to build her freelance health writing business:

> *Every single one of my good clients has come from Upwork. Some of my retainer clients, clients I've been working with for two plus years who I have personal relationships with, have all come from the platform. I think a big proponent of that for me has just been, at the beginning, it took the business-scary side of writing away from me. I didn't have to think about pitching. I didn't have to have a content strategy. I didn't have to know how to send my invoice. All that stuff was handled for me, which I loved. And second of all it taught me really aggressively how to pitch and market myself, because I was sending pitches, because you apply to jobs on Upwork. I was sending these applications to open and receptive ears. I didn't always get a response, but in contrast to sending a cold email into the void, I was getting more responses back. And that really helped me cut my teeth and learn how to say what I do and how to market myself specifically. And that has been super valuable.*

I agree.

Sites like Upwork can provide a solid grounding in the process of hustling, and you will get rapid-fire exposure to the following processes:

- Describing your services
- Bidding on projects
- Engaging with clients
- Managing relationships
- Negotiating rates, turnaround times, deliverables
- Getting client feedback on your writing (this will be low fidelity, but you'll get a feel for what clients appreciate)
- Building confidence in spotting red flags

2. Grow and Nourish Your Network

In 2006, I had no network and was just beginning my freelance journey. Around this time, I discovered the American Medical Writers Association (AMWA). When I was still in job-hunting mode, I noticed this entity called medical writing, but did not really understand what it entailed. It sounded intriguing and tugged at me a little bit since I had been a clinician and taught undergraduate courses on medicine, health, and society as an academic. Finding a professional organization like AMWA was a lightbulb moment for me. I immediately joined and participated in my local chapter (which sadly no longer exists) and met wonderful freelance writers like Genevieve Walker, PhD, and Anita Misra-Press, PhD, both past presidents of the Pacific Northwest chapter.

Join AMWA

Joining an organization like AMWA is like opening a door into your professional home. However, once that door is open, you then need to do the work of initiating and nurturing relationships within your network. One of the easiest ways to kickstart that process is by volunteering. Freelance medical writer Lori De Milto says,

> *Because I volunteered, people got to know and trust me and started giving me referrals without me ever asking*

for any help. When I started out, I was very, very shy. And I would never have even thought of saying, "Hey, I'm looking for this type of work, can you help me out?" or, "What advice do you have for me?" But by volunteering, I didn't have to do that. And that's a very, very easy way to build a strong network without having to do what most people think of as more active and, often for us, uncomfortable networking. Referrals are the easiest way to build a freelance business because when somebody refers you, the client trusts you and is very, very likely to hire you.

Joining AMWA opened the door to CME/CE. Actually, it's not a door: it's a hatch to a secret subterranean bunker.

But once that hatch opened, there was no turning back for me.

3. Find a Mentor

As a result of joining AMWA I also discovered the Alliance for Continuing Education in the Health Professions (ACEHP), which at that time was called the Alliance for Continuing Medical Education, or ACME. Chapter 1 explains why the name changed. Like most professional organizations, ACEHP hosts an annual conference that draws attendance from supporters (representatives from pharmaceutical and biomedical device companies), medical education companies, medical societies, medical schools, hospitals and health systems, and more. ACEHP is organized by member sections aligned with these categories, as well as a section of Professionals with Education Expertise, Resources, and Services (PEERS)—which is a great section for independent writers to join.

I joined ACEHP in 2008 and participated in a mentoring program that matched new with more seasoned members. I'll tell you, it was not a great experience. My mentor was a CME/CE provider who was much older than I was and had worked in the field for many decades.

I thought I would gain some insight from him on how to navigate the field and find clients as a writer.

But at the end of our conversation, the sum of his advice was, *you'll be all right.* At the time, that wasn't helpful. Listen to episode 17 of the Write Medicine podcast for more effective approaches to mentoring and structuring the mentor/mentee relationship. ACEHP refreshed its mentoring program in 2022.

In retrospect, his words forced me to assiduously seek out education and skills-building opportunities. I choose now to see his words as a reflection of what he saw as my expertise. He could see that I was a proficient writer, a published author, and a tenacious researcher. I did not see this then, but over time I have acknowledged the value of these skills and come to realize that I already had most of what I needed to succeed as a freelance CME/CE writer. I had a clinical background, I understood adult learning, and I could write—I had published a couple of books and written research papers, even though my academic discipline is sociology and not in a biomedical field.

So I looked at skills I already had and the path I had taken and saw potential routes into CME/CE based on those skills.

Own Your Current Skills

If you are struggling to see yourself as a freelance CME/CE writer, pause right now and just think about your current skills. You will be amazed at how much intellectual capital you bring to the CME/CE enterprise. Bonus: You will step out more confidently into this exciting field.

4. Build Your Skills

I was drawn to the CME/CE field because of its focus on both education and health care. But I had no experience working in CME/

CE and I had not worked in the pharmaceutical or biomedical device industry, so I didn't really know my way around the field. Although I was excited to have found CME/CE, the field was still a mystery, and navigating its many possibilities felt like wandering through a maze. There were many concepts and topics to learn about, including accreditation (Chapter 2), the education planning process (Chapter 5), adult learning principles (Chapter 6), and assessment and evaluation (Chapter 7). I had no clue about what CME/CE entailed or how I was going to get my foot in the door.

In 2010, I attended an ACEHP intensive on CME/CE basics (the program is still on ACEHP's website). The intensive was very much focused on CME/CE planners, strategists, and business specialists, and focused on topics such as:

- The CME/CE environment
- The ACCME accreditation system and standards for support
- How to plan a CME/CE activity using ACCME accreditation criteria
- The American Medical Association Physician's Recognition Award credit system
- CME/CE professional practice competencies.

As a writer, I felt a little invisible in this intensive. At the time, I thought that was just me! But I have learned that writers in CME/CE are a little bit invisible. In fact, writers are hidden labor in the CME/CE world. We write the needs assessments, the educational activities, the outcomes reports, and the manuscripts, but are seldom acknowledged as partners or collaborators. I strongly urge you to do everything you can to position yourself as a writing partner in the CME/CE work you do. We will talk about how you can do this in Chapter 9.

A decade ago, there were no courses directly related to CME/CE writing (except for a short-lived program run by Johanna Lackner of InQuill Medical Communications, LLC). However, AMWA offered a workshop, "Preparing CME/CE Materials: Concepts, Strategies, and Ethical Issues," hosted by Eve Wilson, PhD, FACEHP. For me, that was the point of no return. You know that feeling you get when the stars align and you know you've landed in the right place? CME/CE is that for me. It's a space where I get to draw on my expertise as an educator, writer, and researcher every single day. "Preparing CME/CE Materials" gave me a solid foundation to build on as a course developed and delivered by a writer for writers. Eve still offers this workshop at annual AMWA conferences, but there has been little expansion on learning opportunities in the CME/CE field specifically for writers.

That is why you need the *WriteCME Roadmap*.

5. Niche Down, Way Down

If you are only just beginning to explore CME/CE writing, it is absolutely OK to start walking on a wide trail with lots of foot traffic versus confining yourself to a narrow path. This is a time to work on different types of projects with different types of clients and learn about the CME/CE field.

At the beginning of a freelance medical writing journey, it's common for writers to take on different types of work and to work for different types of clients. I did this too. In the early years of my freelance medical writing journey, I edited, wrote, researched, and synthesized information for a range of deliverables, including white papers, reports, needs assessments, slide decks, monographs, manuscripts, book chapters, and more. My clients included nonprofit organizations in public health, start-ups in biotech, providers in CME/CE, academics, and individuals who contracted me via Guru.com.

Taking on a broad spectrum of work in the early days of freelancing often stems from uncertainty about how and where to start, so you start anywhere. This needn't be a bad thing. By casting your net widely, you will find what fits your interests and your preferred style of writing. You will learn which clients and medical writing sectors align with your values and the life you want to lead. You will develop a broad knowledge and skill base as well as the flexibility to respond to different situations.

Yet there's a trade-off in confidence and competence from being a generalist. Each fresh project or new client can unleash a cascade of anxieties about whether we are up to the task and potentially leads us down seemingly endless research and prewriting rabbit holes. At some point we begin to harbor a sneaking suspicion that we have spread ourselves thinly across therapeutic areas, specialties, and project types. To switch metaphors here, we can end up feeling less like fisherfolk (casting the net, remember?) and more like goldfish, darting around trying to find bites here and there for our business. Frustration, overwhelm, inconsistent revenue, and cognitive overload ensue.

Thus, at some point in your journey, you might want to consider choosing a narrower path or finding a niche. It is so much easier to marshal your energy, resources, and expertise to serve a niche than it is to spread yourself widely without focus. Your turnaround times will improve, you can command higher rates as a niche expert, and you are more likely to be viewed as a partner or collaborator. It is also easier to ask difficult questions when you cultivate a niche, because you can see the blind spots and more readily spot the red flags. Nourishing a niche (or two) is a way to funnel your energy and target your resources to ensure sustainable revenue for your business. We will explore how to do this in chapter 11.

What Do CME/CE Writers Do?

CME/CE writers offer specialized expertise in synthesizing evidence and simplifying complexity to ensure accessible, accurate content that supports learning, and they are adept at working with faculty to identify key teaching messages. CME/CE writers also develop interactive patient cases, interactive quizzes, pre- and post-activity assessment questions, outcomes reports, white papers, needs assessments, and more. To create high-quality educational content, writers must blend scientific/clinical aptitude, writing ability, and instructional know-how, and grasp the nuances of accredited CME/CE.

Medical writers perform various tasks to develop CME/CE deliverables:

- Conduct literature reviews
- Build interactive patient cases
- Develop and refine learning objectives
- Craft outcomes reports and white papers
- Distill complex research into accessible narratives
- Improve faculty-generated slide decks and presentations
- Identify and substantiate clinical performance practice gaps
- Create engaging pre- and post-activity assessment questions
- Get up to speed quickly with therapeutic areas and disease states

To do these tasks well, writers cultivate expertise in:

- Research proficiency
- Adult learning principles
- Strong writing proficiency
- Scientific and health literacy
- Deep understanding of clinical care
- Logically organizing complex topics
- Storytelling and engaging communication
- Meticulous attention to detail and accuracy
- Quickly absorbing new medical information
- Upholding ethical and accreditation standards
- Integrating the latest evidence and data to content
- Translating medical terminology into plain language
- Collaborating with different stakeholders in the CPD field

- Capacity to work under tight deadlines while maintaining accuracy

CME/CE Market Prospects

What are the market prospects for CME/CE? Many of my students and clients ask whether moving into this field is a viable career option.

The answer to this question is an unequivocal yes.

Physicians and other health professionals require continuing education credits for ongoing learning, licensure, and professional certification. At the same time, the speed at which new therapies are developed and brought to market has accelerated and the number of ongoing clinical trials registered on ClinicalTrials.gov has skyrocketed. Therefore, the demand for ongoing education about therapies and how to use them in clinical practice is robust. In fact, market forecasts suggest there will be an increase in the size and reach of the CME/CE field over the next five years, making it an attractive arena for writers seeking professional growth and opportunities.

CME/CE Market Forecasts[2]

At the time of writing in 2024, the US CME/CE market is expected to reach a market value of $4.23 billion by 2028, representing 6.43 percent annual growth from $2.91 billion in 2022. The Covid-19 pandemic was a major driver of growth in the CME/CE market in 2020–2021 as online, digital, and gamified learning accelerated.[3]

Other market-growth drivers include the consistent evolution of advances in therapeutic areas like oncology, which accounts for a 12 percent market share of the US CME/CE market. Expanding digital health and the incorporation and implementation of technology in clinical practice, including artificial intelligence, are also driving market expansion in CME/CE. And, of course, CME/

CE is a mandatory requirement for health professionals in the United States. Most states require physicians to fulfill a quota of CME/CE credits to maintain an active medical license as well as to maintain, develop, and enhance professional competence and performance. Other health care team members have similar requirements.

It's also worth noting that health care employment is projected to grow by 15 percent to 2029 (from 2019) according to the U.S. Bureau of Labor Statistics.[4] The demand for specialist physicians is forecasted to increase by 45.1 percent between 2019 and 2033, according to the Association of American Medical Colleges.[5]

Private Equity in CME/CE

In the last decade, private equity firms have been busy acquiring multiple health care assets including nursing homes, physician practices, dialysis clinics, hospice operators, and more for the purpose of buy-and-sell for profit[6] The relative market stability of CME/CE during the Covid-19 pandemic has increased its attraction to private equity firms,[7] which have increasingly invested in, acquired, and consolidated health care facilities and biopharma in the United States. Biopharma deals include buyouts, acquisitions, and growth investment in related services such as contract research organizations and CME/CE providers. Why? In part, because business-to-consumer education providers have contact lists and breadth of reach into individual clinical practice offices. Private equity buyers have also acquired CME/CE providers that offer digital content and flexible learning opportunities to clinical learners. Clinical Care Options, Clinical Education Alliance, and CME Outfitters are examples of large or established education providers that were acquired in 2021.[8]

What Does This Mean for You as a CME/CE Writer?

Be aware that this field is ever-changing. A fluid buyout, acquisition, and merger environment means that you could be working with a client one day that ceases to exist the next, as it is absorbed into a larger organization or disappears completely. If the person you have been working with moves to another company, you want to be in a position where they take you with them as their key freelance person. And you want to be able to work with your client's replacement.

The relationship of medical affairs to independent medical education (IME) is also shifting (we will review this in more detail in Chapter 1), and, of course, the emergence of generative artificial intelligence (gen-AI) is another influential driver reshaping CME/CE.

So: you need to keep your eye on what is happening in the field, consistently market to prospects, and maintain robust relationships with current clients.

What's in the Book?

I am writing this book for you because when I fell out of academia and onto the freelance writing path it took some time to figure out a clear direction. I needed a handbook on the CME/CE landscape, a guide to the craft of CME/CE writing, and a desk companion to CME/CE accreditation and compliance.

If you are a new-to-the-field medical writer considering CME/CE as a specialized niche or a seasoned pro ready to add specialized services to your business, *WriteCME Roadmap* is for you. If you work in a medical education company and are responsible for hiring staff to develop CME/CE content, the book provides materials that will help you onboard new hires moving into the CME/CE field.

WriteCME Roadmap will introduce you to the rewarding field of CME/CE and the benefits of specializing in CME/CE for writers. I will share my journey from a clinical background with no CME/CE experience to becoming a skilled CME/CE writer with a sustainable freelance writing business. By sustainable, I mean getting off the feast or famine cycle and settling into a consistent work flow where prospective clients seek me out, I take on projects that are meaningful and substantial, and my business generates the revenue I desire, year on year.

I will demystify CME/CE, review its prospects as a viable career, describe practical steps for breaking into and thriving in the field, and outline the essential competencies you will need for creating impactful educational content that keeps health care professionals updated and improves patient care. I will guide you through the process of getting started as a CME/CE writer. Breaking into the field may seem daunting, and there is no one-size-fits-all approach, but I will share some practical guidance on how to establish yourself, navigate the industry, and launch a successful career. I will also preview strategies for networking, identifying potential clients, and securing projects in the competitive CME/CE industry.

The book is organized in four sections.

1. *Foundations of CME* (Chapters 1-3) covers the basics of CME, including its history, accreditation processes, and ethical considerations.
2. *Developing CME in the Real World* (Chapters 4-6) explores how CME/CE fits into the broader health care landscape and discusses educational planning and adult learning principles.
3. *Crafting Effective Content* (Chapters 7-9) reviews the practical aspects of developing CME/CE, including assessment, various formats, and honing your skills as a CME professional.
4. *Thriving in the CME Ecosystem* (Chapters 10-11) focuses on building a business, maintaining well-being, and continuous professional growth.

Intended for both novice and experienced medical writers interested in CME/CE, *WriteCME Roadmap* covers key topics such as:

- How CME/CE supports health professionals
- Formats, planning processes, assessments in the CME/CE environment
- Core competencies for CME/CE content creation
- Strategies for transitioning existing skills into CME/CE writing
- Building relationships and establishing your professional brand as a CME/CE writer
- Setting rates and negotiating contracts
- Positioning yourself as a valuable partner in the CME/CE enterprise

You will learn about the history of CME/CE; who the main players are in this field; the importance and structure of accreditation; key policies, regulations, and ethical principles; adult learning principles; assessment and outcomes; and associated formats.

While there is no single path into CME/CE, I have created a roadmap for you. You can use this roadmap to find your way in this unfamiliar and complex environment and to map your progress toward the goal of cultivating a CME/CE writing niche.

Are you ready to explore? Let's go!

Foundations of CME/CE

Chapter 1

Understanding CME/CE

Seek first to understand, then to be understood.

— STEPHEN R. COVEY.

Introduction

Even though you are drawn to CME/CE, you might not yet fully appreciate what it is about. I get it. Honestly, it took me a few years to really get a handle on the different stakeholders in this field and understand the terminology.

Let me first tell you what CME/CE is not.

CME/CE is not about promoting or selling pharmaceutical products or biomedical devices. In fact, far from it. CME/CE content must be relevant, accurate, and free from bias that influences (or could be perceived as influencing) the decisions that health professionals make and the care they deliver to patients. In short, content must be fair, balanced, and evidence-based. It is a highly regulated field that comes with a lot of compliance requirements. Chapter 3 explores these requirements in more detail.

This chapter outlines why CME/CE is important in the wider education ecosystem for health professionals. We will trace the development of CME/CE from the early twentieth century to the present and examine the role of CME/CE in the twenty-first century, focusing on its expansion beyond traditional medical knowledge to encompass broader professional responsibilities.

What is CME/CE?

CME/CE is part of a wider education system that helps health professionals (like physicians, nurses, pharmacists, physician assistants, and others) gain and maintain knowledge, techniques, and skills to ensure optimal medical care and outcomes for patients. Indeed, CME/CE is required for health professionals to remain competent in their respective fields and is now an integral part of postgraduate training for health professionals in the United States.[1]

The Accreditation Council for Continuing Medical Education (ACCME) defines CME/CE broadly as,[2]

> *. . . any activity that serves to maintain, develop, or increase the knowledge, skills and professional performance, and relationships that a clinician uses to provide services for patients, the public, or health professions. The content of CME/CE is that body of knowledge and skills generally recognized and accepted by the profession as within the basic medical sciences, the discipline of clinical medicine, and the provision of health care to the public.*

There is a longer version of this answer that we'll get to later in this chapter. But first, let's break down the sometimes confusing terminology in the CME/CE field. For example, we can explore the differences between CME, CE, and CPD.

Terminology

CME is for physicians. Continuing medical education (CME) refers to formal continuing education for licensed physicians to help them maintain competence and learn about evidence-based care to improve patient outcomes. CME is primarily delivered through activities that offer American Medical Association credits, which Chapter 2 explores in more detail.

CE is for health professionals. Continuing education (CE) is an umbrella term that encompasses education for the entire health care team, including physicians, nurses, physician assistants, and pharmacists. CE includes the continuing education that health professionals need for licensure as well as informal learning that may or may not offer formal CE credits.

CPD includes lifelong learning. Continuing professional development (CPD) refers to overall professional lifelong learning that combines education, learning, and practice development across clinical, leadership, business, and other competencies that health professionals need or could benefit from to help them practice as clinicians. CPD encompasses accredited CME/CE as well as other activities that have educational value for physicians but are not certified for credit.

Lifelong learning. Learning is baked into clinical practice for physicians, nurses, pharmacists, and other health professionals. In turn, lifelong learning is a core component of professional identity.[3] Lifelong learning is enshrined in the American Medical Association (AMA) Code of Medical Ethics, and CME/CE is a crucial component of lifelong learning.[4] Education researchers have defined lifelong learning as a continuous process that is self-initiated, is supported by information-seeking skills, is prompted by a sustained motivation to learn, and is also supported by the ability to self-assess and identify one's own learning needs.[5]

AMA Code of Medical Ethics[4]

A physician shall continue to study, apply, and advance scientific knowledge; maintain a commitment to medical education; make relevant information available to patients, colleagues, and the public; obtain consultation; and use the talents of other health professionals when indicated.

◇◇

CME, *CE*, and *CPD* are sometimes used interchangeably to refer generally to continuing education for health professionals. Whatever terms we are using, remember that continuing education is part of an ongoing process—lifelong learning—that helps health professionals maintain competence and learn about new and developing areas of their field.

I will use CME/CE throughout this book, unless I am specifically referring to CME alone. You will also find that many professionals in this field refer to themselves as CME/CPD professionals.

What are the origins of continuing education for the health professions? Let's take a brief look at the history of CME/CE.

History of CME/CE

At the start of the 1900s, medical education operated as a commercial business, rapidly producing inadequately educated doctors who lacked proper oversight and regulation.[6] Informal learning at the century's turn included grand rounds, tumor boards, and morbidity and mortality conferences. In 1906, county medical societies started offering weekly education sessions for practicing physicians.

The publication of the 1910 Flexner Report in the United States,[7] commissioned by the American Medical Association (AMA) and funded by the Carnegie Trust, marks an important moment that changed the course of medical education, including CME.^6 The report documented the mediocrity of medical training at the time, established science as the foundation for medical education, and emphasized the biomedical model as the gold standard for professionalized clinical practice. As a result of the Flexner Report, medical education began to formalize and become more structured. However, the report also recommended harmful directives that marginalized historically Black medical schools and disproportionally impacted Black physicians, who are still underrepresented in medicine relative to their representation in the US population.[8]

From these beginnings, accredited CME in the United States was also born. In the 1920s, brothers Charles and William Mayo developed a Surgeons Club to teach visiting surgeons about new surgical techniques and progress, which evolved into Mayo Annual Clinical Reviews.[9] In 1934, the American Urological Association introduced the first mandatory CME program, and in 1957, the AMA published the first set of CME guidelines and established the Physician's Recognition Award (AMA PRA) credit system for CME (which we will review in Chapter 2).[10]

By the 1960s, CME was mandatory for physicians in the United States, with variations in requirements and regulations from state to state. Many academic centers built CME departments. However, by the 1970s, hospitals, medical schools, and other organizations challenged the predominance of the AMA in CME oversight.[11] As a result, the AMA and six other organizations formed the Accreditation Council for Continuing Medical Education (ACCME) in 1981 as an oversight and regulatory organization for CME, working in concert with the AMA. We will review credit and accreditation in Chapter 2.

ACCME

The six organizations forming ACCME were the American Board of Medical Specialties (ABMS), American Hospital Association, Association of American Medical Colleges, Association for Hospital Medical Education, Council of Medical Specialty Societies, and the Federation of State Medical Boards.

The Alliance for CME (renamed the Alliance for Continuing Education in the Health Professions) was launched in 1974 to build a CME foundation in the United States that brought together publishers, health systems, and academic centers. By the 1980s, the CME enterprise increasingly focused on how to plan and deliver CME to physicians in ways that would ensure learning and behavior change and thus shifted its focus from teaching to learning.[12] ACEHP's name change came about in 2011, when it fully embraced continuing education for other health professionals in addition to physicians. The name change better reflects its broader scope and inclusivity across various health care professions, including nursing and pharmacy.

Continuing Nurse Education

The history of the development of continuing education for nurses in the United States dates back to the early twentieth century. References can be traced back to Florence Nightingale, who emphasized the importance of continuous professional development.[13] Informal continuing education activities, such as lectures and workshops, began to emerge in the early 1900s. Despite Nightingale's advocacy for lifelong learning, substantive education beyond basic nursing training was limited until the mid-twentieth century. The term continuing nurse education (CNE) gained prominence in the middle of the twentieth century, reflecting a shift toward structured and accredited educational activities aimed at enriching nurses' contributions to quality health care and supporting their professional career goals.

Postgraduate courses were among the first organized continuing education initiatives designed for nurses. In the 1920s and 1930s the National League for Nursing Education (now known as the National League for Nursing) began to develop standards for nursing education, including continuing education.[14] The American Nurses Association (ANA) later established the Council on Continuing Education to promote and develop continuing education programs for nurses and developed guidelines for CNE as a foundation for state license renewal in the 1970s.

◇◇

Why is CME/CE Important?

Physicians, nurses, physician associates, pharmacists, and other health professionals (e.g., social workers and psychologists) are required to participate in continuing education to remain competent and maintain professional licensure and board certification.[15] Employers might also have CME/CE requirements.

Keeping Current

CME/CE keeps health professionals up to date on standards of care, new therapies, diagnostic criteria, and evaluation modalities. Since the 1970s, there has been a proliferation of medical information, new technology, state licensing board requirements, standard-of-care issues, outcomes assessment, and utilization review, all of which have fueled demand and shored up an extensive accreditation and regulatory system, as well as the expansion of organizations that provide CME/CE. This system is largely seen as necessary to support knowledge transfer, but it has also shaped a culture in which health professionals are under enormous pressure to remain up to date with rapidly evolving therapeutic agents, technologies, and standards of care. I've interviewed hundreds of clinicians for various CME/CE research projects over the years, and they often compare the experience of information overload to drinking from a firehose.

Patient Safety and Medical Error

The second reason that CME/CE is important is in relation to the wider issue of patient safety and medical error. Over the years, there have been several reports from The Joint Commission, the Institute of

Medicine (such as *To Err is Human*), and other organizations detailing the ways in which health care works against patient safety and pushes clinicians toward error. Although mortality estimates from medical error vary widely, errors can be attributed to omission, commission, or communication. Each year, The Joint Commission publishes a sentinel event data review. In 2022, this review showed that the top two sentinel events reported in 2022 were falls (42 percent) and delay in treatment (6 percent). Communication breakdown was the root cause identified for these sentinel events.[16]

Sentinel Events[16]

The Joint Commission defines a sentinel event as a patient safety event that reaches a patient and results in death, permanent harm (regardless of severity of harm), or severe harm (regardless of the duration of harm).

The health care environment makes it easy for health professionals to get distracted when they are doing their work. CME/CE is a consistent way to ensure that health professionals get access to skills that help them minimize the risk of medical error and optimize patient safety.

Maintenance of Licensure

A third reason that CME is important has to do with licensure. Health professionals must acquire a certain number of credits every year in order to maintain their licensure. Clinical boards for nursing and pharmacy, as well as state medical and osteopathic boards, are responsible to the public for ensuring clinician competence as a condition of license renewal. Since 2010, maintenance of licensure (MoL) has been the framework bolstering the relicensing process for physicians via self-reflection on performance, knowledge and skill acquisition, and performance improvement via feedback.[17] License renewal is required every one to three years.

Most state medical boards require physicians to participate in CME activities for MoL that are practice-relevant, informed by objective data sources, and aimed at improving performance.[18] The specific number of CME credits vary by state board and range from 12 to 150 hours, depending on the board.[19] Some state medical boards also mandate that physicians participate in content-specific CME activities that address state-specific issues or legislative priorities (e.g., opioid prescribing, end-of-life care).[20]

Maintenance of Certification

CME is also important for maintenance of certification (MoC). Once physicians have completed their clinical training and residency, they can pursue specialty board certification. The American Board of Medical Specialties (ABMS) has twenty-four specialty boards that ensure physician competency in providing high-quality specialized patient care through a MoC program, which is also known as continuing or continuous certification. Physicians have to fulfill recertification requirements on a continuing basis via an ABMS MoC program that includes six core competencies defined by ABMS and the Accreditation Council for Graduate Medical Education (ACGME).[20]

ABMS/ACGME Competencies

- Practice-Based Learning and Improvement
- Patient Care and Procedural Skills
- Systems-Based Practice
- Medical Knowledge
- Interpersonal and Communication Skills
- Professionalism

We will dig into competencies in the next section. For now, note that the member board for each specialty defines the requirements and deadlines for their own MoC programs and assesses physician certification status every five years or so. In response to feedback from external stakeholders (e.g., consumers, insurers, and licensing authorities), ABMS developed four specific standards for MoC to better facilitate physician competency.

ABMS/MoC Standards

- Part I Standards — Professionalism and Professional Standing
- Part II Standards — Lifelong Learning and Self-Assessment
- Part III Standards — Assessment of Knowledge, Judgment, and Skills
- Part IV Standards — Improvement in Health and Health Care

Many CME activities meet and contribute to MoC requirements. The Federation of State Medical Boards encourages MoL candidates to comply with the MoC requirements for their specialty field. In turn, board-certified physicians who participate in their specialty board's MoC program are recognized as meeting MoL requirements.[15] Some states also accept physician participation in MoC as a contribution toward the CME credits they need to renew their medical licenses.

Nurses, Pharmacists, and Other Health Care Team Members

Nurses, pharmacists, and other health care team members have their own continuing education requirements.

Nurses and Nurse Practitioners

CNE is important for nurse relicensure in approximately 30 percent of US states. Nurse practitioners must also stay current with their CE requirements to maintain their certification and continue practicing. These requirements typically include a combination of practice hours and CE credits, with specific mandates for pharmacology hours. CNE is also important for specialty certification, while CPD and interprofessional continuing education (IPCE) support lifelong learning and ongoing professional development to help nurses maintain competency.[21] The American Nurses Association (ANA) defines CNE as professional learning experiences that enhance nurses' contributions to health care quality and career advancement, encompassing programs, offerings, and independent studies that meet specific criteria for contact hours.[22]

Most state boards of nursing require nurses to participate in continuing nursing education to maintain their licensure. The specific requirements vary by state and specialty, but most jurisdictions require the completion of a certain number of contact hours within a defined renewal period. As for physicians, educational activities must be delivered by accredited providers and should align with the nurse's area of practice.[23]

Pharmacists

The Accreditation Council for Pharmacy Education (ACPE) requires pharmacists to complete a certain number of continuing pharmacy education credits (CPE) within a set timeframe to maintain their licensure and stay abreast of advancements in pharmaceutical care.[24] Credits should be obtained from ACPE-accredited providers and cover various aspects of pharmaceutical practice.

Physician Assistants/Associates

Physician assistants (PAs) are also bound by continuing education requirements to uphold their licensure. The National Commission on Certification of Physician Assistants (NCCPA) mandates that certified PAs earn and log a minimum of 100 credits of CE every two years.[25] Of these, at least 50 credits must be CME that is designated Category 1 by the American Academy of Physician Associates or by organizations accredited to award *AMA PRA Category 1 Credit*™. Remaining credits can be Category 2. In 2022, the American Academy of Physician Assistants (AAPA) officially changed its name to the American Academy of Physician Associates. Many PAs continue to use the term physician assistant rather than physician associate.

Pro Tip

When you are developing continuing education content for nurses, physician associates, and pharmacists, make sure that the materials you create focus on topics that are relevant to the clinical practice of these specific health professionals.

Interprofessional Continuing Education

When I trained as a trauma operating room (OR) nurse, my professional socialization included learning what it means to be an effective OR team member. At the Western Infirmary in Glasgow, Scotland, nurses were expected to understand each person's vital contribution to the team's overall function and trained to appreciate the roles and responsibilities of every member of the team. I know that other members of the team—and here I specifically mean surgeons and anesthetists—did not have this training, with the result that nurses pretty much had to keep the OR teamwork show on the road.

Education in Silos

Health care team members are often trained and educated separately. This is not ideal. For one thing, this separation reinforces competing professional identities and territorial behaviors among professions. Separate training just makes it harder for everybody to fully understand the roles and responsibilities of their fellow team members, let alone use this knowledge to actually work together across health systems—a skill that is increasingly required to support change management in health care.[26] These knowledge and skill gaps become a barrier to communication, coordination, and collaboration.

Enter interprofessional continuing education (IPCE) as a critical approach to fostering collaboration and teamwork among health care professionals. The roots of team-based care date back to the 1940s,[27] strategy for effective resource use and addressing the chronic health care needs of an aging population.[28] The Covid-19 pandemic further highlighted the importance of teamwork in health care as it required the rapid creation of teams and disrupted existing teams as they were redeployed to meet changing needs in health systems.

The Health Care Team and the Need for IPCE

Team-based care is associated with improved clinical outcomes, enhanced care coordination, and patient safety.[29] High-functioning teams are more efficient in managing chronic diseases, leading to increased job satisfaction among health care professionals. The skills required for successful interprofessional collaboration, such as effective communication and teamwork, are not innate, and health professionals are not routinely educated about how to develop and apply these skills. Moreover, despite its proven benefits, health care professionals have historically been educated in silos, with little emphasis on collaborative care. As a result, the opportunities for health care professionals to learn about the roles and responsibilities of other team members are few and far between. This segregated education often translates into hierarchical clinical practice that, combined with professional jargon, can undermine respect, trust, and collaboration.[30] An accumulating body of evidence suggests that when health care professionals communicate effectively and collaborate as an interprofessional team, they can improve care processes and clinical outcomes, enhance patient satisfaction, and reduce costs.[31]

Defining IPCE

The overarching goals of IPCE are to foster interprofessional interactions, improve health outcomes, and deliver better-coordinated patient care. The UK Centre for the Advancement of Interprofessional Education (CAIPE) first developed the definition of IPCE, which has been widely adopted by the World Health Organization and the Interprofessional Education Collaborative in the United States, and is used by Joint Accreditation for Interprofessional Continuing Education™. IPCE involves a common learning process in which practitioners from different professions and specialties learn from and about each other and have opportunities to practice IPCE skills in an environment that acknowledges professional identities but defuses professional hierarchies.[32-33] IPCE is distinct from multidisciplinary education, which involves health professionals learning separately about patient needs and the work of other health care disciplines.[34]

The Interprofessional Education Collaborative (IPEC) has outlined four core competency domains required for interprofessional collaborative practice:[35]

1. Values and Ethics
2. Roles and Responsibilities
3. Communication
4. Teams and Teamwork

IPCE that supports team-based care is a critical component of health care quality and safety.[36] Evidence suggests that IPCE leads to better understanding among health care professionals, respect for each other's roles, and collaboration for optimal health outcomes. Organizations that offer IPCE report better staff retention and 12 percent fewer medical incidents.[36-37]

Examples of IPCE in Practice

Several programs exemplify the principles and practices of IPCE:

- **TEAMSTEPPS™.** A training program developed by the Department of Defense and the Agency for Healthcare Research and Quality to improve team performance in health care.[38]
- **StoryCare.** StoryCare.com is a library of story-based simulations based on TEAMSTEPPS™ designed to improve patient safety and satisfaction. The materials include authentic stories to teach team members about best practices in communication and the potential consequences for patients and health professionals when interprofessional communication and teamwork break down.

- **Schwartz Rounds.** Structured discussions for health professionals to explore the social and emotional challenges they face in caring for patients.
- **Project ECHO®.** Project Extension for Community Healthcare Outcomes (Project ECHO®) is a virtual tele-education and capacity-building program that shares knowledge and best practices via a collaborative hub-and-spoke knowledge network.

Future Directions and Opportunities in IPCE

Joint Accreditation for IPCE (revisited in Chapter 2) offers a unified mechanism to incentivize participation in IPCE and to accredit organizations that promote collaboration, teamwork, and design and that deliver continuing education by the team, for the team. As health care continues to evolve, emerging trends in IPCE include shifts toward more personalized learning experiences, the growing importance of data-driven decision-making, and the integration of artificial intelligence in training. These developments present opportunities for writers to create educational materials that support IPCE.

Pro Tip: IPCE Needs Assessments

The first critical step is assessing the interprofessional learning needs of your target audiences. Useful questions to guide needs assessments include:

- What patient care challenges does the team face that proper coordination and collaboration could help address? Common examples include care transitions, preventable readmissions, diagnostic errors, suboptimal patient education, etc.
- Where do breakdowns currently occur in team communication or delivery of coordinated care?

- What skills gaps related to interprofessional collaboration have been identified? What underlying knowledge gaps contribute to these?
- What are some specific roles, responsibilities, or contributions of individual team members that others may not fully understand?
- What tools, systems, or resources to support team-based care are lacking?

Multiple data-collection methods can help answer these questions, including focus groups, observations, surveys, analysis of quality improvement data, and patient feedback. Comparing insights across clinical and nonclinical team members is invaluable.

Competency-Based Education

Let's dig into the idea of competency. In response to studies and reports that pointed out deficiencies in ongoing physician knowledge and behaviors, medical education shifted toward competency-based medical education (CBME). In 1999, the ABMS and the ACGME developed six core competencies for physician residency training in 1999 that were endorsed in academic medicine in 2014.[39]

CBME emphasizes the mastery of specific skills and knowledge with the goal of improving patient outcomes rather than measuring the number of hours that learners are exposed to instruction. Also known as outcomes-focused learning, CBME provides a personalized and flexible learning experience that accommodates individual learning needs. This approach includes milestones and entrustable professional activities (EPAs) to provide a structure for teaching, learning, and assessment.[40]

In the early 2000s, interest in CBME intensified after a series of Institute of Medicine (IOM) reports identified specific problems in health care delivery and pointed to CBME as one of many potential solutions. In *Crossing the Quality Chasm*, published in 2001, the IOM proposed sweeping changes to health care delivery that included principles for performance, patient–provider relationships, and payment.[41] A subsequent IOM report, *Health Professions Education: A Bridge to Quality* highlighted the need for substantive changes in professional education curricula to better align with the evolving demands of health care delivery and quality improvement.[42]

The report emphasized interdisciplinary teamwork and the need for robust proof of ongoing clinical proficiency through rigorous testing by licensing boards and certification bodies. The report also suggested core competencies for health professionals and spurred a more general shift toward competency frameworks for all health professions as well as outcomes-driven CME/CE. These recommendations were further endorsed by subsequent resorts from the IOM, such as *Redesigning Continuing Education in the Health Professions* (2010), and the Macy Foundation (*Continuing Education in the Health Professions* in 2008 and *Lifelong Learning in Medicine and Nursing* in 2010).

As a result, CME/CE in the United States and across the world have increasingly focused on competency-based education design in medicine, dentistry, pharmacy, and nursing.[43] Concomitantly, outcomes frameworks have shifted to assess whether clinicians achieve competencies that range from knowledge to patient outcomes and are adequately prepared for the complexities of modern health care delivery. That said, competency-based education is challenging to implement and remains the topic of considerable discussion in academic and professional literature.

As Graham McMahon, president and CEO of ACCME, notes, “Health professionals are strategic and effective learners, with a thirst for deep, scientific/analytical knowledge as well as the practical steps they need to take to apply knowledge and skills in clinical practice.”[44] Although health professionals routinely receive multiple marketing and social media messages with information about pharmaceutical and biomedical devices, simple information exchange has relatively low value for physicians. Rather, education lies at the core of clinical implementation.

Pro Tip

When developing content for competency-based CME/CE, keep the following tips in mind:

1. Focus on creating materials that emphasize the practical application of knowledge and skills rather than just acquiring information.
2. Use case studies, simulations, and interactive exercises to help learners develop and demonstrate the specific competencies required for effective clinical practice.
3. Align your content with established competency frameworks and learning objectives and consider incorporating assessments that measure the mastery of these competencies.
4. Remember to invest in your own competency development as a CME/CE writer. This book should help!

Who is Involved in Creating CME/CE Content?

Patients are at the heart of health care and therefore are the primary focus for all CME/CE. The work we do in this field is grounded in supporting health professionals deliver quality care that improves patient outcomes. As a result, creating substantive CME/CE content is a team sport.

So, who is involved in creating CME/CE content? Accredited education providers have been accredited by ACCME or one of the other accreditation bodies to design, deliver, and evaluate educational activities for health professionals. CME/CE providers are either accredited themselves or partner with accredited providers to certify activities for credit. Chapter 2 reviews accreditation in more detail. For now, note that education providers have overall responsibility for developing gap analyses, needs assessments, and education strategy, as well as for driving instructional design, vetting faculty, and designing assessment and outcomes frameworks.[45]

Working as a CME/CE writer involves working with many different types of education providers as well as different personnel across provider organizations. Understanding who these key players are can help you be more effective in developing educational content that is targeted, compliant, and impactful. Several internal team members within CME/CE provider organizations might review your work.

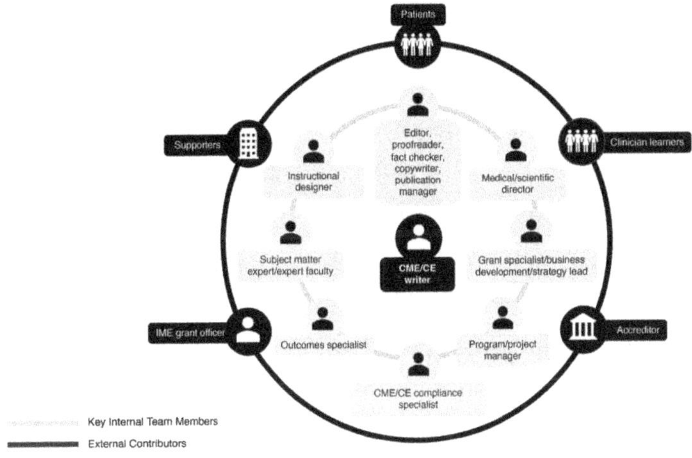

Key Parties Involved in Creating Education Content

Key Internal Team Members

- **Medical/scientific director.** Medical or scientific directors (SD) work for education providers. They liaise with faculty and develop strategy and direction for educational content. The SD is often the main point of contact for the medical writer, providing content feedback and ensuring that the content aligns with the project's goals. MDs/SDs also often make CME/CE content and liaise with business development to create proposals/needs assessments.

- **Grant specialist/business development/strategy lead.** Business development folks look for grant opportunities. They stay abreast of emerging therapies and changes in their specialty landscape and conduct competitive intelligence. They develop and maintain relationships with subject matter experts (faculty) and independent medical education (IME) personnel in pharmaceutical and device companies (supporters). They also determine budget parameters, identify pertinent research related to grant opportunities, and shape messaging to align with supporter interests.
- **Program/project manager.** Program managers who work for education providers support business development and coordinate between business development, faculty, writers, and other internal teams. They focus on educational format, logistics, and costs, by tracking program progress and budgets and developing processes and protocols to streamline content development. They also confirm if content ideas are feasible. Program or project managers are likely to be the client with whom writers work most closely.
- **CME/CE compliance specialist.** This expert ensures CME/CE meets accreditation standards for independence and support. They review content for compliance, fair balance, and accessibility of references.
- **Outcomes specialist.** The person in this role creates data-collection tools, such as pre- and post-education surveys, and analyzes results. They assess whether the content in the education activity links to measurable outcomes.
- **Subject matter expert/expert faculty.** Medical writers may interact directly with faculty experts who develop content. Faculty often join initial planning and debrief calls with the

internal CME/CE team to understand direction and decision rationales. Although faculty are responsible for preparing and presenting their own content in CME/CE activities (including the learning objectives, presentation materials, and interactive involvement with participants), as the writer, you are likely to be tasked with helping faculty wrangle their content into shape or working with them to develop content from scratch.

- **Instructional designer.** Instructional design (ID) involves creating engaging and effective online, in-person, or simulation-based learning experiences to change knowledge and behavior. Instructional designers strategically select the most appropriate content delivery methods and use storytelling and tools like Articulate Storyline and Camtasia to build interactive content and simulations that include practice scenarios and feedback. The overarching process instructional designers follow is the ADDIE model—analyze, design, develop, implement, and evaluate.
- **Editor, proofreader, fact checker, copywriter, publication manager.** Not everyone occupying these roles will work in CME/CE, but many will, or in CME/CE adjacent roles (e.g., medical publishing). At some point the companies they work for will need freelance help with manuscripts, slides, posters and reports for conferences, educational activities, advisory boards.

As noted by Audrie Tornow, managing partner at Excalibur Medical Education,

> *The business development person is going to bring that idea back in house to the team, and that team may be made up of the editor, the program manager, perhaps the owner of the organization, someone from their CME/CE department. Ultimately, they're all trying to contribute to what they think a grant and a needs assessment could encompass.*

External Contributors

Beyond the core CME/CE team, external stakeholders have a relationship to needs assessments and educational content:

- **Accreditor:** Groups like ACCME ensure CME/CE meets educational quality standards. Content and format must adhere to strict accreditation criteria.
- **Clinician learner:** The target audience guides content shaping through surveyed needs and learning format preferences. CME/CE providers use clinicians' engagement with the educational content or activity and the outcomes reported from those activities to demonstrate value to supporters.
- **Pharmaceutical/device supporter:** These companies fund grants for education in their therapeutic areas. They want to support education providers who know how to develop educational content that bridges practice gaps in ways that adhere to accreditation standards.
- **IME grant officer:** IME grant officers are typically tasked with the strategic alignment of educational initiatives with the broader goals of the health care system and the pharmaceutical company's vision. This alignment demands a deep understanding of both the medical field and educational strategies that can effectively address the identified gaps in health care practice.

CME/CE Around the World: A Global Perspective

CME/CE is increasingly global. However, there are important regional differences in how CME/CE is credited, accredited, and funded. While the United States has a well-established system for CME/CE, in many parts of the world (such as Canada, the European Union, the United Kingdom, and Australia) medical education is embedded within the broader concept of CPD. As noted earlier in this chapter, CPD refers not only to enhancing medical knowledge and skills, but also the development of skills and attitudes related to a broader range of functions associated with working as a physician, including managerial, communication, and information technology functions.[46]

In these countries, members of professional organizations (such as Royal Colleges) are required to formally assess their learning needs, document their participation in continuing education activities, and record how CPD participation contributes to outcomes in their practice.[47] While CPD frameworks vary across different regions, quality improvement, patient safety, and public concerns about practitioner accountability are primary drivers of CPD.

Accreditation Organizations in Other Parts of the World

ACCME recognizes six CME/CE organizations outside the United States as substantially equivalent to the ACCME's accreditation system, including organizations in Canada, Europe, Oman, Qatar, and Germany:

- The Royal College of Physicians and Surgeons of Canada
- The Committee on Accreditation of Continuing Medical Education (Canada)
- The European Board for Accreditation in Cardiology
- The Oman Medical Specialty Board as part of the Ministry of Health of the Sultanate of Oman
- The Qatar Council for Health Practitioners
- The Federation of the German Chambers of Physicians

In Europe, individual countries often have their own CME/CE systems that are led by different entities (e.g., physicians, universities, politicians). It varies considerably whether CME/CE is compulsory or voluntary; how it is implemented and organized; the types of activities eligible for CME/CE credit; whether CME/CE is accredited, and if so, whether activities or providers are accredited; and whether there are sanctions or incentives for participation.[48] For example, while CME/CE is formally compulsory in Austria, France, Italy, and the United Kingdom, sanctions are not enforced against noncompliant physicians in practice, and private sponsorship of CME/CE is permitted.[49]

In France, where CME/CE has been compulsory since 1996 and primarily driven by legislation such as the Act on Patient Rights and Quality of Care 2002, both medical societies and private CME/CE providers plan and deliver CME/CE.[50] Belgium and Norway offer financial incentives to enhance CME/CE participation for specific categories of physicians.[51] In France, Germany, Italy, Spain, and the United Kingdom, medical societies, medical associations, and employers are the main CME/CE providers.

The European Accreditation Council for CME/CE (EACCME®) is a pan-European accreditation system, but education implementation is driven by national requirements. Germany has a compulsory and regulated CME/CE system supported by formal sanctions, though physicians can choose the type of CME/CE activity they want to participate in to accommodate their learning styles. Doctors in Germany pay for their own education since industry funding is restricted.[50] In contrast, CME/CE in Spain is voluntary. EACCME® launched new accreditation criteria in 2023 (3.0). However, the Good CME Practice group (gCMEp) has criticized these standards for using ambiguous definitions. The authors of a 2023 article in the *Journal of CME* note:[52]

> *The new standards do not differentiate between "medical communications agencies", where content is required to be reviewed and controlled by the industry supporter, and education providers who work under arms-length grant agreements with no input from the supporter.*

In sum, while CME/CE is increasingly global, recognize that there are significant differences in how health care is structured and delivered across different countries, which impacts the organization and delivery of CME. If you find yourself working with global education providers, considering the following tips will help you navigate the diverse landscape of global CME/CE.

Pro Tip

1. **Regional Differences:** Medical education systems and CME/CE/CPD frameworks vary across regions, with some countries having compulsory CME/CE and others having voluntary systems. Be aware of the nuances in how CME/CE is implemented, organized, accredited, and incentivized in different parts of the world.
2. **Stay Informed on Accreditation Systems:** Familiarize yourself with accreditation bodies and systems in various countries. Understanding these systems can help ensure compliance and quality in CME/CE content development.
3. **Adapt to Local Requirements:** The expectations and preferences of learners for CME can differ substantially across regions in terms of format, language, and content. Tailor your writing to align with the specific needs and regulations of different regions. Understanding the local context and involving local experts is crucial for organizing effective global CME activities.

Does CME/CE Work?

While CME/CE is mostly mandatory and health professionals value it, its effectiveness is hard to research. Extensive research over the past twenty years has demonstrated that CME/CE has a positive effect on clinical decision-making, physician performance, and patient health outcomes.[53–54] These effects are more evident when CME/CE is goal-oriented and interactive, involves multiple exposures and multimedia formats, includes feedback, and is focused on outcomes that physicians consider important to their practice.[55–56] A meta-analysis of the 220 articles in the ABMS Evidence Library supporting the maintenance of certification program showed that 129 activities demonstrated a positive impact of CME/CE on physician performance and patient health outcomes.[55] That said, challenges in measuring the effectiveness of CME/CE remain. We will examine these in Chapter 7.

What's the Difference Between CME/CE, IME, and Company-Led Education?

Pharmaceutical and biomedical device manufacturers create many different types of content for health professionals to promote their products, inform clinicians about their products, and provide learning and skill development. This content is regulated by the U.S. Food and Drug Administration (FDA), as authorized by the Food, Drug, and Cosmetics Act (FDCA 1938) and the Office of Prescription Drug Promotion (OPDP). The FDA regulates the production, sale, and distribution of drugs, medical devices, and cosmetics, and protects the public from adulterated and misbranded products that are manufactured in the United States. The OPDP protects public health by ensuring that promotional content for prescription drugs is truthful, balanced, and accurately communicated.[57]

While Marketing functions in pharmaceutical and biomedical device manufacturers create promotional materials, Commercial Operations and Medical Affairs functions are responsible for creating scientific and educational materials. Medical Affairs teams mostly focus on company-led disease state education as well as Independent Medical Education (IME), while Commercial is usually the lead for product-specific or company-led education and collaborates with Medical Affairs for scientific accuracy.

Promotional Content

Promotional materials advertise or market a specific manufacturer's product to health professionals and the public. The Commercial function within industry is responsible for promotional assets. Content is promotional if the manufacturer's product is mentioned. The FDA requires pharmaceutical companies to monitor their content and submit their promotional materials to the FDA for review via an FDA 2253 Form. HCPS can report to the FDA any instances of potentially false or misleading prescription drug promotion via the FDA Bad Ad Program.

Company-Led Education

Company-led education (also known as industry-led) is nonaccredited education in which a pharmaceutical or biomedical device company organizes and pays for the creation of scientific content. Company-led education includes speaker programs, webinars and satellite symposia at conferences, disease awareness campaigns for health care professionals, and other activities that support scientific information exchange. Company-led education is considered non-independent because manufacturers can influence the content and speaker selection. Pharmaceutical companies often hire agencies and medical communications (medcomms) agencies to create education assets.

Speaker programs. Speaker programs are typically events sponsored by companies where a health care professional speaks about a product or disease state on the company's behalf.

Medcomms. Medical communications agencies (medcomms) are distinct from medical education companies, which are often ACCME-accredited education providers or work with accredited companies to produce CME/CE. Medcomms agencies collaborate with Medical Affairs to produce information that informs health professionals about drug products and their benefits and risks to patients. This information is packaged as education and delivered to health professionals via advisory boards, conferences, speaker programs, and publications such as literature reviews and manuscripts. These education and training materials are subject to internal medical, legal, and regulatory (MLR) review by pharmaceutical companies (the medcomms' clients).[58]

Independent Medical Education

The term independent medical education (IME) emerged in the late 2000s. IME provides a safe harbor to ensure that education content is independent and not influenced by pharmaceutical and biomedical device manufacturers. Independent education providers develop IME, which industry can fund via education grants or sponsorship. IME can also be accredited or nonaccredited. IME teams manage accredited CME grants or nonaccredited sponsorships separately from other Medical Affairs activities. The education IME supports needs to align with not only insights about learner needs and practice gaps derived from external data (which we will review in Chapter 5), but also the company's priorities and scientific goals based on internal data from various departments. As a result, supporters develop rigorous grant planning processes to ensure that the education, skills training, and performance improvement they fund aligns with their therapeutic area strategies and the overarching goals of health care improvement.

Industry-supported scientific and educational activities that are nonpromotional and educational are not subject to regulation under the FDA, nor are they subject to MLR review.[59] For instance, disease awareness communications are not subject to FDA regulations unless they "effectively promote" a drug or medical device.[60] However, non-promotional scientific and educational activities are typically subject to some level of medico-legal review.

Grants. The process of grant planning in IME involves stakeholders across different departments and functions, stringent compliance norms, and an in-depth understanding of educational needs in health care. Grants are funds awarded to support a program, meeting, or activity over which the grantee (an education provider) has control and discretion over the content, and the grantor (the commercial supporter) has neither influence nor receives benefit beyond acknowledgement of support.

Sponsorship. Sponsored programs or activities are funded by manufacturers who receive a defined benefit in exchange for support, such as advertising in the program materials or an exhibit booth.

Accredited CME/CE. There are two types of CME/CE. Accredited CME/CE, the focus of this book, is under the oversight of accreditation organizations (reviewed in Chapter 2).

Nonaccredited CME/CE. Nonaccredited education refers to educational programs that originate within IME. The content is nonpromotional and not influenced by the pharmaceutical industry itself. The purpose of nonaccredited CME/CE is to educate health professionals on how to use new therapies and indications and to inform them about products and services sold by commercial companies.

The Role of MAPs[61]

Medical Affairs professionals (MAPs) are responsible for scientific strategy, company-led education, and IME. They are responsible for understanding the details of a pharmaceutical or biomedical device company's products and how they apply in clinical practice. MAPs liaise internally with regulatory, research and development, and medical liaisons. They interact with external groups such as health professionals, knowledge experts, payers, academia, government departments, and patient organizations. They develop and share clinical and scientific data with these groups via training, education materials, and advisory boards. MAPs typically work with external agencies and medical education companies to create educational content and are increasingly involved in developing and measuring the impact of nonaccredited medical education.

Funding for CME/CE

Sources of funding for CME/CE have shifted over time. Funding for CME/CE activities comes from various sources, including the pharmaceutical industry, registration fees, physician employer support, advertising, private donations, and government grants. ACCME publishes an annual report that reviews funding and other metrics in the CME/CE field. In 2022, the most recently published report available, commercial support accounted for 26 percent of total income for CME/CE providers in the ACCME system.[62] Funds for CME come from Medical Affairs as part of its discretionary spending. As such, commercial funding for CME can be very vulnerable to budget changes with the pharmaceutical and biomedical device industry.

In the 1950s and 1960s, CME/CE programs were primarily funded by universities, medical schools, and professional organizations. Commercial support was minimal.[63] In the 1970s, as part of its effort to ensure the safe and effective use of prescription drugs, the FDA required pharmaceutical companies to provide educational programs about their products to health care professionals.

The pharmaceutical industry's involvement in funding CME/CE grew substantially in the 1980s and early 2000s. Pharmaceutical manufacturers could collaborate with ACCME-accredited education providers to present a session at a medical society or specialist association meeting. This collaboration included professional societies, medical schools, or one of the many large for-profit medical education and communication companies (MECCs) to develop the content (also described as publishing/education companies).[64] Some physicians were critical of this arrangement between commercial interests, as they were called at the time, and accredited CME/CE on the grounds that CME/CE providers funded by pharmaceutical companies were incentivized to favorably present the funder products.[65] This perception was further fueled by studies in the 1980s, which suggested industry funding of education had the potential to introduce commercial bias into educational content and influence prescribing behaviors.[66] Despite these criticisms, by 2006 MECCs, professional societies, and university CME/CE providers derived 50 to 65 percent of their funding from pharmaceutical companies.[65] In 2006, commercial support for CME/CE totaled $1.2 billion (61% of total income for providers of CME/CE).[62]

In response to growing awareness of the financial interdependency between CME/CE providers and commercial industry, ACCME introduced new guidelines in 2006 designed to establish stronger barriers between funding and program planning processes.[67] These guidelines imposed restrictions on speakers who received substantial support from industry, limiting their participation in CME/CE conferences and, in particular, prohibiting their use of industry-prepared informational or educational materials in the guise of CME/CE. Heightened government scrutiny of CME/CE funding in the early 2000s and subsequent ACCME guidelines led to a decline in industry funding. By 2018, commercial support had decreased to about 25 percent of total CME/CE funding.

The debate about the appropriate role of industry funding in CME/CE continues. Some critics argue that as long as accredited CME/CE continues to be heavily funded by the pharmaceutical industry, we should consider it drug promotion.[68] However, multiple layers of compliance and regulatory codes exist to protect CME/CE from commercial influence, including, most recently, ACCME's 2020 *Standards for Integrity and Independence in Continuing Education and Independence in Accredited Continuing Education.* Chapter 3 describes the requirements in place to prevent bias. But first, let's review what the field means when it is talking about credit and accreditation.

Key Takeaways

- CE refers continuing education for health professionals to maintain competence and improve patient outcomes and includes CME, CNE, and CPE

- CME/CE is distinct from promotional or marketing activities by pharmaceutical companies
- CME/CE has evolved from informal learning into a highly regulated field
- Key players include patients, accreditors, education providers, supporters, and health professionals
- CME/CE is crucial for keeping health professionals up to date
- CME/CE must be independent from commercial influence
- Understanding the history and ecosystem of CME/CE is important for writers
- Multiple stakeholders are involved in creating CME/CE content

Chapter 2

Credit and Accreditation

Education is not preparation for life; education is life itself.

— JOHN DEWEY

Introduction

We all want to trust that health professionals will stay current with new therapies and treatments. Accreditation is a quality assurance system to maintain the integrity and quality of the CME/CE activities that help clinicians stay current with standards of care. This chapter provides an overview of what accreditation is, how it has evolved, and describes the credit system that rewards clinicians for participating in CME/CE.

What is Accreditation?

Accreditation is a system to ensure that educational content is independent from commercial influence and is trustworthy (i.e., evidence-based). The goal of accredited CME/CE is to provide evidence-based education that improves clinician competence and patient outcomes and measures these changes via established evaluation methodologies.[1] Accredited CME/CE is also a potential mechanism for advancing health care imperatives and accelerating translational medicine.[2] Accreditation bodies, like the Accreditation Council for Continuing Medical Education (ACCME), play a crucial role in maintaining the integrity and quality of educational offerings for health professionals. Accreditation bodies have established rigorous guidelines and standards to guarantee that CME/CE content remains relevant, current, and independent from commercial influence. By adhering to these strict accreditation standards, educators ensure that the content they provide is fair, unbiased, and centered on enhancing the knowledge and skills of health care professionals. Ultimately, this focus on quality and independence in education translates to better patient care and a stronger health care system overall.

The Evolution of Accreditation Standards

Current accreditation standards emerged in response to congressional probes into the influence of the pharmaceutical industry in educational programming. In 2005, the Senate Finance Committee reviewed the CME/CE grant-issuing practices of the twenty-three largest manufacturers in response to allegations that drug companies were using grants to promote drugs "off-label."[3] Senator Charles Grassley questioned pharmaceutical company policies around CME/CE grant policies and procedures, including the role of sales and marketing personnel in originating or evaluating grant requests.[4]

The Committee reported that the pharmaceutical industry not only funneled more than $1 billion per year into funding CME/CE programs, but also had a tendency to fund programs that favored their own products and devices.[3] Senators Max Baucus and Charles Grassley wrote a letter to then ACCME chief executive, Dr. Murray Kopelow, noting that, at best, such funding created a bias in CME/CE activities toward the agenda of pharmaceutical companies and potentially tainted the integrity of education. At worst, pharmaceutical manufacturers were using CME/CE grants to influence clinical decision-making, especially decisions about which therapies to prescribe, as well as to bias clinical protocols and promote off-label products. The Finance Committee subsequently urged the ACCME to improve its oversight of CME and establish mechanisms to ensure the independence of education from commercial interests (referred to in ACCME's 2020 Standards as ineligible companies).[5]

The Role of Accrediting Bodies

In the United States, the ACCME sets out the ethical and compliance guidelines for creating CME/CE content, in alignment with established U.S. Food and Drug Administration (FDA) and the U.S. Department of Health and Human Services (HHS) Office of the Inspector General (OIG) independence criteria (which we will review in more detail in Chapter 3). ACCME's 2020 *Standards for Integrity and Independence in Accredited Continuing Education* specify the types of organizations that can provide education, the types of content that they can create, and the criteria for creation.[6] These standards are designed to ensure that accredited CME/CE is based on valid content, free from commercial influence, and serves the needs of patients and the public.

Continuing education for health professionals is a broad field that encompasses not only physicians but multiple health professions and associations. Thus, ACCME collaborates with seven other accreditation bodies in the United States that represent multiple health professions and have adopted ACCME's *Standards for Integrity and Independence.* ACCME also collaborates with accrediting bodies worldwide, like the European Accreditation Council for Continuing Medical Education, and provides guidance to organizations in Europe, the United Kingdom, Canada, and Asia.

Accreditation Organizations in the USA

Accreditation Council for Continuing Medical Education	Regulates CME/CE activities and approves organizations as accredited CME/CE providers

Accreditation Council for Pharmacy Education	Sets standards for pharmacist education and accredits professional degree programs and continuing education
American Academy of Family Practitioners	Established the first physician credit system and requires physician members to complete 150 hours of CME every three years
American Academy of Physician Associates	Accredits CME for physician assistants/associates
American Nurses Credentialing Center	Sets criteria for accredited nurse professional development and continuing education
American Osteopathic Association	Requires physician members to complete 120 CME/CE credit hours every three years
Association of Regulatory Boards of Optometry/Council on Optometric Practitioner Education	Accredits optometric CE necessary for license renewal
Joint Accreditation for Interprofessional Continuing Education	Accredits organizations to provide CE for multiple professionals through a single application process
Commission on Dietetic Registration	Accredits providers to grant continuing education for registered dieticians and dietetic technicians

Joint Accreditation

Joint Accreditation for Interprofessional Continuing Education (IPCE) accredits health care systems, specialty societies, medical schools, and other organizations that promote collaboration, teamwork, and design and deliver continuing education by the team, for the team.[7] ACCME, the Accreditation Council for Pharmacy Education (ACPE), and the American Nurses Credentialing Center (ANCC) are founding organizations of Joint Accreditation for IPCE, which collaborates with additional accreditors.

Joint Accreditation for IPCE Organizations

Accreditation Council for Continuing Medical Education	American Nurses Credentialing Center
Accreditation Council for Pharmacy Education	American Academy of Physician Assistants
American Psychological Association	American Social Work Boards Accredited Continuing Education
American Dental Association Commission for Continuing Education Provider Recognition	Board of Certification for the Athletic Trainer
Council on Optometric Practitioner Education/Associated Regulatory Boards of Optmetry	Commission on Dietetic Registration

Can Any Organization Be Accredited?

ACCME makes a distinction between organizations or entities that are eligible for accreditation and organizations that are ineligible.

Ineligible Entities. Entities that are ineligible for accreditation include marketing, medical communications agencies, and pharmaceutical companies themselves, as well as education providers that are owned, in whole or in part, or otherwise influenced or controlled by manufacturers or other ineligible companies. ACCME also defines an entity as ineligible if it has begun a governmental regulatory approval process (e.g., submission of an investigational new drug application [IND] to FDA for drugs or the initiation of the premarket approval [PMA] process for devices).[6]

Eligible Entities. There are many types of accredited education providers including schools of medicine, medical specialty societies, insurance companies, commercial medical education companies, hospitals and health systems, nonprofit physician membership organizations, and more. Hospitals and health systems are the largest group of education providers in the accredited CME/CE ecosystem.

Accreditation Criteria

ACCME has established Core Accreditation Criteria and additional criteria to support Accreditation with Commendation.

Core Accreditation Criteria

- **CME mission and program improvement.** The education provider has a mission, gathers and analyzes program-based data, and improves programs to meet its CME mission.
- **Educational planning and evaluation.** The education provider supports CME by identifying educational needs; develops activities to change competence, performance, or patient outcomes; selects appropriate learning formats; designs education to align with physician competencies; and analyzes change.

Criteria for Accreditation with Commendation

- **Promotes team-based education.** The education provider engages interprofessional teams, patients, and learners in the health professions.
- **Addresses public health priorities.** The education provider uses health and practice data for health care improvement, addresses public health, and collaborates with other organizations.
- **Enhances skills.** The education provider optimizes communication and procedural skills and creates individualized learning plans with support strategies.

- **Demonstrates educational leadership.** The education provider engages in scholarship, supports CPD for the CME/CE team, and is creative.
- **Achieves outcomes.** The education provider improves performance, health care quality, and patient/community health.

You'll find the full set of criteria at: https://accme.org/accreditation-rules/accreditation-criteria.

What Counts as Accredited Education?

The ACCME defines CME as:[9]

> *. . . any activity that serves to maintain, develop, or increase the knowledge, skills and professional performance, and relationships that a clinician uses to provide services for patients, the public, or health professions.*

Physicians can participate in CME activities that focus on building knowledge, developing medical and surgical skills, and cultivating broader professional capabilities, such as practice management (e.g., for physicians who manage service lines or health care facilities), teaching methods (e.g., for physicians teaching in medical schools), and coding and reimbursement.

Health professionals have freedom to choose CME/CE activities but need to consider cost, credibility, convenience, and content-relevance in their selection processes. ACCME includes many different formats and activities for accredited CME/CE, such as live conferences, seminars, workshops, and grand rounds; online activities that involve enduring print, video, or audio materials; educational activities based on reading and reviewing articles in peer-reviewed medical journals (journal-based CME/CE); research/publishing; and quality improvement initiatives.

We'll explore these formats and activities in more detail in Chapter 8.

CME Credit

Accreditation is one part of the CME/CE framework. Credit is another. The organizations that oversee clinical standards and ethics in medicine, including the American Osteopathic Association (AOA), the American Medical Association (AMA), and the American Academy of Family Physicians (AAFP), established lifelong learning as a premise for these standards. These organizations also established credit recognition systems to reward clinicians for participating in lifelong learning, enhance the objectivity and quality of CME/CE, and track compliance with regulatory requirements.[10]

AMA. The AMA has a long history in CME oversight. AMA *Principles of Medical Ethics* established the grounding principles for CME, which emphasizes the ethical responsibility of physicians to pursue lifelong learning and facilitate the education of others. The AMA established a Committee on Medical Education in 1847, which became the AMA Council on Medical Education in 1901. The elected physician members comprising this body formulate policy recommendations on medical education, which are then passed to the AMA House of Delegates for consideration through the AMA Board of Trustees.

In 1968, the AMA established the Physician's Recognition Award (AMA PRA) as its CME credit system.[10] This credit was designed to reassure the American public that its physicians are maintaining competence through regular learning activities. *AMA PRA Credit*™ is generally held as a marker of high standards in education and awards credits to physicians who participate in 150 hours of CME/CE every three years.

The *AMA PRA Credit*™ system offers two types of credit. *AMA PRA Category 1 Credit*™ is awarded by an accredited CME provider or the AMA and includes live and online activities, test-item writing, and manuscript review. Physicians who participate in educational activities that meet certain criteria (e.g., research, peer review) can self-claim and self-document *AMA PRA Category 2 Credit™*. Learn more about the *AMA PRA Credit™* system at www.ama-assn.org.

AOA. The AOA was formed in 1887 to advance the osteopathic medical profession. It is the primary certifying body for doctors of osteopathic medicine (DO) and is the accrediting agency for osteopathic medical schools in the United States.[10] The AOA established a credit system in 1973 for physicians with an osteopathic degree.

AAFP. The AAFP was the first medical specialty society to require its members to participate in CME. In 1947, AAFP established the first physician credit system in response to increasing specialization during and following World War II. This CME credit system required physicians to complete 150 hours of CME every three years to maintain AAFP membership.[10] AAFP has equivalency credit agreements with the AMA, AOA, and the College of Family Physicians of Canada. For instance, AAFP Prescribed Credit is accepted as *AMA PRA Category 1 Credit™* toward the Physician's Recognition Award (PRA) and the AAFP accepts *AMA PRA Category 1 Credit™* as Elective Credit.[10]

In the United States, only organizations accredited by the ACCME or a recognized state medical society can award *AMA PRA Credit™* to physicians. Accredited CME providers must comply with ACCME accreditation standards and offer activities that align with AMA credit system standards in order for the credits to be certified. Aside from some events directly certified by the AMA itself, only accredited providers can designate credits for educational activities. Additionally, the AMA maintains international partnerships for certain activities meeting its standards to ensure additional eligible credit opportunities for member physicians.

The International Association for Continuing Education and Training (IACET) accredits continuing education for all health professionals.

Core Requirements for AMA PRA Category Credit™ Certification

To be certified for CME credit by the AMA, education providers must meet AMA PRA core requirements, format-specific requirements, and requirements for designating and awarding *AMA PRA Category 1 Credit*™:[11]

1. The content of CME activities must conform to the AMA/ACCME definition of CME.
2. The activity must address an educational need (knowledge, competence, or performance) that underlies the professional practice gaps of that activity's learners.
3. The CME activity must present content appropriate in depth and scope for the intended physician learners.
4. The CME activity must utilize one or more learning methodologies appropriate to the activity's educational purpose and/or objectives.
5. The CME activity must provide an assessment of the learner that measures achievement of the educational purpose and/or objective of the activity.
6. The activities must present content appropriate in depth and scope for the intended physician learners; have an educational purpose; aim to maintain, develop, or increase the knowledge, skills, and professional performance that a physician uses to provide services for patients, the public, or the profession.
7. The CME activity must be planned and implemented in accordance with the ACCME *Standards for Integrity and Independence in Accredited Continuing Education.*
8. CME activities must meet the requirements for one of the established learning formats, such as live activities, enduring materials, or journal-based CME.

How Physicians Claim CME Credit

Physicians claim CME credit by participating in accredited CME activities that are offered by organizations accredited by ACCME, AAFP, or AOA to award *AMA PRA Category 1 Credit*™.[12] Physicians can also claim Category 1 Credit™ directly from AMA-designated activities and can self-report Category 2 Credit™. Category 2 Credit™ includes professional development activities that offer learning experiences that are relevant to the physician's practice.

Physicians can also claim credit by participating in quality and performance improvement activities, point-of-care learning, maintenance of certification activities (MOC), and clinical data registries. The American Board of Medical Specialties (ABMS) requires physicians to take CME to maintain board certification. Some states also accept physician participation in MoC as a contribution to the CME/CE credits they need to renew their medical licenses.

US-based physicians can claim *AMA PRA Category 1 Credit*™ in systems outside the United States by attending international conferences or congresses that meet AMA guidelines for CME. AMA also converts select CME credits issued by the European Union of Medical Specialists/European Accreditation Council for Continuing Medical Education, the Royal College of Physicians and Surgeons of Canada, and the Qatar Council for Healthcare Practitioners to *AMA PRA Category 1 Credit*™.

How Other Health Professionals Claim Credit

Continuing education for nurses is generally measured in terms of contact hours rather than credit hours. The American Nurses Credentialing Center (ANCC) accepts *AMA PRA Category 1 Credit*™ for recertification. Many US state boards of nursing accept ANCC contact hours and relicensure. Nurses and other nonphysician health professionals can participate in activities that are designated for

AMA PRA Category 1 Credit™ and apply those credits toward their CE requirements for recertification. Pharmacists claim continuing pharmacy credits (CPE) through the Accreditation Council for Pharmacy Education (ACPE). States vary tremendously in the content requirements for each profession.

Pro Tip[11]

What is the correct AMA credit designation statement?

As a writer, if you are working on a needs assessment, grant proposal, or content, you should see this language somewhere in the content:

The [name of accredited provider] designates this educational activity for a maximum of [number of credits] *AMA PRA Category 1 Credit(s)*™. Physicians should only claim credit commensurate with the extent of their participation in the activity.

How and when does the AMA trademark need to be used?

The complete phrase in italics with trademark symbol (*AMA PRA Category 1 Credit*™) is required the first time it is mentioned in a publication (e.g., grant proposal, syllabus). The complete phrase is also required in every designation statement and on certificates, if issued.

Conclusion

The intricate scaffolding of accreditation and credit systems have evolved to uphold the trustworthiness of CME/CE.[13] Rigorous accreditation oversight helps champion education that addresses authentic practice gaps and proactively builds public assurance that clinicians pursue regular learning that is responsive to emergent health care needs. In the past, physician credit systems were time-, participant-, and knowledge-based. Physicians showed up, provided feedback on the value of the education activity, and were given credit for their attendance. Over time, credit systems have shifted to include competency-based learning, quality and performance improvement, and point-of-care learning. These accreditation and credit systems exist within wider ethical and regulatory frameworks that have emerged to ensure that industry-funded education is protected from commercial influence. Let's explore these in Chapter 3.

Key Takeaways

- Accreditation ensures quality and independence of CME/CE
- ACCME is the main accrediting body in the US
- Joint Accreditation facilitates interprofessional continuing education
- Credit systems reward clinicians for participation in lifelong learning

Chapter 3

Compliance and Ethics

Education without values, as useful as it is, seems rather to make man a more clever devil.

— C.S. LEWIS

Introduction

How can CME/CE medical writers balance the need for accurate scientific representation with the pressure to create content that aligns with pharmaceutical industry interests? You would think there was no need to even ask this question, but you'd be wrong. I once worked on a CME/CE project where a supporter complained that faculty did not give sufficient attention to the supporter's therapy in a live preconference education session. Subsequently, the education provider asked me to include additional material about the supporter's product in the downloadable slide deck "to keep the supporter happy." This behavior flouts a fair and balanced approach to content, threatens content integrity, and damages the regulatory firewall.

History of Federal Regulations

There are many laws and federal policies that regulate relationships, entities, and structures in CME/CE. You don't have to know the ins and outs of all of them, but you should have a general understanding of broad principles and their implications for developing compliant, ethically sound CME/CE content.

Until fairly recently, medicine has largely been a self-regulating profession that internally develops and enforces standards of professional practice. Several laws now exist to prevent improper financial relationships from influencing medical decision-making, protect the integrity of federal health care programs, and ensure that patient care is driven by clinical considerations rather than financial gain.

Many of these laws were established in the late 1990s or early 2000s in response to federal concerns about relationships between pharmaceutical manufacturers and physicians, conflicts of interest that could arise in the context of Medicare's prescription-drug benefit program, and exchanges of information or service between health professionals and pharmaceutical manufacturers. In the early 2000s, for instance, physicians still received gifts from pharmaceutical companies, including pens, memo pads, meals, educational trips (take the family skiing in Colorado! Cruise Alaska!), consulting fees, and research grants.[1] The pharmaceutical industry was able to sweep physicians away to exotic places to educate—or persuade—them on how to use new therapies and medical devices.

But, as French sociologist Marcel Mauss noted, the gift is never free.[2] Gifts to physicians, however small, have the potential to bias decision-making and undermine public trust in medicine. In practice, these gifts have biased decision-making. They still do. One recent study published in the *Journal of the American Medical Association* showed that physicians receiving a low-dollar meal gift from a pharmaceutical company promoting a particular drug were more than twice as likely to prescribe the drug being promoted than other similar drugs.[3] The number of times they prescribed the drug also increased directly in proportion to the number of meals provided.

There are several cases in which clinicians have selected therapies or made drug purchasing decisions that have resulted in substantial personal or group practice profit. One notable case involving TAP Pharmaceuticals and the drug Lupron sparked changes in legislation.

Lupron[4–5]

Two internal whistleblowers in 2001 at Takeda Chemical Industries and Abbott Laboratories, known collectively as TAP Pharmaceuticals, told federal officials that TAP was engaged in illegal drug sales practices. The case found that TAP encouraged urologists to bill Medicare for the average wholesale price of Lupron, a widely used drug. This arrangement led to significant profits for urologists who were receiving the drug at no cost or at a discounted rate. The investigation also uncovered that TAP had been hiring physicians as consultants without requiring any actual consulting services from them. The company was also reported to have offered educational seminars that included free travel for clinicians and educational grants, raising questions about the ethical boundaries between educational support and promotional activities. TAP agreed to pay $875 million to settle the health care fraud charges against them.

While industry provides crucial support for scientific research and innovation, financial interests also pose threats if allowed to directly influence clinical activities and prescribing behaviors. Physicians have historically been the main prescribers in the health care ecosystem. The TAP/Lupron case and numerous others put the relationship between physicians and pharmaceutical manufacturers under intense scrutiny and increasingly subject to federal oversight. The rest of this chapter will review this.

What is the Regulatory Firewall?

The U.S. Federal Drug Administration (FDA) allows pharmaceutical and biomedical device manufacturers to award grants to third-party organizations for accredited or IME activities, providing they are strictly focused on education versus promoting pharmaceutical products and medical devices.[6] The FDA and the Department of Health and Human Services Office of the Inspector General (OIG) view educational grants that are supported by pharmaceutical manufacturers as a risk area for potential fraud and abuse. But they also recognize that pharmaceutical grants supporting IME generally pose little risk of fraud or abuse and provide a valuable way for physicians to enhance their knowledge and skills and stay up to date on diagnostic and treatment advancements.

Nonetheless, the OIG, the FDA *Guidance for Industry*, and the PhRMA Code have established policies that require a clear separation between educational content and promotional activities, prohibiting direct influence over the educational material by companies.[6–8]

Separation of marketing and medical activities. Strict regulations require that commercial activities within pharmaceutical organizations be detached from medical education activities. This separation is crucial to prevent the promotion of therapeutic products from influencing medical education.

Unrestricted educational grants. Pharmaceutical companies can support independent CME events through unrestricted educational grants and sponsorships. These grants should come with no strings attached, meaning that the company providing the grant should not have any control over the content, faculty, or materials used in the CME activity.

Prohibition of direct influence. The FDA enforces guidelines that prohibit pharmaceutical and device companies from directly influencing the content or faculty of CME programs they fund. Companies are not allowed to offer financial support for travel, lodging, or personal expenses of nonfaculty health care professionals attending CME events, nor can they compensate for the time spent by health care professionals participating in the event.

No direct meals or entertainment. Companies should not directly pay for meals at CME events. If a CME provider chooses to provide meals at a company-funded CME event, the CME provider must pay for the meals from the financial support received and the food must be provided for all participants. Additionally, companies should not offer entertainment or recreational items to health care professionals in relation to CME events.

Compliance with ACCME standards. Financial support for CME should be in line with the standards established by ACCME or other accrediting entities. This includes ensuring that the CME provider retains independent judgment and control over the selection of content, faculty, educational methods, materials, and venue.

The FDA does not have a system in place to monitor the compliance of educational activities and programs. That job falls to education providers to review their internal compliance processes and financial arrangements with health professionals to detect potential violations of federal law and to maintain accreditation status. Violation of compliance can be self-reported or reported by a third party to the ACCME.

ACCME requires accredited CME providers to establish a robust firewall policy to prevent commercial influence on CME content and activities that include the following components:[9]

- Independence regarding decisions about the disposition and disbursement of commercial support
- Disclosure from everyone who is in a position to control the content of an education activity of all relevant financial relationships with ineligible companies

- Mechanisms to identify and resolve all conflicts of interest prior to the education activity being developed and delivered to learners
- Policies regarding relationships between education providers and their other business development activities
- Written policies and procedures governing honoraria and reimbursement of out-of-pocket expenses for planners, teachers, and authors
- Direct payment of honoraria or reimbursement for out-of-pocket expenses from the education provider to any teacher or author
- Product-promotion material or product-specific advertisements of any type are prohibited in or during CME activities

The Stark Law and the Anti-Kickback Statute

Pharmaceutical and medical device companies, as well as other commercial entities, are major financial supporters of accredited CME/CE activities. Both Stark Law and the Anti-Kickback Statute (AKS) are designed to prevent overuse of services, eliminate improper influences on health care decisions, and to prevent financial incentives from influencing medical decisions, ensuring that patient care decisions are based on medical need rather than financial gain.

Stark Law

The Stark Law, also known as the physician self-referral law and named after Congressman Pete Stark, is designed to prevent conflicts of interest in physician referrals.[10] The law prohibits physicians from referring patients to receive care or "designated health services" payable by Medicare or Medicaid from entities with which the physician (or an immediate family member) has a financial relationship, unless an exception applies. This civil law does not carry criminal penalties, but violations can result in significant fines and exclusion from federal health programs.

Anti-Kickback Statute (AKS)

The AKS is a criminal law that prohibits the exchange (or offer to exchange) of anything of value, not just cash, in an effort to induce or reward the referral of federal health care program business. This statute prohibits offering or accepting kickbacks and makes it illegal to knowingly and willfully offer, pay, or provide gifts, payments, or anything of value to induce an individual or entity to recommend or prescribe a product or service that is reimbursed by the government.[11]

The AKS is broad and applies to a broad range of participants in the health care system, including doctors, procurement staff, and marketing/advertising/sales personnel. Violation of the AKS is a felony with serious penalties, and it also results in liability under the False Claims Act (FCA).

The AKS provides safe harbors with clear guidelines for defining practices and structuring business relationships to avoid implicating the AKS. Organizations must ensure that their arrangements precisely meet the conditions outlined in the safe harbor to benefit from this protection.

Implications for CME/CE Content, Funding, and Structure

Stark Law underscores the importance of being transparent about content sources and avoiding content that could be perceived as promoting self-referral practices that violate the statute. When developing CME/CE materials, writers should ensure that any discussion of services, products, or treatments is evidence-based, balanced, and free of any suggestion that might encourage or endorse a self-referral arrangement that could be construed as noncompliant with Stark Law.

Both Stark Law and the AKS are designed to reduce potential conflicts via financial relationships, rewards, or referrals between physicians and entities providing designated health services. When CME/CE providers seek funding for and develop educational activities, they typically consider the parties involved in education to ensure compliance with these laws.[12] They assess funding sources, faculty relationships with pharmaceutical companies, and monitor the design and delivery of CME/CE content to avoid any potential violations of the law. They exercise due diligence to ensure the independence and objectivity of the educational content and to ensure it is free from any influence that could be perceived as a violation of these laws.

Off-Label Uses

I remember listening to a dinner conversation about off-label uses between two seasoned medical writers at an AMWA conference in 2010 or so. I had been writing needs assessments and a little activity content by then and had already taken Eve Wilson's workshop on CME.

But I did not understand off-label use, how it differs from off-label marketing, or why these terms are important to understand in developing CME/CE content.

Here is why:

Off-label use. Off-label use refers to prescribing or using a drug or medical device for an indication, dosage, purpose, or patient population not approved by the FDA. Prescribers have latitude to use drugs and medical devices off-label, as long as they believe such use will benefit the patient and base their decisions on "firm scientific rationale."[13] Off-label prescriptions account for between 20 and 30 percent of prescriptions overall.[14] Prescribing health professionals can discuss off-label uses with individual patients as well as at medical conferences with other providers. However, they are not allowed to promote off-label use to the general public, to a general practice, or to groups of physicians.[14] Discussion of off-label uses of approved products is permitted in independent, nonpromotional educational activities, such as accredited CME/CE, as long as the discussion is scientifically balanced and clearly labeled as off-label.

Off-Label Use

How do we know if health care providers are using a medication off-label? Where is the best place to find current treatment options to double-check if medications are being used off-label? About 20 percent of drugs are prescribed off-label, according to the National Task Force on CME/CE Provider/Industry Collaboration.[15] The best place to find up-to-date information about drug labeling is the FDA Label Database,[16] especially the searchable Drug Approvals and Databases.[17] NIH/NLM's DailyMed database is also easy to search, easy to read, and overall very user friendly.[18]

Off-label promotion. Off-label promotion or marketing involves the illegal act of promoting or advertising the use of a drug or device for anything other than its FDA-approved use.[14] Off-label promotion is considered "misbranding" and is prohibited by the FDA. Pharmaceutical and device manufacturers are not allowed to engage in any form of marketing that encourages off-label use, such as providing promotional materials, organizing seminars, or sharing information with health professionals about off-label uses. Pharmaceutical companies can be prosecuted for promoting their products off-label under the False Claims Act (FCA), which imposes liability on individuals and entities that defraud governmental programs, including Medicare and Medicaid, by knowingly submitting false claims for payment or by promoting off-label products.

The False Claims Act[14]

The FDA's limitations on promoting off-label uses in CME/CE activities are designed to ensure that medical education remains independent and evidence-based, free from the influence of promotional activities that could compromise patient safety and public health. Pharmaceutical companies can be prosecuted for promoting their products off-label under the False Claims Act, which imposes liability on individuals and entities that defraud governmental programs, including Medicare and Medicaid, by knowingly submitting false claims for payment or by promoting off-label products.

◇◇

The FDA's restrictions on discussing off-label uses in CME/CE activities include the following:[13–14]

1. **Prohibition of direct promotion.** Pharmaceutical and device manufacturers are not allowed to directly promote off-label uses of their products during CME activities. This includes activities such as providing promotional materials, organizing seminars, or engaging in any form of marketing that encourages off-label use.
2. **Physician's freedom to prescribe off-label.** While manufacturers are restricted from promoting off-label uses, physicians are legally allowed to prescribe drugs for off-label uses. However, the FDA prohibits manufacturers from influencing or encouraging physicians to prescribe their products for off-label uses.
3. **Regulatory oversight.** The FDA closely monitors and enforces regulations related to off-label promotion. Companies that engage in off-label marketing can face (and often have faced) legal consequences, including lawsuits, fines, and other penalties.

In summary, the FDA's limitations on promoting off-label uses in CME activities are designed to ensure that medical education remains independent and evidence-based, free from the influence of promotional activities that could compromise patient safety and public health. Any educational content that refers to off-label use must be clearly identified as such. As a writer, you need to be clear about the approved indications for therapies and devices and ensure that any mention of off-label use in a live meeting or enduring materials emphasizes it as such.

HIV/AIDS[19]

A case using the FCA and the AKS is ongoing on behalf of the federal government against two medical sales reps for Tibotec Therapeutics, a subsidiary company of Johnson & Johnson that later rebranded as Janssen. The reps are charged with marketing HIV drugs by presenting misleading messages to physicians about lipid neutrality, efficacy and safety, mechanism of action, and dosing schedule. The reps say that upper management encouraged them and the national sales team to use the allegedly misleading marketing messaging. The cases also accuse Janssen of providing kickbacks to physicians associated with its speaker program via honoraria amounts that were tied to the volume of prescriptions they wrote for the HIV drugs. At the time of writing, this case is still ongoing.

The PhRMA Code

In 2002, the Pharmaceutical Research and Manufacturers of America (PhRMA) developed a *Code on Interactions with Health Care Professionals* to govern the interactions between pharmaceutical companies and health care professionals, including those related to CME/CE.[8] The PhRMA Code is based on the principle that a health professional's care of patients should be based solely on each patient's medical needs and the health care professional's medical knowledge and experience.

The PhRMA Code emphasizes the importance of providing health care professionals with accurate, balanced, and scientifically rigorous information about prescription medicines. It outlines the principles for appropriate marketing of medicines, ensuring that patients have access to the products they need and that the products are used correctly for maximum patient benefit. The Code also addresses how scientific and educational information should be provided to health professionals, how pharmaceutical manufacturers should support medical research and education, and how to obtain feedback and advice about products through consultation with medical experts. The PhRMA Code was last updated in August 2021.

Physician Payments Sunshine Act

The Physician Payments Sunshine Act (PPSA) was introduced in 2021 to increase transparency around the financial interactions between drug and medical device manufacturers, physicians, and teaching hospitals, and to expose financial relationships that might influence clinical decisions.[20] The grants that manufacturers give to accredited education providers are excluded from the PPSA, providing that the manufacturer does not require, instruct, direct, or otherwise cause the education provider to make payments or transfers of value to educational program faculty, speakers, authors, or attendees.[21]

The Centers for Medicare & Medicaid Services (CMS) oversees this initiative via an Open Payments program, which requires manufacturers to annually report any payments or other transfers of value to health care providers.[22] The Open Payments database is available for public viewing. The PPSA encourages physicians to actively review and correct their records to maintain the accuracy of the data. Before information in the database about payments is publicly disclosed, physicians can examine and dispute their records.

Disclosures of Conflicts of Interest

The laws and policies described in this chapter refer to conflicts of interest (COI). What are these and why are they important?

Trust

COIs arise in health care when health professionals are in situations where they might be persuaded or induced to choose one specific drug or device over another because they stand to gain financial, reputational, or some other benefit as a result of that choice. COIs have the potential to breach trust, which is part of the social contract glue that binds patients to health professionals. Patients trust their health care providers to serve their best interests and make clinical decisions based on the best available evidence. In turn, health professionals are obliged to make decisions that serve their patients, rather than their own financial or reputational interests.

Definition of a Conflict of Interest

COI typically refers to financial conflicts, although other types of COI are possible. COI occurs when an individual (e.g. a subject matter expert, content creator, or faculty) has both a financial relationship with an ineligible company and the opportunity to affect the content of an educational activity. This relationship can compromise the educational activity's objectivity, balance, and scientific rigor, leading to biased information that may not serve the best interest of learners or patients. Managing and disclosing COIs is crucial to maintain the integrity, objectivity, and scientific rigor of educational content.[23]

While the phrase COI is used, the ACCME prefers the wording "financial relationships with ineligible companies." As defined in Chapter 2, ineligible companies are those whose primary business is producing, marketing, selling, re-selling, or distributing health care products used by or on patients. The accredited provider must determine if the collected financial relationships are relevant. If so, they must be mitigated and disclosed to learners.

Who Should Disclose

Anyone who is involved in developing education content should disclose their financial relationships.

1. **Speakers/authors.** Individuals who are responsible for planning, presenting, or authoring content for CME/CE activities.

2. **Planning committee members.** Those involved in the conceptualization, development, and review of the educational activity. This includes you, the writer.
3. **Content reviewers.** Individuals who review CME/CE content for accuracy, balance, and the presence of commercial bias.
4. **Staff.** Organizational staff involved in the planning and implementation of the activity.

What Should Be Disclosed

The AMA and ACCME define a financial relationship as any relationship in which an individual benefits by receiving a salary, royalty, intellectual property rights, consulting fee, honoraria, ownership interest (e.g., stocks, stock options, or other ownership interest, excluding diversified mutual funds), or other financial benefit from an ineligible company.[24] Education providers develop in-house forms to collect COI information that all individuals working on content, including writers, must disclose. This information includes the following relevant financial relationships with any an ineligible company that could potentially influence the content of the educational activity:

1. **Remuneration.** Salary, stock ownership, stock options, royalties, consulting fees, honoraria, or reimbursement for speaking.
2. **Gifts.** Endowments, sponsorship of trips, support of training (such as fellowships), and other sponsorships.
3. **Research support.** Company support for research, including equipment, biomaterials, discretionary funds, and support of office or research staff.
4. **Leadership positions.** Holding office in a company, such as positions on the board of directors or scientific advisory board.

Processes for Disclosure[9]

1. **Disclosure statement submission.** Prior to their involvement in the activity, folks involved in planning or presenting/authoring

a CME/CE activity complete and submit a disclosure statement of relevant financial relationships with ineligible companies.

2. **Review and mitigate relevant financial relationships.** The CME/CE provider reviews all disclosed financial relationships to determine relevant relationships and, if so, takes steps to mitigate those relationships. This could involve changing the role of the individual in the CME/CE activity, altering the content, or implementing other measures to ensure the activity's integrity.
3. **Disclosure to learners.** All disclosed financial relationships should be shared with learners before the educational activity begins via printed materials, verbal announcements, or on digital platforms.
4. **Content validation.** Presentations must be fair, balanced, and based on scientific evidence. As we discussed earlier in this chapter, any discussion of unlabeled (off-label) or investigational use of products must be clearly disclosed to the audience.
5. **Peer review.** CME/CE content is subject to external peer review prior to publication or going live to evaluate validity, ensure fair and balanced content, and review for bias or the perception of bias. Technically peer review is not required per ACCME, although it is certainly best practice and is considered an accepted mitigation protocol for an identified relevant financial relationship.

ACCME created a handy tool for identifying, mitigating, and disclosing relevant financial relationships.[24]

Why COI is Important

The manifest reason for disclosure is to maintain separation between commercial influence and educational content. The profit motive is a powerful incentive for many people and the pharmaceutical industry is largely a for-profit industry with strong interests in maximizing that profit. Many subject matter experts and expert faculty work with pharmaceutical manufacturers outside the CME/CE context as advisory board members, speakers, and clinical trial investigators. They own stock or equity and might receive consulting fees or patent royalties.[25] When the people creating educational content also have a stake in the therapies or devices that are the focus of that content, one might assume a COI.

You might own stock or equity too. If you own stock or equity in the pharmaceutical manufacturer supporting a CME/CE activity, you need to disclose your ownership as a potential COI.

The broader ethical question is whether COI disclosures work. If I am expert faculty contributing to an accredited CME/CE activity and disclose financial, advisory board, and research relationships with multiple commercial entities, does this disclosure add confidence to the trustworthiness of the content? Or is it simply smoke and mirrors?

To ensure transparency and avoid even the perception of COI, some academic centers and health systems, like the Mayo Clinic, forbid faculty from accepting honoraria as part of their CME/CE contributions. This divestment strategy ensures that academic faculty are not entangled with the pharmaceutical industry in ways that could undermine public and professional trust in medicine.

Trust, Integrity, and Fair and Balanced Content

As with conflict of interest, federal regulations emphasize the importance of developing content for CME activities that is fair and balanced. "Fair and balanced" means that the content does not promote the therapies, interventions, or devices of one pharmaceutical company over another.

From time to time, medicine, science, and the pharmaceutical industry contend with lapses in public trust, often through industry relationships with health professionals and health systems that have pushed acceptable boundaries and sought to influence clinical decision-making and prescribing behaviors. According to Graham McMahon, MD, president and CEO of the ACCME, integrity is the foundation for continuing education that clinicians can trust to improve their practice and that the public can trust as a source for improvement in patient care. CME/CE providers can foster trust and content integrity by delivering relevant, high-quality content that is fair and balanced and aligns with clinician needs. As reliable curators of evidence, CME/CE plays an important role in elevating expertise over misinformation through rigorous, impartial education that is designed through a transparent process and supported by credible, trustworthy sources of evidence.

The 2020 ACCME *Standards for Integrity and Independence in Accredited Continuing Education* were developed to address emerging threats to the integrity of CME/CE, particularly in contexts where industry seeks to sway clinician prescribing behaviors.[9] The standards ensure the strict separation of education from promotion, independence from industry influence, and affirm the importance of accurate, balanced content. Multiple health profession accreditors have adopted these standards to uphold independence as the cornerstone of accredited CME/CE.

ACCME 2020 *Standards for Integrity and Independence in Accredited Continuing Education*

The standards aim to:[9]

- Protect CME/CE from commercial bias and marketing influence from pharmaceutical and medical device companies.
- Ensure recommendations are based on scientific evidence and serve patient care needs, not industry interests.
- Require CME/CE providers to identify and mitigate relevant financial relationships between faculty/planners and industry.

- Prohibit employees of pharmaceutical and device companies from controlling CME/CE content, with few exceptions.
- Allow commercial support from industry for CME/CE only if certain independence rules are followed.
- Require clear separation between accredited education and marketing activities before/after CME/CE events.
- Limit industry influence on decisions about CME/CE planning, delivery, and evaluation.
- Mandate disclosure to learners about relevant faculty/planner financial relationships and commercial support.

◇◇

The ACEHP recently developed a formal code of ethics that speaks to the integrity of CME/CE.[26] It sets standards for behavior, intention, equity, and applicability for the work of CME/CE professionals, including:

- Create evidence-based content
- Promote the value of continuing education
- Protect the integrity of continuing education
- Embrace the social justice dimensions of continuing education
- Develop and support activities that help learners meet educational needs
- Design interprofessional activities to advance patient safety, teamwork, and quality improvement
- Engage and support learners in their own professional development and promote collaborative practice
- Participate as essential stakeholders in the legal, regulatory, and ethical framework of continuing education

While the ACCME does not police individual CME/CE activities, it ensures the integrity of continuing medical education by providing oversight of the CME/CE field through its accreditation and standards-setting process.

Ties That Bind

It is generally accepted in CME/CE that pharmaceutical manufacturers are instrumental in developing new tests, treatments, and devices. This field, alongside academic medicine, views industry as important partners in educating health professionals about therapies, devices, and interventions, provided they do so in a way that does not influence clinical decision-making, treatment selection, or referral to specific clinicians or health care facilities.[25]

But it is important to be aware that commercial interests are baked into the health ecosystem. For instance, the opioid epidemic in the United States demonstrates how the pharmaceutical industry established ties with multiple entities, including clinicians and health systems that provide direct care to patients, as well as politicians, regulators, and other entities that indirectly influence health care delivery.[27] Financial and nonfinancial ties between industry and the wider health ecosystem are deeply intertwined, complex, and extensive. In 2009, the Institute of Medicine published *Conflict of Interest in Medical Research.* This report, alongside other journal articles at the time, documented the range of industry influence on the wider health care ecosystem and the various ways that health care providers, researchers, clinical care facilities, journals, professional societies, and other health care organizations collaborate with pharmaceutical, medical device, and biotechnology product manufacturers to deliver patient care, conduct research, and provide clinical education.[28]

Sometimes this labyrinthine set of relationships and tacit assumptions creeps into the CME/CE content creation process. For instance, as writers, we need to be aware that when pharmaceutical manufacturers issue RFPs for proposals to design and deliver educational programs or activities, they have internal objectives that they expect the education they support to meet. The business and sales managers within education provider organizations know this. Their role in securing funding via the grant development process involves a delicate dance to ensure content remains firmly within the 2020 ACCME standards framework, yet also implicitly appeals to supporter interests. At times, they might zealously or tacitly communicate these interests to writers.

Recognize any requests from business or sales strategists to over-egg a needs assessment with reference to the potential supporter's therapy or device as counter to the principle of developing fair and balanced content. Similarly, when needs assessments are narrowly focused on a specific therapy versus objectively identifying clinical and professional practice gaps, content is already skewed toward supporter interests. Writing extensively about clinical trial data for one particular therapy is a common way that content gets skewed.

Established Ties That Bind[29]

These deeply connected and intertwined relationships between the health care ecosystem and medical products remain. Medical product ties include money or items of financial value, like supply chain price negotiation, journal reprints, or consultancy, speaker, and key opinion leader fees. Nonfinancial ties include direct-to-consumer advertising to patients, gift authorship to clinicians or researchers, or the offer of access to data. A scoping review of published manuscripts and articles that mapped the ties between different sectors and stakeholders in the health care ecosystem found an extensive network of medical product industry ties to research, health care education, guideline development, formulary selection, and clinical care through nonprofit entities such as patient advocacy groups, health professionals, the market supply chain (e.g., payers), and government (e.g., public officials). Ties were established

> and maintained with individual health professionals (in 78 percent of the included studies), publications (56 percent), clinical care (29 percent), health professional education (27 percent), guideline development (6 percent), and formulary selection (1 percent). Policies for conflicts of interest exist for some financial and a few nonfinancial ties; publicly available data sources seldom describe or quantify these ties.

Compliance Tips for Writers

Focus on evidence. Ensure that all CME/CE content is rooted in the latest evidence-based guidelines and research findings. Evaluate and reference all scientific evidence to support the claims you or faculty make. When collaborating with faculty as subject matter experts, ensure that the information they provide is accurate and supported by evidence. Trust no one. Check everything. Avoid making unsubstantiated claims about the safety or efficacy of medical products or services. I know you won't—just be aware.

Maintain neutrality. Strive for balanced discussions of therapeutic options, including a fair representation of risks and benefits, without giving undue emphasis to any product or service that could benefit specific providers or entities. When referring to therapies, use generic versus brand names, and avoid using brand colors in graphics or illustrations.

Avoid promoting specific providers. Content should not implicitly or explicitly suggest that learners refer patients to specific providers of designated health services, especially if there is a financial relationship that could be construed as falling foul of the Stark Law.

Follow the money. A little understanding of financial relationships goes a long way. It is not your job to police your clients or employers, but be aware of the financial relationships between educational content supporters and service providers as we discussed earlier in this chapter.

Disclosures should be clearly stated in CME/CE materials to inform learners of these relationships.

Writers as Bricks in the Firewall

Chapter 3 has described several policies in place to ensure that the content being used to educate health professionals is free from bias and commercial influence. These policies also establish a regulatory framework that CME/CE professionals must remain compliant with and provide oversight to reduce the potential for conflict of interest.

Medical writers are instrumental in developing content for the purpose of educating health professionals on how to provide care for and treat patients. As such, we are bricks in the firewall between industry and education, charged with maintaining content accuracy, independence, and integrity. It's our job to ensure that content meets the requirements of accreditation, so we need to be meticulous in the sources we review and use to create content, and conscientious about developing the content. Some companies also have explicit policies that disallow writers from working on both sides of the firewall; that is, in both CME and promotional content.

Stay informed about the regulatory requirements and industry standards related to the development of CME/CE content. Check the CME Coalition (www.cmecoalition.org/) and ACHEP (www.acehp.org) for updates. This includes understanding the legal and regulatory framework governing promotional activities, off-label use, and appropriate referencing of scientific evidence. Be diligent in your research, transparent in your sourcing, and committed to upholding the highest standards of ethical conduct. By doing so, you will contribute to the dissemination of reliable, evidence-based information that supports health care professionals in delivering optimal patient care, while remaining compliant with the FDA and other relevant regulations.

Key Takeaways

- Multiple laws and regulations govern CME/CE
- Commercial influence must be strictly separated from educational content
- Off-label use discussions are permitted, but must be clearly labeled
- Conflict of interest disclosures are crucial
- Stay informed about relevant laws and regulations
- Maintain a strong ethical compass in content creation

Developing CME in the Real World

Chapter 4

The Context of Health Care

America's health care system is neither healthy, caring, nor a system.

— WALTER CRONKITE

Introduction

This chapter explores the health care landscape (including shared decision-making, quality improvement, and health systems as learning systems) as not only the context that informs educational content but also the setting in which learning occurs.

The Context of Health Care

Health professionals across disciplines face immense pressure in today's fast-paced health care environment. The combination of packed schedules, administrative burdens, technological demands, and resource constraints leaves little time for full deliberation and introduces increased risk for errors or lapses in clinical decision-making and judgment. Physicians conduct back-to-back patient appointments with 15 minutes or less allotted per person, relying on electronic health records and prescription systems to keep up with the clinical information firehose. Nurses manage overloaded patient assignments while continually receiving alerts for new diagnostic results and medication orders. With extended shifts and overtime becoming the norm, exhaustion compounds the effects of ongoing stress.

Health care workers, including nurses and physicians, face stressful conditions that can lead to fatigue and increased risk of errors due to interruptions and distractions during critical tasks. Lack of adequate resources, poor ergonomic design, and exposure to health hazards like infectious diseases further contribute to stress and physical exhaustion among health care professionals.

The load on clinician cognitive bandwidth means even minor additional stresses can negatively impact information processing, analytical thinking, and decision-making. For example, an alert from a patient monitor, a question from a family member, or a missing lab report easily breaks concentration when a physician attempts a complex diagnosis. Likewise, a brief workplace conflict or momentary lack of focus may lead to mistakes in dosing medications or assessing patient vital signs. An abundance of technology has not alleviated time pressures. In many cases, it has made them worse. Without systems changes to improve work-life balance, support team collaboration, and reduce unnecessary tasks, clinicians will continue to face overload and burnout.

As a writer and CME/CE professional, it is important to be aware that health professionals operate in dynamic situations that require quick, in-the-moment decision-making. They constantly have to make risk assessments in diagnosing and treating patients. Additionally, the increasing prevalence and complexity of chronic disease involves prolonged management with multiple primary and specialist providers, as well as across hospital and community settings that require care coordination and collaboration. None of this is easy, even after years of professional training.

Supporting the Health Care Team

In addition, the concept of the health care team has become increasingly crucial. Modern health care delivery relies on a diverse, interdisciplinary team of professionals, each bringing unique skills and perspectives to patient care. This team may include physicians, nurses, pharmacists, therapists, social workers, and specialists, all working collaboratively to provide comprehensive, patient-centered care. The shift towards team-based care is driven by the recognition that no single professional can effectively manage all aspects of a patient's health, particularly in the context of chronic diseases and complex health conditions.

Patients as Active Partners

Patients are at the core of the health care team with unique insights into their own health, values, and preferences that are crucial for effective care planning and delivery. Patients are not passive recipients of care, but active partners in the decision-making process. This shift is reflected in concepts like shared decision-making and patient engagement, which emphasize the importance of patient input in treatment choices. Patients bring valuable perspectives regarding their symptoms, treatment effects, and quality of life that complement the clinical expertise of health care professionals. Moreover, patients often serve as the bridge between various health care providers, especially in fragmented care systems, and play a critical role in care coordination, medication management, and implementing lifestyle changes. As CME/CE professionals, it is essential to consider how educational content can support health care professionals in effectively engaging patients as team members. This might involve developing communication skills, understanding health literacy challenges, or learning strategies to empower patients in self-management.

What Health Professionals Do

What do health professionals do? This sounds like a silly question, especially if you have a clinical background, as many medical writers and other CME/CE professionals do. It might also sound silly if you have been a patient. But it's not silly in the context of CME/CE. As we have seen in earlier chapters, health professionals have different training, roles, responsibilities, and professional identities that all contribute to the type of continuing education content they need. Each profession has its own credentialing and accreditation bodies, too.

Health Professional Roles and Responsibilities

Health Professional	Role	Responsibilities
Physicians (MD, DO, MBBS)	Diagnose diseases and conditions and treat patients	• Conduct physical exams • Order and interpret diagnostic tests • Diagnose and treat illnesses/ injuries • Prescribe medications • Counsel patients • Perform surgical and medical procedures • Supervise residents, fellows, students • Conduct research
Advanced Practice Registered Nurse (NP, CNS, specialty nurses)	Practices independently without physician oversight in some states	• Conduct exams • Diagnose and treat acute/ chronic illnesses • Prescribe medications • Manage patient care • Provide preventive care • Collaborate with physicians

Health Professional	Role	Responsibilities
Pharmacist (RPh, PharmD-Retail)	Dispenses medications/ provides medication-related education	• Fill prescriptions • Counsel patients on medication use • Monitor drug interactions/ allergies • Recommend OTC products • Manage pharmacy operations
Pharmacist (RPh, PharmD-Hospital)	Manages therapies, educates providers and patients on dosing, titration, side effect management	• Review and verify medication orders • Prepare and dispense medications • Collaborate with health care team on patient medication management • Monitor patient responses to medications • Make recommendations on drug therapy • Educate patients
Physician Assistant/ Associate	Licensed clinicians who practice medicine	• Examine patients • Diagnose and treat illnesses • Develop treatment plans • Assist in medical procedures and surgeries • Order and interpret tests • Prescribe medications in some states

Health Professional	**Role**	**Responsibilities**
Nurse (LPN, RN)	Provide care and support	• Provide bedside care • Monitor patient health • Administer medications and treatment • Educate patients and families about care • Monitor/manage treatment-related side effects • Assist with ADLs • Collaborate with health care team
Medical Assistant	Performs clinical and administrative tasks	• Room patients • Record medical histories and personal information • Measure vital signs • Assist with patient examinations • Prepare blood samples for laboratory tests • Collect samples for testing • Sterilize instruments • Administer medications • Schedule appointments
Dietitian	Provides nutrition and diet-related advice	• Assess patient nutritional needs • Develop and implement dietary plans • Educate patients on healthy eating habits

Health Professional	Role	Responsibilities
Occupational Therapist	Assist patients in developing, recovering, or maintaining daily living skills	• Analyze patient needs • Develop individualized treatment plans • Teach skills for daily living and working
Physical Therapist	Helps patients improve movement/ mobility and manage pain	• Develop rehabilitation plans • Guide patients through exercises • Use techniques to alleviate pain and improve mobility
Social Worker	Provides support and resources to patients and families	• Assess patients' social and emotional needs • Connect patients with community resources • Provide counseling and support

Sources: Classifying health workers: Mapping occupations to the international standard classification. Geneva: World Health Organization; 2019; aapa.org; Ulrich A. Continuing education writing: Know your clinician audience. AMWA Journal. 2023;38(2):43–46

It is easiest to write content that resonates with your audience when you have a deep understanding of their pressing needs and issues. If you have a clinical background, you will likely be on the receiving end of CE content. As someone with clinical experience, you have a clear understanding of the context for which CME/CE content is designed. With this profound understanding of the needs of CME/CE learners, you will be able to write better CME/CE content that captures relevant information in a practical and applicable way.

If you are unfamiliar with the roles, responsibilities, and workplace environment of the target audience you are writing for, ask your colleagues or the faculty involved in the project for a rundown. The World Health Organization provides a detailed list of health professionals and outlines their roles within the health care system.[1] While this list is over a decade old, it is still a useful starting point. The following resources also provide information that will help you learn more about your target audience.

- American Medical Association (ama-assn.org)
- American Nurses Association (nursingworld.org)
- American Academy of PAs (aapa.org)
- American Pharmacists Association (pharmacist.com)
- American Physical Therapy Association (apta.org)
- Center for Health Interprofessional Practice and Education, University of Texas at Austin

If you do not have clinical experience, you must *imagine* what your audience is thinking, feeling, and experiencing. You will need to put yourself in your audience's shoes via audience analysis that at the very least explores the professional background, educational needs, and learning preferences of the audience, and understands their workplace environment, demands, and challenges.

Pro Tip

Eketarina Chachnikova, a medical writer and pharmacist, recommends searching YouTube for recordings of medical webinars and conferences to get access to "insider" information about health professionals. She recommends the list of channels with relevant content from MyMedPharmInfo. I also recommend reading memoirs and lived experience accounts written by physicians, nurses, and other health professionals. Here are some of my favorites:

Jay Baruch, *Tornado of Life*

Jerome Groopman, *How Doctors Think*

Paul Austin, *Something for the Pain: Compassion and Burnout in the ER*

Christie Watson, *The Language of Kindness: A Nurse's Story*

Rachel Clarke, *Breathtaking: The UK's Human Story of Covid*

The Changing Health Care Landscape

Quality in health care has long been subject to scrutiny by policymakers, economists, and politicians, with persistent gaps between evidence-based clinical recommendations and the care that is actually delivered to patients. A seminal RAND study on practice patterns reported that up to 45 percent of patients do not receive recommended care.[2] Many other studies affirm the persistence of too many unplanned readmissions, medication errors, and hospital-acquired infections, as well as suboptimal delivery of primary and secondary prevention of the major diseases that account for chronic conditions. A series of reports from the National Academy of Medicine since 2000 have shone a spotlight on medical errors, gaps in quality, safety, and efficiency, and disparities in the health care system.[3–5] In response to these reports and other drivers, the organization, delivery, and reimbursement of health care in the United States has undergone a seismic process of transformation since 2010. Health care in the United States is an extraordinarily complex environment characterized by at least three notable trends.

Accelerating Science and Innovation

First, therapeutic innovations have accelerated, diagnostic and care management options have multiplied, and biomedical knowledge continues to accumulate at an unprecedented rate. Science moves quickly. Every year, several times a year, a flood of clinical data is presented at conferences and published in peer-reviewed publications. Technology is also transforming health care. Digital health (e.g., electronic health records, social media, mobile apps, wearables, telemedicine, and more), technology-enabled health care (e.g., novel drug delivery solutions and 3D printing), advances such as proteomics in neurology, micro-RNA-based therapies in cardiology, and precision-editing techniques (such as genomics and next-generation sequencing in oncology) have all revolutionized prediction, prognosis, and treatment. Health professionals are expected to stay up to date with the science and the rapid acceleration of therapeutic innovations and make decisions about which therapies to select and how to treat patients. They are also expected to master clinical informatics, systems and human factors engineering, process improvement and safety science, implementation science, health care economics and financing, and leadership.[6]

Health Care Reform

Second, in response to an increasing emphasis on objective clinical outcomes measures as indicators of quality in health care (e.g., readmission rates, patient safety, and care processes), the Institute for Healthcare Improvement's Triple Aim framework identified three goals—better care, better health, and lower cost for all—that have shaped legislative, payment, and care delivery reform since 2010. A series of legislative changes, including the Affordable Care Act (ACA), the Medicare Access and CHIP Reauthorization Act of 2015 (MACRA), the Merit-based Incentive Payment System (MIPS) which is part of the Quality Payment Program (QPP),[7] and the Health Information Technology for Economic and Clinical Health Act (HITECH), placed increasing emphasis on care coordination, team-based care, and patient engagement.

The National Quality Framework reinforced the importance of the effective and timely translation of biomedical research and clinical data into clinical practice, as well as the integration of best practices to organizational, reimbursement, workforce, and information systems.[8] Reimbursement redesign shifted care delivery from a fee-for-service to a fee-for-value model of physician reimbursement via performance metric-based programs such as Medical Advantage, Meaningful Use, and the Patient Quality Reporting System. These risk-bearing, coordinated care models emphasize cost-effectiveness and outcomes-based care. Patient care also transitioned from a physician-centric, hospital-based system to one that encourages new resource- and cost-sharing models to ensure organizational efficiencies (e.g., accountable care organizations). Patients, too, are increasingly part of the decision-making picture, coming to the clinic armed with not only questions that their physicians must be prepared to answer but also personal data generated via mobile health apps and information gleaned from online searches.

As a result, health professionals face enormous pressures to deliver value and bend the cost curve by creating greater efficiencies in care delivery and make cost-efficient care decisions. This pressure is further compounded by staffing shortages and clinical burnout. The National Council of State Boards of Nursing (NCSBN) paints a dismal picture of the current nursing landscape. A 2023 report by NCSBN estimated that 100,000 registered nurses (RNs) left the workforce in 2021–2022 due to stress, burnout, and retirement.[9] Another 610,388 RNs intend to leave the workforce by 2027 for the same reasons. The situation in medicine is just as dire. A competitive intelligence report by Definitive Healthcare estimated that 117,000 physicians left the workforce in 2021 alone due to retirement, burnout, and pandemic-related stressors, with the largest exodus seen in internal medicine, family practice, and emergency medicine.[10]

Information Technology

Information technology is a third factor to consider that affects not only health care delivery and practice, but also the reporting requirements for health professionals on performance indicators, as well as how and when they engage with CME/CE. The ACA, MACRA, and HITECH expanded health information technology as a tool to improve quality through collecting data (for instance, incidence and patient registries) via electronic health records.

Private Equity and The Financialization of Health Care

Health care delivery and ownership is shifting away from independent physician-owned practices toward consolidated models. The percentage of primary care physicians and specialists in practices owned by hospitals or health systems doubled between 2010 and 2018.[11] Private equity firms have actively acquired several specialty groups—over 350 comprising 5,700 physicians across 1,400 plus sites from 2013 to 2016, according to one recent analysis.[12]

Private equity ownership of physician practices and specialty groups and the emphasis on high financial returns for shareholders has potential consequences for health care delivery.[12] The degree of investment required to ensure health care quality and delivery could be displaced, while the emphasis on generating revenue could result in hiring clinicians at lower cost.[13]

The profit motive in US health care is not new. We touched on this briefly in Chapter 1, which noted the incursion of private equity to the field of CME/CE. Private equity is part of a broader process of corporatization and financialization that has been transforming health care in the United States for decades.

Financialization refers to the increasing influence of financial markets, motives, strategies, and elites in society, with a growing number of financial actors driving the health care sector, including commercial and investment banks, private equity, venture capital, and other types of investors.[14] Increasingly, financial considerations play a more significant role than hospital operations in revenue generation, and financial intermediaries and investors view health care organizations as profit-making and wealth-extraction vehicles.[15] The involvement of private equity firms in health care transactions has further contributed to the dismantling and dissection of health care property and service lines as salable assets rather than as services designed to deliver patient care.[16]

The financialization of health care in the United States has significant implications for health equity, patients, and clinicians. Overall, financialization represents a shift from viewing health care as a social good that can improve population health and reduce inequities.[16] Instead, health care is increasingly managed as a commercial venture. Deepening inequities, escalating health care costs, and limiting access to care for many individuals, particularly those from low-income groups, are among the likely consequences of this shift.[15] Clinicians in for-profit, corporately owned health systems face incentives to increase revenue, which can result in overtesting, overdiagnosis, and unnecessary treatments—key targets for the American Board of Internal Medicine Foundation's *Choosing Wisely* campaign.

The influence of financial institutions in the health care industry raises concerns about the ethical and social implications of profit-oriented decision-making, and its potential to compromise patient outcomes and exacerbate health disparities.[14] CME/CE professionals should be aware of the implications of financialization for clinical practice and patient well-being and stay apprised on research, advocacy, and policy interventions that address this development in health care.

Evidence-Based Medicine

Evidence-based medicine (EBM) represents an important milestone in modern medicine that sought to bring more certainty to clinical care. EBM is a systematic approach that involves the conscientious and judicious use of the best available evidence to guide clinical management.[17] The concept of EBM emerged in the early 1990s and gained significant traction due to its emphasis on quantification, statistics, and evidence-based decision-making in health care. David Sackett, a clinical epidemiologist at McMaster University in Canada, pioneered the EBM movement, and Gordon Guyatt, also at McMaster, gave the movement its name.[18] EBM's popularity was rapid, with a surge in publications and dedicated resources like textbooks, journals, and online portals focused on how to appraise evidence and integrate research into clinical practice.[19]

The power of EBM lies in its insistence on using empirical evidence, rather than expert opinion and tradition, as the basis for informed clinical decision-making. Scientific methodology, critical appraisal of a hierarchy of clinical evidence from animal and laboratory studies, the randomized control trial (RCT), and patient values are the foundations for EBM.[20] Overall, the widespread adoption of EBM has transformed the health care landscape by fostering a commitment to lifelong learning, encouraging the rigorous evaluation of scientific literature, and facilitating the implementation of clinical practices supported by the most robust available research findings. EBM is the driver behind the expansion of the Cochrane principles and database as well as other tools and best practices, including protocols, algorithms, and clinical practice guidelines.[21]

Criticisms of EBM

Nonetheless, EBM has sparked debate within the medical community. Critics of EBM point to challenges in what constitutes the "best available evidence" and warn against misusing or over-relying on p-values, publication bias, and problems of validity within systematic reviews and meta-analyses.[22] Additionally, difficulties arise when evidence is inconclusive, inconsistent, irrelevant to clinical realities, or of poor quality. Critics also note that biological variations can hinder the extrapolation of research findings to specific patients and pose challenges for the application of research findings to individual patients.[21] While clinical judgment is paramount in these scenarios, critics fear that EBM's emphasis on internal validity and RCTs as evidentiary gold standards has sidelined the role of clinical judgment, expert knowledge, and patient values in decision-making.[23] The RCT as gold standard also makes it challenging to address the complexities of health care implementation.

There is a call for EBM to evolve toward a more comprehensive understanding of health and health care as complex, nonlinear phenomena that requires a broader range of methodologies beyond traditional RCTs.[21] It's also worth noting that CME/CE has evolved as an excellent mechanism for teasing out the real-world implications of RCT data and the complexity of tailoring evidence-based practices to individual patient needs and values.

Shared Decision-Making

You will often hear CME/CE professionals talking about shared decision-making (SDM) as though it is a new concept. SDM has become increasingly significant in the context of health care reform and the policy shift to value-based care and reimbursement, but it's not really new. In fact, SDM was proposed as an ideal model of treatment in the late 1990s.[24] At its core, SDM is a two-way process of communication that involves clinicians and patients working together to achieve common aims. SDM has made its way into health policy too, as a mechanism to reduce health care practice variations and overuse of treatment options without clear benefit.[25]

The idea is that in a SDM model of care, at least two participants (provider and patient) share information, try to arrive at a consensus about treatment, and work together to reach an agreement on the treatment plan. Including patients in SDM involves discussions about their circumstances and preferences and explores the treatment benefit they anticipate, the support they might require for treatment adherence, and the side effect burden they are willing to bear. In oncology, for instance, effective SDM can lead to better outcomes, improve treatment adherence, reduce care variations, and enhance satisfaction for both patient and providers.[26] In cardiology, SDM can reduce decision conflict for patients and increase their knowledge as a basis for taking an active role in their health.[27]

Although SDM has made its way into some clinical practice guidelines, it is not as widespread in clinical practice as you might think. For one thing, SDM can be hard to execute in the moment. However, several tools support SDM, which is helpful to know about as a CME/CE professional.

A small sampling of these tools includes:

- **GURULZ™**, a decision support tool designed to reduce disparities in health care coverage by arming patients and health care providers with information about their coverage options to support real-time decision-making
- **Prescription to Learn®**, a personalized health GPS that *Cancer101* designed to guide patients with cancer through treatment decision-making
- **The National Quality Task Force Shared Decision-Making Action Brief,** which promotes the value of SDM.[28]

As SDM becomes an increasingly promoted model of patient care and a mechanism for improving value-based outcomes, medical writers should understand the concepts, tools, and challenges involved to effectively communicate its core principles and support its wider adoption in clinical practice.

Understanding Health Systems

Health care is increasingly understood as delivered in the context of interconnected and dependent health provider, patient, and payer systems.[29] Understanding these systems and overarching health care priorities is crucial for effective problem-solving and education design in CME/CE (Chapter 5 describes systems thinking). Per the IHI's Triple Aim, improving population health, effective stewardship of health care resources, and improving the patient care experience continue to be primary goals for health systems.[30] Other critical priorities to enhance the effectiveness and accessibility of health systems include tackling racial disparities, expanding telehealth and in-home services, building integrated systems, and adopting value-based care models.

The quality of health care services is a fundamental aspect of health systems performance, encompassing dimensions like safety, effectiveness, timeliness, patient-centeredness, equity, and efficiency.[31] Quality health care involves delivering the right care, at the right time, in the right way, to the right person; while avoiding overuse, underuse, or misuse of services.[32] The American Board of Internal Medicine Foundation's

Choosing Wisely campaign highlights the overuse and duplication of unnecessary tests, treatments, and procedures in the health care system and offers tools for patients and providers to initiate conversations about tests and procedures.[33]

In the context of health systems, quality is assessed at two levels: the level of health services (focusing on individual care quality) and the level of the health care system as a whole (evaluating overall system performance).[34] Factors that influence quality include appropriate care and resource under- and overuse, misuse, and waste, which can all result in needless delays in treatment or patient harm.[31] The measurement of quality in health care involves collecting and analyzing a plethora of data on care processes and outcomes, patient-reported outcome measures, and patient satisfaction and experience of care, which are components of the CMS Hospital Value-Based Purchasing Program.

Health Learning Systems[35]

Health systems are also learning systems in which individuals are constantly learning and adapting to new challenges. The Agency for Healthcare Research and Quality defines a learning health system as:

> *. . . a health system in which internal data and experience are systematically integrated with external evidence, and that knowledge is put into practice.*

Learning systems require a shared understanding of what the organization is trying to achieve and a commitment to working together to achieve it. As Andrew Barry of Curious Lion has noted, shared vision is a key element in creating a culture of learning and involves having a North Star that everyone in the organization is working toward. It's not enough to have a vision that is created by the marketing team or the top brass; shared vision has to be something that everyone is invested in and feels ownership of. Based on Peter Senge's work (*The Fifth Discipline*), shared vision means that everyone on the team or in the organization must be aligned around a common purpose and needs to understand how their individual contributions fit into that larger vision.

But a shared vision is just the beginning of a learning culture. Other building blocks need to be in place, like peer-to-peer learning, experimentation, and a willingness to take risks and make mistakes. It's also important to create an environment where people feel safe to ask questions and challenge assumptions.

Patient-Reported Outcomes Measures[36]

CMS defines patient-reported outcomes as "*any report of the status of a patient's (or person's) health condition, health behavior, or experience with health care that comes directly from the patient, without interpretation of the patient's response by a clinician or anyone else.*" Patient-reported outcome measures (PROMs) are vital tools in both research and clinical settings, offering direct insights from patients about their health status, treatment experiences, and various issues like symptom severity, functional problems, psychological issues, treatment satisfaction, and health-related quality of life. PROMs are categorized as either generic (assessing any disease or general population), or disease-specific (focusing on particular health conditions). Their development ideally involves input from those with lived experiences of the condition, and agencies like the FDA emphasize the importance of including patient perspectives.

Properly used, PROMs can significantly contribute to shared decision-making, clinical trials, guideline development, pharmaceutical labeling, and health policy, serving as crucial endpoints in clinical and epidemiological studies.

Quality Improvement

You are probably well aware that, although the United States spends more than any other industrial nation on health care, we continue to lag on important indicators of quality and patient outcomes. As a result, the ACA ushered in a suite of reforms and initiatives designed to improve health care quality, decrease costs, and improve patient outcomes.

Quality improvement (QI) is one such initiative that is increasingly important as hospitals, health systems, and large physician practice groups pursue greater efficiency and value in the services they provide. QI initiatives aim to optimize patient care by improving structural components like equipment availability, facility conditions, and staffing levels, as well as improving care processes like hand-hygiene practices and adherence to clinical guidelines. These efforts are designed to impact outcome indicators and, ultimately, patient outcomes.

The Institute for Healthcare Improvement defines QI as a systematic method to test, implement, and evaluate a designated program of change using specified measures of improvement.[37] Using rapid-cycle test methodology like Plan-Do-Study-Act, QI identifies a need for improvement, determines the necessary steps to implement change, establishes metrics to measure progress, and immediately implements small tests of the changes needed for improvement.

Conclusion

By now you should have a clearer sense of the dynamic and complex environments that health professionals work in and the factors that drive decision-making and clinical practice. Health professionals are also notoriously short on time. Learners need to be able to access educational content at speed, at the point of care, or in between other activities. This means CME/CE content must be designed to be meaningful, interactive, immersive, and motivating. For instance, Allison Kickel, CEO of Bonum CE, designs social media-delivered CME/CE in a tweetorial format so learners can engage in educational content on their phone, on the go, and in the moment of need.

Who or what decides which information is relevant as part of education? That is where the education planning process comes in, which we will explore in Chapter 5.

Key Takeaways

- Health care is a complex, dynamic environment with many pressures
- Team-based care and patient engagement are increasingly important
- Quality improvement, value-based care, technology, and data are driving changes in health care
- Understand the daily challenges faced by health care professionals
- Recognize the importance of interprofessional collaboration

Chapter 5

Planning Education

Education is not the filling of a pail, but the lighting of a fire.

— WILLIAM BUTLER YEATS

Introduction

Developing CME/CE activities requires thoughtful planning that identifies genuine clinical and professional practice gaps, defines clear learning objectives, and designs interactive education formats relevant to learners. Education providers engage in planning cycles that take their own business goals into account as well as emerging therapies and conversations between their sales team (strategists, business directors). This chapter explores the education planning process, how needs assessments fit into this process, and what writers need to know to be effective partners.

Planning CME/CE Activities

The education planning process is often extensive and future-focused. Education providers are typically looking months ahead to determine where to put their efforts and submit proposals for funding.

Key education provider personnel such as grant specialists or business strategists review what is happening in areas where they focus their education efforts (e.g., new therapies, guideline or policy changes, new diagnostic criteria) by:

- Scanning the horizon; developing landscape, environmental, or comprehensive needs assessments
- Having conversations with independent medical education supporters
- Developing partnerships with academia or nonprofit organizations
- Responding to requests for proposals (RFPs)
- Reviewing the literature
- Listening to clinicians about their self-reported needs
- Looking at hot topics and presentations at health care meetings

Education providers use all this information to plan education with specific, strategic goals.

In CME/CE, PDSA (plan, do, study, act) and ADDIE (analysis, design, development, implementation, and evaluation) are the two most common models that education providers use to plan education designed to transform knowledge, skills, and behaviors. The PDSA model is a widely recognized framework for continuous quality improvement in various settings, including CME/CE activities. PDSA encourages an incremental approach to evaluating learning that allows educators to iteratively refine activities and programs.[1] Measuring and analyzing outcomes informs subsequent iteration. ADDIE is widely used in instructional design to build learning content in a linear, sequential approach.

These models are premised on three essential questions:

1. What are we trying to accomplish?
2. How will we know that a change is an improvement?

3. What change can we make that will result in improvement?

These education planning models are not unique to CME/CE and are used in instructional design, public health evaluation, quality improvement, and training and development. See the Appendix for a link to a downloadable AHRQ/PDSA toolkit.

CME/CE providers consider a variety of elements when they design effective educational activities. First, they conduct a needs assessment, gap analysis, and root cause analysis to identify the clinical and performance gaps and educational needs of the target audience. Writers are often hired to develop needs assessments. Next, providers must identify learning objectives and clearly define what participants should know, or be able to do, after successfully completing the educational activity (the intended outcomes). Providers select appropriate and engaging instructional methods that are aligned with the learning objectives and develop an outcomes analysis framework and assessment tools to measure the effectiveness of the CME/CE activity. Completing the cycle, outcomes data often serve as a basis for identifying new or remaining gaps and developing future education.

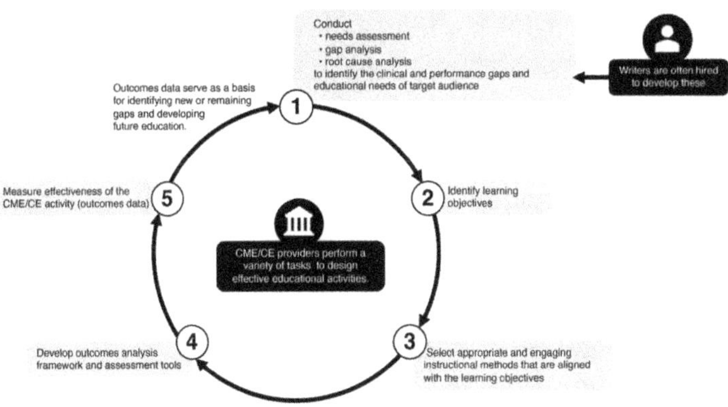

Education Planning Process

Grant Proposals and the RFP Process

Education providers often submit grant proposals to IME departments by invitation based on conversations that grant specialists or business strategists have with IME personnel. IME departments also issue RFPs to solicit grant proposals from education providers. These RFPs focus on emerging therapies, such as a compound that is in the early phase (Phase 1 or Phase 2) of investigation, agents that are newly approved by the U.S. Food and Drug Administration, or, most commonly, on established agents with new Phase 3 data or a new indication. RFPs also focus on social, cultural, or public health initiatives such as equity in clinical trial participation or cultural competence in diabetes management. RFPs are also often generated to focus on a disease state that is not that particularly widespread or well-known among clinicians.

Understanding what has stimulated an RFP is additional information that can help you develop a lean, agile needs assessment. Established medical writer Kristen Dascoli recommends talking to your client to understand why they are responding to an RFP and to also try to learn more about the supporter's educational interests and goals. She recommends reviewing the supporter's earnings, call transcripts, and their medical grant transparency reports. She says:

> *I've used both to tease out key data and educational patterns, ensuring that the scope and focus of my current grant-request proposals align with the commercial supporter's latest interests. Is this something that every medical writer should do? Maybe not. But I consider it a part of how I provide my clients with the optimal opportunity to win IME grant funding for their educational initiatives.*

Submitting a grant proposal in response to an RFP is a detailed process that requires meticulous attention to the supporter's guidelines and expectations. Education providers also submit unsolicited proposals to request supporter funds on a rolling basis or as part of planning within a medical society, health system, or health care member organization.

IME personnel review hundreds of educational grants every year and are looking for precise and data-driven needs assessments that align with the organization's strategic goals. They look for effective education projects to fund that align with their internal objectives, offer a good return on investment, and provide robust data and outcomes. Reviewers are looking for very specific needs assessments versus large, rambling literature reviews. They are interested in detailed descriptions of clinical practice and performance gaps, accompanied by learning objectives that align with the identified gaps.

Although IME departments invest considerable effort into developing RFPs, not all are well-written. Unfocused, unclear, or disorganized RFPs potentially point to dispersed internal priorities at the supporting company. Some RFPs will also include a laundry list of requests and accompanying learning objectives. As the writer, ask your client questions to clarify which aspects of the RFP they want to prioritize in the needs assessment. This will help ensure your work aligns to their expectations.

Structure of a Grant

The format of grant proposals and RFPs has remained remarkably consistent over the years. While education providers and supporters have their format preferences, common elements include a table of contents and an executive summary of the whole grant request that includes:[2]

- Summary statement of need (why the education is needed)
- Description of the gaps
- Education to bridge the gaps
- Learning objectives

- Anticipated outcomes as a result of the education
- Activity agenda

Proposals will also include a description of the target audiences for the education, the outcomes assessment and evaluation framework or plan, the number and type of credits that participants will receive on completion of the education activity, information about the education provider and any partners that are collaborating on the grant, and why the provider is a good fit for this particular education. The needs assessment is often included in the appendix with an abbreviated version in the main body of the proposal. Including a table is an effective and highly visual way to communicate the alignment of gaps, education needs, learning objectives, and outcomes.

Providers typically have boilerplate information they include in grant proposals. As the writer, sometimes you will be asked to include this language and fill in proposal gaps with insights from your needs assessment research.

AI in Grant Writing

The National Institutes of Health peer review process prohibits the use of generative artificial intelligence (gen-AI) technologies for developing grant applications.[3] Major journal networks and the scholarly publishing community also either prohibit the inclusion of AI-generated text in submitted work or discourage the submission and publication of content created by AI technologies. While the CME/CE field has not yet issued protocols or statements for using gen-AI to develop needs assessments, grant proposal, or educational content, gen-AI raises concerns about content integrity.

Needs Assessments

Needs assessments are core documents in CME/CE planning, grant proposal development, and education design.[4–5] While definitions of needs assessment vary by purpose, at its core a needs assessment gathers information about—and offers analysis on—the difference between is and ought. In CME/CE, these differences typically refer to gaps between current clinical practice or performance (is) and optimal practice (ought). ACCME's *CE Educator's Toolkit* says this about needs assessments:[6]

> *Needs assessments help accredited education providers develop effective education to keep health professionals current in their practice and to support lifelong professional learning. The overall goal is to develop education that improves patient outcomes.*

As any supporter or education provider will tell you, a well-constructed needs assessment is the foundation of successful CME/CE grant applications and justifies why an educational activity should be developed. The needs assessment should clearly articulate the educational and practice gaps within the target audience, provide the rationale for education, and propose a feasible plan to address these gaps. By zeroing in on evidence-based practice gaps and defining how education will close them, medical writers are instrumental in developing needs assessments that secure funding.

Evidence Sources for Professional Practice Gaps[7]

Writers charged with developing a particularly targeted needs assessment typically draw on a range of sources to build up a detailed picture of what the need is for education, including an analysis of clinical practice and professional performance gaps. Inferred needs are derived from changes in the health care landscape and in ways of delivering health care. Verbalized needs are also called felt or expressed needs, and typically come from health professionals themselves. Proven needs are typically based on objective data sources and should form the core evidence for need. Clinical practice or expert consensus guidelines and peer-reviewed clinical evidence (e.g., the most recent data from phase three clinical trials) represent standards and criteria that promote the highest quality of clinical care, performance, and patient outcomes.

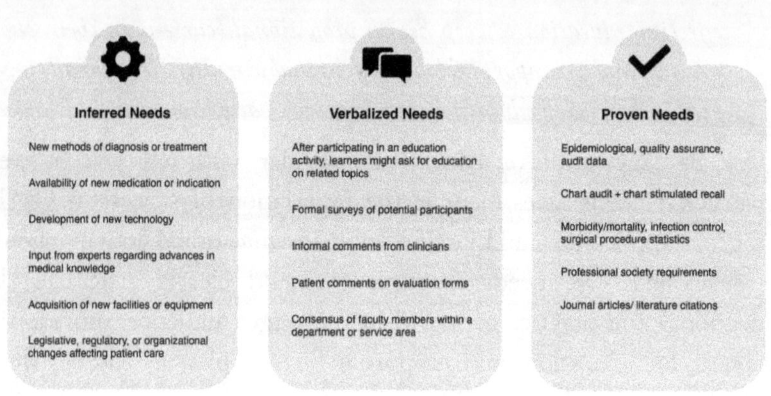

Inferred Needs
New methods of diagnosis or treatment
Availability of new medication or indication
Development of new technology
Input from experts regarding advances in medical knowledge
Acquisition of new facilities or equipment
Legislative, regulatory, or organizational changes affecting patient care
Verbalized Needs
After participating in an education activity, learners might ask for education on related topics
Formal surveys of potential participants
Informal comments from clinicians
Patient comments on evaluation forms
Consensus of faculty members within a department or service area
Proven Needs
Epidemiological, quality assurance, audit data
Chart audit + chart stimulated recall
Morbidity/mortality, infection control, surgical procedure statistics
Professional society requirements
Journal articles/ literature citations

Categories of Need [4-5]

The Needs Assessment Process

The needs assessment process involves a thorough analysis of the current state of knowledge and practices in the relevant medical field, followed by the identification of specific areas where educational interventions can bring about significant improvement. Education providers have often conducted internal preliminary research and developed a tentative sketch of what they perceive as the gaps and learning objectives. They will ask writers to do additional research to substantiate the gaps. However, it is often the case that education providers do not provide writers with much direction. In these circumstances, asking good questions is key.

Your job as the writer is to tell a well-supported story that shows the reader the need for education and the consequences of not developing the education. As Michelle Rizzo shared on the Write Medicine podcast,

> *Needs assessments don't need to be a huge data dump. I've read so many needs assessments, and they all start out the same way, with the prevalence and incidence, and it's just fact after fact*

after fact thrown at the reader. There's no story woven in there. You have to pull the reader in. Otherwise, they're not going to care. And you've got to make it readable in a way that will draw their interest. The reader has not gone through your thought process. The reader has not gone through your research level; he or she is coming in cold and doesn't know what you know. So you've got to be on their side. You've got to be able to step outside yourself, put yourself into someone else's shoes, and look at it the way they're looking at it.

Project Startup

When clients start to think about generating a needs assessment, they will usually be able to share supporting materials with the writer to help them build it, along with a written backgrounder or briefing document that includes the following:

- What the topic is
- Statements about gaps and education need
- Draft learning objectives
- Outcomes results from previous education on a similar topic
- Evaluations
- Links to previous educational activities that have covered the particular topic
- A proposed agenda for the educational activity
- Proposed faculty
- A description of the outcomes assessment framework
- Interview quotes from subject matter experts/key opinion leaders

Pro Tip: Questions to Ask

- Sometimes the scope of the needs assessment can seem very broad. Ask the client which topics they really want to focus on and that will potentially be part of an educational program. As an informed writer, you can also make suggestions along the lines of:

- Here's what I'm seeing in my research.
- Do you want me to include this topic? Or is this something for another program?

- Always ask clients if they have outcomes data from previous activities. This information reveals gaps in education the provider has covered in the past and which types of education activities have demonstrated improvement in whatever outcomes are being measured—knowledge, confidence, competence, performance.
- Ask clients if they have other materials that could help this particular needs assessment, including:
    - Existing reference list
    - PDFs from prior literature searches
    - Member surveys
- There's usually something you can use from existing material that a client provides. For instance, evaluation data from previous activities often include participants' responses to open-ended questions. You can mine this material for illustrative quotes to add more substance and flavor to the needs assessment you are working on.

What Are Clinical Practice Gaps?

CME/CE is heavily invested in designing education to create learning and behavior change that will achieve specific and desired results, improve health care quality, and enhance patient outcomes. The needs assessment is essentially a story of transformation that needs to capture current knowledge, competence, and performance (what clinicians currently know and are doing in practice) and what they *should* know and do according to the best available clinical evidence and professional recommendations. This disconnect between what clinicians actually know and do and what they should know and do is referred to as clinical practice or performance gaps. Practice gaps are the building blocks of CME/CE. When you have identified a gap, it's helpful to describe the reason the gap exists, such as lack of knowledge, low awareness, or lack of skill.

Defining Gaps

A clinical (or performance) practice gap is a gap between is and ought—between what is happening in practice and what should be happening according to current evidence, clinical practice guideline recommendations, quality indicators, and other sources of trustworthy, validated data. The ACCME defines a gap as "*the difference between health care processes or outcomes observed in practice, and those potentially achievable on the basis of current professional knowledge.*"[8]

Pro Tip

Most of your effort as a writer developing a strong needs assessment will focus on conducting and synthesizing research to substantiate practice gaps. Your key task as a writer is to collect evidence to support the following assertions:

- A gap exists.
- The gap is caused by knowledge, skills, attitude deficits that are amenable to education.

- The gap can be narrowed via education.

Gap statements should be concise yet provide context.

- Including percentages or data can help clarify if there is a measurable gap between current and optimal practice.
- Avoid blaming language like "clinicians fail to . . ." as it can set a negative tone. Use judgment on word choice based on evidence.
- Be as specific as possible when narrowing down populations, problems, and education needs.

One way to think about a gap analysis is through a series of questions.

1. What is the gap/problem?
2. Who has the gap/problem? Be as specific as possible: Primary care providers? Nurses? Specialists (e.g., oncologists)? Pharmacists?
3. When does the gap/problem occur? At what point in a workflow or clinical process?
4. Where is the problem occurring? In certain settings (e.g., community vs. academic centers)?
5. Why is this gap occurring/why is this a problem? What factors contribute to the gap?
6. What is it they are doing, or not doing, that makes this a problem?
7. How is education going to address the gap/problem? By attention to knowledge, skills (competence and performance), attitudes, or something else?

Julie Dirksen's five common gaps to learning are helpful ways to think about what the learner (clinician) needs to learn to move closer to a desired/recommended practice or performance outcome:[9]

- Knowledge gaps

- Skill gaps
- Motivation or attitude gaps
- Environmental gaps
- Communication gaps

Learning Objectives

Learning objectives are critical action statements that connect identified practice gaps and educational needs to the anticipated outcomes learners should achieve from the education. These outcomes range across various domains including knowledge, competence, performance, and impacts on patient and community levels. As writers developing needs assessments, we should aim to craft clear, actionable learning objectives that align with the principles of effective instructional design.

When writing learning objectives:

1. Make them actionable with only one clear action statement per objective. Avoid long, convoluted statements with multiple clauses or actions.
2. Ensure learning objectives are measurable so education providers can evaluate if learners achieved the intended outcome.
3. Use action verbs that target the desired outcome level—knowledge, competence, performance, patient outcomes. Refer to Bloom's Taxonomy for guidance on verb selection.
4. Make sure the objectives are relevant and supported by the educational content and activities planned.
5. Follow the SMART criteria (specific, measurable, achievable, relevant, time-bound) when possible.

Bloom's Revised Taxonomy

Bloom's Revised Taxonomy provides a framework to write objectives targeting different cognitive levels from basic knowledge/recall to more advanced application, analysis, and synthesis. While knowledge-based objectives are common in CME/CE, the ideal is to develop higher-order objectives that build competence and impact performance.

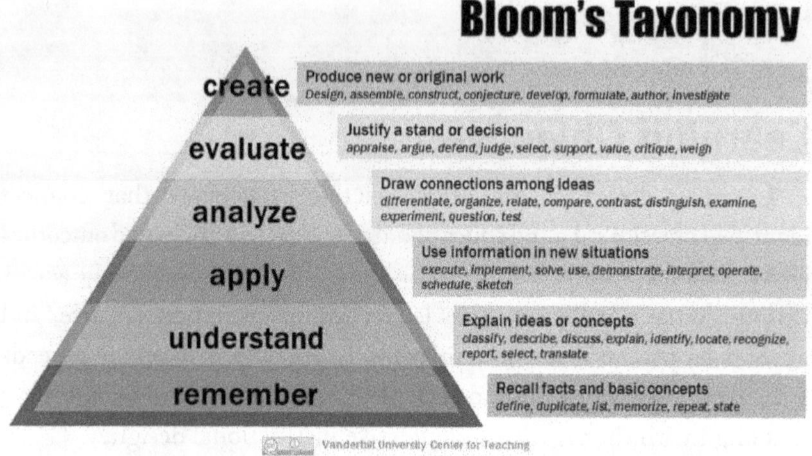

Vanderbilt University Center for Teaching, CC BY 2.0 <https://creativecommons.org/licenses/by/2.0>, via Wikimedia Commons

While many learning objectives in CME/CE focus on knowledge acquisition, the ultimate goal is to design education that enhances competence and positively impacts clinical performance. This shift requires a move beyond knowledge-based objectives to include those that foster skill development, critical thinking, and practical application in clinical settings.

As needs assessment writers, our role is to carefully analyze gaps/needs and craft objectives that clearly articulate what learners should be able to do differently after the education. Well-designed objectives form the foundation for developing effective instructional activities.

Peer Review

What happens to content after it is developed? Who decides when it is ready for consumption? This is where peer review comes in. Peer review in CME/CE involves the evaluation of educational content, activities, or manuscripts by experts in the field to ensure accuracy, relevance, and quality. The process typically includes professionals with expertise in the subject matter under review, who assess the educational materials based on established criteria to determine their suitability for CME/CE accreditation or publication. Peer reviewers help maintain the integrity and standards of CME/CE programs by providing constructive feedback, identifying areas needing improvement, and ensuring that the content aligns with current best practices and evidence-based guidelines. Note that internal policies for the use and process of peer review vary greatly by organization.

Quality Improvement CME/CE

Quality improvement education (QIE) is a form of education designed to improve process, performance, and practice at a systems level. As we saw in Chapter 4, quality improvement became a major focus in health care delivery in the 2010s. The IOM and other organizations began to see CME/CE as a mechanism to improve clinical practice and performance. In response, CME/CE providers began to think more critically about designing education to address quality, health systems, and cost savings, which led to a white paper on the topic. *The Quality Improvement Education (QIE) Roadmap: A Pathway to Our Future* mapped out a strategic path for QIE to improve the performance of health professionals on quality measures, enhance care coordination, and improve patient outcomes.[10]

IME professionals also began to grapple with questions about measuring QIE. I worked with a team at Genentech to develop a white paper about an outcomes model to evaluate improvements in quality resulting from education interventions and measure outcomes at a systems level.[11] The model was not widely adopted but was an excellent exercise in developing an industry-related white paper (see Chapter 8 for more details on white papers).

What Does QIE Look Like?

QIE interventions typically focus on specific clinical care issues, like improving foot care for patients with diabetes, reducing readmissions, and increasing preventive screening rates in primary care. Clearly defined metrics are essential at baseline to benchmark and evaluate the success of a QIE intervention. Metrics are often multidimensional and include organizational, process, outcome, and patient measures, such as those developed by the Physician Consortium for Performance Improvement (PCPI), the Healthcare Effectiveness Data and Information Set (HEDIS), or endorsed by the National Quality Forum (NQF). QIE interventions might also include a logic model to establish benchmarks for measuring progress.

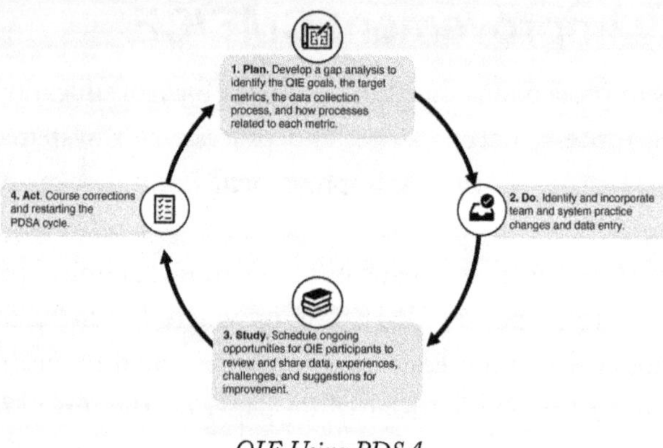

QIE Using PDSA

Pro Tip

Implementation science is the theoretical foundation of QI (which we'll touch on later in this chapter), of which there are many models, including Six Sigma, Lean Six Sigma, Continuous Quality Improvement, Total Quality Improvement, or PDSA.[12] I have been involved in several QIE projects with member associations and medical education providers that focused on hematological cancers, cardiovascular disease, HIV, and respiratory diseases.[13–16] They are robust projects that demand writing, research, and collaboration skills. CME/CE writers with these skills are well-placed to develop online and enduring materials to support QIE initiatives and revise that content throughout the QIE cycle to address emerging needs.

Performance Improvement CME

The AMA launched performance improvement (PI) CME in 2005.[17] PI-CME uses evidence-based measures developed by entities like the National Committee for Quality Assurance (NCQA) and the Physician Consortium for Performance Improvement (PCPI) to benchmark care quality and highlight concrete areas for clinical advancement. These benchmarks provide standardized ways for health professionals to identify and address areas needing improvement.

PI-CME uses these measures as a baseline, enabling physicians and other health care providers to assess their current practice against established targets and pinpoint steps for improvement. PI-CME contrasts with standard CME/CE models by tightly linking learning goals with defined performance deficits.

The process of PI-CME typically unfolds in three stages:

1. Learning about specific performance measures
2. Assessing current practice against these measures
3. Participating in educational activities aimed at improving performance in targeted areas

This cycle concludes with a reassessment using the same performance measures.

Pro Tip

As a specialized niche within medical education, PI-CME is closely aligned with specific clinical goals. Education is tailored to help health professionals meet these objectives. Medical writers can contribute to PI-CME by crafting online or print content to support the process and by developing individualized feedback summaries that align health care providers' self-assessments with current evidence and performance indicators. The evolving methodologies in outcomes evaluation present further opportunities for writers in this dynamically changing landscape of medical education.

Organizational CME/CE

ACEHP's *Educating the Educator* curriculum includes a focus on systems and organizational thinking as a required competency for education planning, including an understanding of:

1. Learners in the context of health care systems
2. Barriers to optimal care
3. The role of the interdisciplinary team
4. Identification of organizational needs and goals
5. The role of CPD in health care systems

Many CME/CE professionals believe that the field must evolve to address health care delivery through education aimed not only at individuals but also health systems. As Chapter 3 described, the health care landscape in the United States has changed significantly. In the 1980s, patient care was largely delivered in independent hospitals, physician offices, or group practices, and reimbursed on a fee-for-service basis. At the time of writing in 2024, patient care occurs in many different contexts, including hospitals that are part of consolidated systems or chains, investor-owned practices, managed care organizations, accountable care organizations, medical homes, retail clinics, community health centers, and urgent care and surgical centers.[18]

Indeed, when Curtis Olson, PhD, was editor of the *Journal for Continuing Education in the Health Professions*, he made twenty predictions in an attempt to shift CME/CE from a knowledge update model to improving clinical practice.[19] Further, in 2020, the IOM highlighted flaws in the structure and rationale of continuing health professions education in its report, "Redesigning Continuing Education in the Health Professions." As reviewed in Chapter 1, this report called for a greater emphasis on interprofessional continuing education.

Systems Thinking

Systems thinking involves looking at how everything fits together (e.g., providers, patients, administrators), and how feedback is created within the system. Systems thinking is an approach to problem-solving that examines how various components within a complex system interrelate, rather than analyzing individual parts in isolation. In health care, embracing wider perspectives is crucial when addressing multifactorial quality, cost, and health access dilemmas. For instance, hospital readmission rates may stem from fragmented discharge processes, inadequate community resources, clinician burnout, or social barriers patients face. Systems thinking mandates tracing how these elements interconnect. It then informs integrated solutions accounting for bigger pictures. Implementing transitions clinics supplying wraparound postdischarge services exemplifies interventions recognizing clinical and social determinants. Overall, systems thinking signifies expanding lenses beyond siloed views to catalyze change through comprehensively aligned actions across health ecosystem layers.[20]

On an individual program level, systems thinking means carefully examining root causes behind professional practice gaps and designing tailored educational interventions to drive change. For example, if a hospital identifies a trend of increased hospital-acquired infections, a systems-thinking approach to CME/CE would go beyond simply offering courses on infection control procedures. It would examine the underlying causes, such as staff workflow, communication channels, environmental factors, and existing protocols. The CME/CE program might then integrate training on teamwork and communication, systemwide safety culture, and effective use of technology alongside clinical best practices in infection control.

Implementation Science

Implementation science (IS) refers to the systematic study of methods that promote integration of research evidence and clinical expertise into health care practice and policy.[21] This framework focuses on understanding factors that facilitate or hinder widespread adoption, sustainability, and scaling of evidence-based interventions in real-world settings. IS draws on several change theories, including the theory of planned behavior, the transtheoretical model of change, and principles of cognitive psychology, as well as PDSA, Six Sigma, systems theory, and diffusion of innovations.[18]

An example of IS in practice is the integration of new guidelines for diabetes management into a primary care setting. Suppose research identifies a new, more effective medication regimen for type 2 diabetes. IS would study how best to introduce this regimen into everyday clinical practice. This could involve developing and testing interventions to educate health care providers about the new regimen, addressing barriers to its adoption (like cost or accessibility of the new medication), and creating systems to monitor and evaluate the uptake and effectiveness of the new treatment protocol in various patient populations. The goal is not just to inform practitioners about a new development, but to actively facilitate and study its integration into routine care, thus bridging the gap between research and practice.

Conclusion

The education planning process in CME/CE is a complex and multifaceted endeavor that requires careful consideration of various factors, including the identification of genuine clinical and professional practice gaps, the definition of clear learning objectives, and the design of engaging and relevant educational formats. Needs assessments serve as the foundation for successful grant applications and justify the development of educational activities. Medical writers are instrumental in the gap analysis/needs assessment process by conducting thorough research, synthesizing evidence, and crafting compelling narratives that highlight the need for education and its potential impact on patient outcomes.

As we have seen, CME/CE has traditionally focused on updating clinician knowledge and skills, which remains essential for medical professionals to meet various professional requirements. However, its role in health care improvement is evolving, and scholarship in the CME/CE field continues to explore models and frameworks that support CME/CE as a strategic tool in behavior, practice, and systems change and improvement.

Key Takeaways

- Educational planning involves needs assessment, gap analysis, and learning objectives
- PDSA and ADDIE models are commonly used in CME/CE planning
- Outcomes measurement is crucial for demonstrating effectiveness
- Grant proposals and RFPs are important aspects of CME/CE development
- Master the process of conducting needs assessments and gap analyses
- Learn to develop clear, measurable learning objectives
- Understand how to align content with desired outcomes

Chapter 6

Adult Learning Principles

[Learning is] . . . a process that leads to change, which occurs as a result of experience and increases the potential for improved performance and future learning.[1]

Introduction

When we think about learning, we might think what we're doing in CME is simply sharing information. However, *how* the information is shared can have a huge impact on whether (and how much!) the learner understands, retains, and applies it. As Chapter 1 noted, education for the health professions has increasingly moved toward a competency-based model. To address competencies, CME providers rely on evidence-based practice and adult learning principles (ALPs) to guide content development that supports knowledge retention and helps learners apply what they are learning to align with their professional roles and responsibilities.

A wide set of processes and characteristics shape learning, including cognition, memory, brain structure and function. But learning is more than cognition. Sociocultural, professional interests, organizational contexts, and social/emotional factors (e.g., demographics, technology, stress) also shape learning.[2] Moreover, learner actions, instructional design, and even learning environments determine which interventions result in better learning and behavioral outcomes.

Technical writing skills will make you a good CME writer, but to create great content, you must go a step further. To excel in the field of CME writing, you must have a strong awareness of adult learning principles and the characteristics of adult learners. In fact, adult learning principles form a core ACEHP *Educating the Educator* knowledge domain for professionals involved in CME/CE content development, including writers. Adult learning scholarship and learning science have generated multiple theoretical approaches to learning that draw on cognitive psychology, sociology, neuroscience, anthropology, behavioral economics, and other academic disciplines.[3–4] These approaches explore how we acquire and apply knowledge and build skills and competencies, and they offer a treasure trove of insights to help CME writers create more effective content for learners.

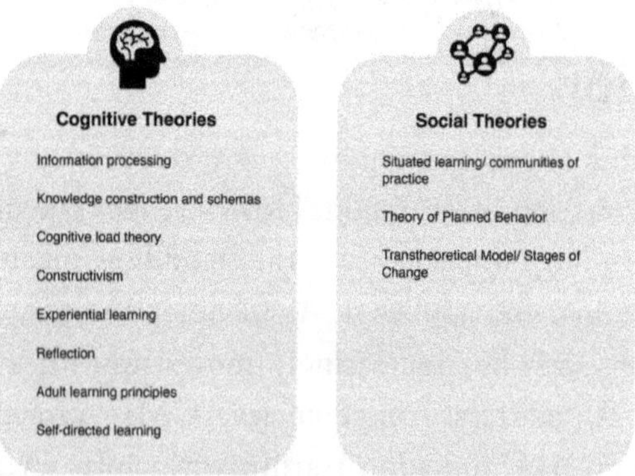

Cognitive Theories
Information processing
Knowledge construction and schemas
Cognitive load theory
Constructivism
Experiential learning
Reflection
Adult learning principles
Self-directed learning
Social Theories
Situated learning/ communities of practice
Theory of Planned Behavior
Transtheoretical Model/ Stages of Change

Adult Learning Theories

The Learning Process

What is learning? Here are three critical components to consider:[1]

1. Learning is a fluid process, not a product. The learning process involves information intake, internal processing, and output.
2. Learning involves change in knowledge, beliefs, behaviors, or attitudes that unfolds over time.
3. Learning is not something done to learners, but something learners do.

Education providers draw on both psychological and social theories that explain the learning process, and use frameworks such as andragogy, self-directed learning, and problem-based learning to design their programs and activities.

Andragogy and Adult Learning Principles

When I first started creating CME content, I worked with a client who had built an online learning platform supported by adult learning principles as described by Malcolm Knowles. Although I had been teaching in higher education for over a decade, I wasn't aware of Knowles or his work. It turns out that he has had a huge influence on the professional development of medical education generally and the way CME approaches learning design.

Knowles was a mid-twentieth-century educator who differentiated adult learning (andragogy) from child learning (pedagogy) and distilled this philosophy of learning into key characteristics. He argued that for education to resonate with adults, it must center on the learner, directly relate to their practice, and align with their expected outcomes. The andragogy model of education argues that adults approach learning with distinct needs and preferences, including a desire for education that is relevant, problem-oriented, and immediately applicable in their professional context. Learners seek not just knowledge but actionable skills for tangible results.[5]

As a humanistic philosophy of learning, andragogy assumes that individuals are primed for self-actualization and ongoing development.[6] This philosophy emphasizes the importance of the human capacity to reason, which we use to gain insights about the problems we face and weigh the benefits and costs of various actions to address those problems.

The characteristics Knowles assumed are key to adult learning are:[2]

1. **Autonomy/self-direction.** As adult learners we prefer to manage and self-direct our own learning journey, choosing what and how we learn. We want to be in control and have a say over when, what, and how we learn.
2. **Experience.** We bring a wealth of experiences to the learning process, which helps us contextualize and internalize new information. We rationalize, analyze, synthesize, and develop new ideas or tweak old ones through the filter of our own experiences.
3. **Relevance and readiness.** As adult learners, we need to know why we have to learn something and be ready to learn it.
4. **Problem-oriented.** Adults learn best when we have a real or immediate problem to address. We prefer learning activities that help us reach substantive goals, focus on solving real-world problems, and help us apply new skills.
5. **Motivation.** Intrinsic values such as personal growth, self-esteem, and satisfaction motivate learning.

As an adult learner yourself, you can probably relate. We don't just want to know how to do something. We want knowledge and skills we can apply right now to get the specific results or outcomes we are looking for. We learn best when we are doing tasks, solving problems, and applying what we are learning. We seek learning that is relevant to our professional needs or social roles, and our willingness or readiness to learn comes from perceiving the relevance of this knowledge or skill. Similarly, adult learners in CME want access to education that is relevant to their real-world clinical challenges and offers solutions they can apply in their daily clinical setting.

These adult learning principles are not in themselves a theory of learning. Rather, they are a set of guiding principles for education design that include the following characteristics:[7]

1. **Create psychological safety.** Create conditions that support characteristics such as trust, respect, and openness.
2. **Involve learners in planning.** Solicit input for needs assessments or provide options for learning.
3. **Provide self-assessment.** Invite learners to diagnose their own needs for learning.
4. **Set objectives.** Allow learners to create their own learning objectives and goals.
5. **Identify pathways.** Help learners create learning pathways that allow them to meet their objectives.
6. **Support learners.** Provide resources and tools to help learners implement their learning plan.
7. **Evaluate.** Establish opportunities for self-evaluation.

Criticisms of Andragogy

While andragogy has been influential in adult education, it faces several significant criticisms.[8] One primary concern is its oversimplification of the differences between adult and child learners, which fails to capture both groups' complex and varied learning behaviors. Additionally, the lack of robust empirical evidence supporting Knowles' assumptions has led to calls for more rigorous scientific validation of andragogical principles.[8]

Further critiques highlight andragogy's cultural bias, reflecting a Western, individualistic perspective that may not be universally applicable.[8] The inconsistent application of andragogical principles in practice and questions about its historical and philosophical foundations also contribute to skepticism. These criticisms underscore the need for a more nuanced, evidence-based approach to adult learning that addresses the theory's limitations while building on its valuable insights.

Motivation

Motivation is a core adult learning principle. Many theories centralize motivation as a psychological construct that drives goal-oriented activities like learning, such as self-determination theory, expectancy-value theory, attribution theory, and social cognitive theory. These theories often have different definitions or emphasize different aspects of motivation.[9] In CME, the most common concept of motivation pertains to intrinsic and extrinsic motivation, which is tied both to the anticipated value of a learning task and the expectancy of success in completing the task.

Intrinsic motivation. Motivation for adult learners can be driven by the interest, pleasure, and satisfaction of learning itself. In turn, when learners have a sense of control over their learning, their sense of intrinsic motivation increases. They are likely to persist and not give up. Essentially, when we understand why we are learning, we are more motivated to learn.

Extrinsic motivation. Extrinsic motivation to learn is driven by external factors. For instance, we might be motivated to learn something new because we want to grow in our professional roles, get a promotion, or stay abreast of competitors. Other factors can also be drivers of extrinsic motivation, including making new friends, relieving boredom, taking a break from the routine of home or work, meeting CME credit requirements, or learning new skills to meet clinical practice demands or improve patient care.

◇◇

Growth Mindset in Adult Learning[10-11]

Adopting a growth mindset can boost motivation. Growth mindset in adult learning is based on Carol Dweck's research on the idea that intelligence and abilities can be developed through effort, learning, and persistence. As adults we often come to learning with entrenched beliefs and fixed mindsets shaped by years of experiences, successes, and failures. Changing these established beliefs may require targeted interventions and consistent reinforcement. Emphasizing growth mindset in education activities can boost learners' motivation to learn and increase their resilience when facing challenges. Cultivating a growth mindset can also lead to better academic outcomes for adult learners and greater willingness to engage in continuous learning and self-improvement.

◇◇

Self-Directed Learning

Self-directed learning (SDL) is a learner-centered approach that helps learners to take responsibility for their own education by actively engaging in the learning process, setting goals, and identifying resources to achieve those goals. SDL is a guiding principle across the medical education continuum and in cultivating lifelong learning skills among health professionals.[7] In theory, SDL enables learners to develop the autonomy and motivation needed to continuously update their knowledge, adapt to new information, and enhance their clinical practice -- in short, to be the lifelong learners that medicine, pharmacy, and the nursing profession all require of its members.

However, not all learners respond to self-directed learning or are motivated to learn what they need to know.[12] This deficit makes a well-constructed, evidence-based needs assessment so important. Learners might also be overwhelmed by the volume of resources and options in a learning management system (LMS), which can lead to decision paralysis and hinder effective learning.

Cognitive Learning Theories

Cognitive learning theories liken the brain to a computer and focus on information intake, processing, storage, and retrieval.[7]

Memory, Maps, and Cognitive Load

Cognitive learning theories offer a unique perspective into the internal mechanics of learning and how people process, structure, and retrieve information. As we absorb information through our senses, we use our working or short-term memory to process and organize it into increasingly complex schemas or maps.[13] Our cognitive load (which includes intrinsic and extrinsic load) affects this processing, determining the volume of information we can handle and the effort required to process it. Cognitive load theory focuses on how learning can be optimized to help us effectively process, structure, and retrieve information, like metacognition.

Learning engages our brains in encoding, organizing, and consolidating perceptions and experiences to retrieve them later in the correct context and for the appropriate purpose.[14] By integrating new information with previous knowledge through cues and context, our short-term and long-term memory work together to embed it more deeply into our internal archives or memory traces. Forgetting and unlearning are also integral parts of acquiring new information.

Learning and Forgetting

Introduced to psychology in the 1930s, learning curve theory posits that proficiency and efficiency increase with experience as individuals engage in repetitive tasks.[15] The more a task is performed, the quicker and more proficiently it can be completed over time. A German psychologist, Hermann Ebbinghaus, identified the forgetting curve and demonstrated that the time it takes for people to forget things they have learned is much shorter (hours and days vs. months and years) than we would like to believe.[16] Many factors contribute to forgetting, such as how the material is presented, how meaningful the material is to learners, level of difficulty, and physiological factors like sleep.

Learning and forgetting curves are important in adult learning because they provide a framework for understanding how proficiency and performance evolve over time with practice and experience. In the context of CME, the learning curve concept can help educators track learners' progress, identify challenges, and adapt training programs to meet individual needs effectively. Spaced repetition is a learning technique that involves reviewing information at increasing intervals to enhance long-term retention. By spacing out review sessions over time, spaced repetition leverages the psychological spacing effect to strengthen memory recall and promote durable learning. When learning is spaced out over time, we tend to remember more material, more deeply. By recognizing that learning is a gradual process, and that improvement takes time, educators can design activities with realistic goal setting, personalized support, and tactics to enhance motivation and engagement.

Constructivism

Constructivist learning theory, advocated by scholars like Jean Piaget and Lev Vygotsky, defines learning as an active, constructive process that focuses on making sense of reality.[17] As learners, we are not passive recipients of information. Instead, we actively participate in learning, building, or constructing knowledge based on our experiences and our reflections on those experiences. Central to constructivism is the idea that we add new experiences to our existing foundation of understanding, creating unique knowledge structures. By engaging in social activities, discussions, and interactions, learners construct meaning and deepen their understanding of concepts. Constructivism highlights the importance of active engagement in learning, contextual learning experiences, and the personal construction of knowledge through individual perspectives and prior knowledge.[7]

Experiential Learning

What and how we learn is also shaped by our experiences, values, and beliefs. John Dewey was an American philosopher of the pragmatism school who believed adults learn better when they draw on lived experiences to evaluate new concepts—a principle he called the continuity of experience. Continuity of experience suggests that we connect new information or experiences to knowledge and experiences we have already acquired and reflect on the implications of what we're learning for the future. Dewey saw education as a process in which we are constantly developing skills through experience.

David Kolb saw education in this way too, as expressed in the theory of experiential learning. Experiential learning is distinguished from cognitive theories of learning because experience and perception are central to the learning process, which Kolb viewed as a transformative cycle.[18] Experiential learning emphasizes hands-on experiences, active engagement, problem-solving skills, and the ability to adapt knowledge to new contexts.

Experiential learning is widely used across the medical education continuum.[7] This approach often includes activities that involve self-appraising or reflecting on current practice, identifying a problem in that practice, and problem-based learning as an individual or within in a team. More recent research affirms that learners retain information better once they have the opportunity to apply their new knowledge.[19] Project ECHO is a good example of experiential learning in practice.

Project ECHO

Project ECHO is a "hands-on" learning model (described in Chapter 1) that is structured to help participants apply existing knowledge to clinical situations while also generating new knowledge and skills.[20] Learners engage in case-based learning and knowledge sharing and actively apply their knowledge and skills to real-world scenarios.

The model builds in opportunities to reflect on experiences and collaborate with experts via telementoring to address complex health care challenges. The experiential ECHO model is designed to foster critical thinking, problem-solving abilities, and expertise development in learners so they can navigate real-world challenges, think innovatively, and continuously improve their knowledge and skills in their professional setting.

Metacognition and Reflection

Metacognition involves understanding one's own knowledge and thought processes and is considered important in transformative learning theories, such as those associated with Jack Mezirow.[21] Metacognitive skills like reflection are crucial in adult and professional learning as they help adult learners plan, monitor, evaluate, and modify their learning strategies effectively. Reflection has many definitions in the education literature, including looking back on one's experience (reflection-on-action), reflecting in the moment as one is performing a task (reflection-in-action), and thinking about thinking.[22-23] By reflecting on our thinking, monitoring our learning behaviors, evaluating our performance, and making necessary adjustments, we develop a deeper understanding of our cognitive abilities and can improve our learning outcomes.[22]

Reflection plays a vital role in professional practice and CME as it allows adult learners to make sense of their experiences and integrate new knowledge into existing frameworks. This deliberate attempt to understand and learn from situations informs future actions and decision-making.[23] The significance of reflective practice as a key to learning, especially for professionals, has been influenced by the works of John Dewey and Donald Schön, author of *The Reflective Practitioner*. Additionally, reflection is an essential part of David Kolb's experiential learning cycle, emphasizing the importance of reflecting on experiences to facilitate effective learning and growth. By reflecting on what they have learned and what they can do better next time, learners can continuously improve their skills and knowledge.[24]

Reflection allows learners to:

- Assess their effectiveness as clinicians
- Identify strengths and weaknesses
- Clarify areas that need improvement
- Develop skills
- Act with agency and take responsibility for their learning

In CME, self-assessments or reflection questions can help learners reflect on their own work or performance, identify gaps in their knowledge and practice, and measure what they know or are doing in relation to certain criteria or to their peers.

Behavior Change Theories

Behavior change theories, such as the Theory of Planned Behavior, the Transtheoretical Model of Change (TTM, also known as Stages of Change theory), and Self-Determination Theory, emphasize the importance of intention and process in behavior change.

The Theory of Planned Behavior. The Theory of Planned Behavior is based on the idea that intent to change behavior precedes actual change. Intent to change is influenced by attitudes, beliefs, motivation, subjective and social norms, and an individual's perceived control of a situation.[25] For instance, to improve handwashing behaviors in hospital settings, educational interventions need to convince individuals to regularly wash their hands. Education activities could include social influences (highly regarded peers), showing the connection between lack of handwashing and infection rates, providing motivation (stories of success), and easily accessible reminders to wash hands.[26]

TTM/Stages of Change. TTM describes an individual's readiness and willingness to change and explains how individuals move through different stages of change; from precontemplation to contemplation, to preparation, to action, and to maintenance.[27] Processes of change are techniques that help people make and maintain changes, including weighing the benefits against the costs of change.

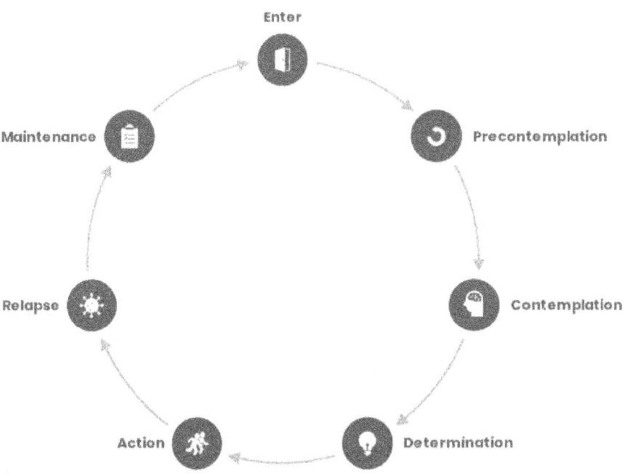

Transtheoretical Model of Change

TTM and Sleep Apnea CME

A CME intervention used TTM to address clinicians' practices regarding the screening and management of obstructive sleep apnea (OSA).[28] The intervention addressed different stages of change by incorporating tailored behavior change messages into CME activities to meet clinicians wherever they were at in their readiness to change their practice behaviors.

Here is how the education addressed each stage of change:

- **Precontemplation**. In this stage, clinicians are not yet considering a change in their practice behavior within the next six months. The educational content focused on raising awareness about the significance of OSA and its health implications. Messages highlighted the underdiagnosis of OSA and its consequences, aiming to motivate clinicians to start thinking about the importance of screening and managing this condition.

- **Contemplation**. For these clinicians, the CME content provided information on the benefits of early identification and treatment of OSA and addressed common barriers to change, such as perceived time constraints for screening or lack of familiarity with diagnostic tools.
- **Preparation**. The educational interventions for clinicians who intended to change their behavior in the next thirty days included specific strategies for integrating OSA screening and management into routine practice, such as practical tips for using screening tools.
- **Action**. The CME content for clinicians who had recently adopted new best practices focused on reinforcing their new behaviors and providing support for any challenges they might encounter.
- **Maintenance**. For clinicians who had adopted new screening behaviors for more than six months, the educational content focused on encouraging continued adherence to best practices (e.g., sharing success stories from other clinicians).

Self-Determination Theory

Self-determination also lies at the heart of behavior change. Self-determination theory emphasizes competence, relatedness, and autonomy as the core of the behavior change process.[29] Andrew Barry, CEO of Curious Lion, observes that for people to change their behaviors, they must start with a clear picture of their current reality, be dissatisfied with it, have a vision of what success or a better future could look like, and make a clear pathway to get there. Educators in CME have called on self-determination theory to guide the development of learning activities that address workforce imbalance by attracting and recruiting physicians to less-attractive specialties in medicine. By incorporating self-determination theory principles to CME, educators can create a learning environment that fosters intrinsic motivation, engagement, and optimal learning outcomes for learners.[30]

Behavioral Economics

One of the highlights of the 2019 ACEHP Annual Meeting in National Harbor, Maryland, was David Asch's keynote address on behavioral economics. CME is largely premised on the assumption that building knowledge provides a foundation for clinicians to make rational decisions about their clinical work. Asch challenged this assumption, suggesting that individuals often make irrational decisions or behave irrationally despite broadening their knowledge. But educators can use these irrational decisions or behaviors because they often occur in predictable patterns.

This is where behavioral economics comes in.

Behavioral economics posits that a variety of factors (including social context, emotional processing, and cognitive biases) influence our choices and actions.[31] By addressing these factors, educators can create "sticky" learning experiences that shape habits, behaviors, and practices. Tools such as nudges, choice architecture, and social incentives can be employed to guide health care providers toward evidence-based decisions and actions.

Here are some ways that behavioral economics might be incorporated into CME:

1. **Identifying educational needs and performance gaps.** In addition to assessing competence and performance, needs assessment can also examine the social contexts in which

health care is delivered, the emotional pathways through which clinicians process information and make decisions, and the cognitive biases that influence decision-making. This holistic approach can help frame interventions more effectively.

2. **Cultivating partnerships.** Collaborating with organizations that understand both behavioral economics and learning science, such as patient safety and risk management groups, can enhance the design and delivery of CME interventions. These partnerships can complement existing collaborations with quality improvement (QI) experts, as exemplified by the Quality Improvement Education Roadmap.
3. **Leveraging technology.** Technology plays a crucial role in blending behavioral economics and learning science to create sustainable behavior change. For example, electronic health records (EHRs) can be used to display best practice alerts and proactive care alerts at the point-of-care, encouraging individual reflection and reinforcing evidence-based practices. When coupled with a team-based approach to learning, technology can facilitate discussion, connection, and change across entire health care teams.

Emotions in Clinical Decision-Making[32]

We probably assume that clinical decision-making is a rational, algorithmic process. It can be. *Clinical decision-making and judgment* is a core competency for physicians and was originally defined as a "hypothetic-deductive process of determining patients' problems" that follows Bayesian logic. Clinicians are trained in clinical reasoning as well as shared decision-making. However, not only are clinical decisions often made in contexts that are emotionally charged; emotions are also unacknowledged drivers of decision-making.

Self-Efficacy

Self-efficacy is an important concept in the Theory of Planned Behavior, TTM, and social cognitive theory. In these theories, self-efficacy is a motivational construct that bridges the gap between knowing and doing,[33] and is most foundational in social cognitive theory. Self-efficacy refers to the confidence a person has in their ability to make and sustain changes in situations that could trigger a return to previous behaviors. Self-efficacy affects how adults approach challenges, tasks, and the persistence they exhibit in the face of adversity. Environmental variables affect self-efficacy, such as role models and social experiences. Personal beliefs also shape self-efficacy. Confidence and self-efficacy are closely intertwined, with self-efficacy essentially reflecting an individual's confidence in their ability to achieve a desired outcome. High self-efficacy means not only feeling confident in knowing something but also in one's capacity to apply that knowledge effectively in practice.[33]

Education can build self-efficacy by including opportunities for observation and social comparison—for instance, via activities that let learners watch peers complete a task, record and watch themselves complete a task, or view vignettes that include peers or patients talking about their experience. Including rewards in game-based educational activities can also build self-efficacy.

Activities and Approaches That Build Self-Efficacy

1. **Vicarious learning.** Learning through others' lived experiences, such as listening to experts share lessons learned and mistakes made. This approach provides learners with role models and a sense of context.
2. **Simulation.** Opportunities to practice open-ended decision-making in a simulated environment allows learners to apply their knowledge and skills in a safe setting. This hands-on experience builds confidence.

3. **Didactic instruction.** While not always viewed as engaging, listening to expert lectures can be valuable for some learners in providing foundational knowledge and sparking further self-directed learning. This contributes to the knowledge component of self-efficacy.
4. **Writing out intentions.** The physical act of writing out concrete plans for implementing changes helps learners elaborate on their goals and strategies. This detailed planning increases commitment and confidence in ability to follow-through.
5. **Reflection on experience.** Thinking back on past performance and identifying areas of strength provides positive reinforcement. Learners who answer pre- and post-test questions correctly both before and after an educational activity feel affirmed in their knowledge and abilities.

As we will see in Chapter 7, self-efficacy is used as an indicator of how likely learners are to translate new information into practice. In CME, self-efficacy also informs peer-to-peer learning in communities of practice. The more connected we feel to our peers and the better we know them, the more likely we are to share, be open, and exchange ideas and information.

Social Theories

Psychological theories and frameworks treat learning and behavioral change as individual, cognitive pursuits. Rooted in a belief in the unique human capacity to reason, these views prioritize individual insight and decision-making processes based on evaluating the costs and benefits of actions. However, learning also has social and collective components that involve interaction between oneself, others, and the environment. Sociological and anthropological theories emphasize that learning is a social process in which the experience of others, not only one's own, provide examples for us to think through and learn from.

Social Cognitive Theory

Albert Bandura was a psychologist who argued that learning occurs in a social context with a dynamic and reciprocal interaction of the person, environment, and behavior. Essentially, we learn by observing and modeling the behaviors and actions of other people. If these new behaviors are reinforced, they are more likely to persist over time. Similarly, self-efficacy affects which behaviors we attempt and continue. When self-efficacy is bolstered, learners are more likely to see learning challenges as attainable or as opportunities for mastery.[34]

Situated Learning

Situated learning is a form of experiential learning that emphasizes the importance of context, authentic experiences, social interactions, and collaboration in the learning process. Developed by Jean Lave and Etienne Wenger, situated learning is most effective when learners have opportunities to apply new knowledge and practice skills within meaningful and relevant contexts.[35] This integration emphasizes the importance of connecting theoretical knowledge with practical application, ensuring that learners can effectively apply what they know in real-world situations. Social participation enhances learning. Learning is also more meaningful when learners are part of a community of practice, which is defined as:

> *a persistent, sustained social network of individuals who share and develop an overlapping knowledge base, set of beliefs, values, history and experiences focused on a common practice and/or mutual enterprise (p. 496).*[36]

We all belong to personal and professional communities of practice; groups and situations in which we learn together, exchange ideas with others, and encounter different ways of thinking—yoga, creative writing, or music classes; discussion boards; and professions like medicine and nursing. When health professionals learn in real-world (or simulated) settings, they are more likely to integrate knowing what (declarative knowledge) with knowing how (procedural knowledge).

◇◇

Peer-to-Peer Learning[37]

Peer-to-peer learning is an example of social learning. Members of a community of practice learn from each other through peer-led discussions and collaborations through which they share diagnostic approaches, treatment strategies, and outcomes to enhance their problem-solving skills and clinical decision-making abilities within the community. Journal clubs, Tweetorials, interactive workshops, and case study reviews are all examples of peer-to-peer learning.

◇◇

Active Learning

Overall, cognitive and social theories emphasize learning as an active endeavor in which adults learn best when they are actively involved in the learning process. Active learning is learner-centric and involves engaging learners in purposeful activities that promote critical thinking, discussion, and active participation.[7] In CME, educators can enhance learner engagement, motivation, and the application of knowledge in real-world contexts by incorporating active learning strategies to CME activities and programs.

Despite the evidence to support active learning in CME/CE,[38] the adoption of active learning strategies in this field has been rather slow.[39] Active learning involves strategies that require learners to "construct," understand, and comprehend the knowledge derived from their educational experience "*while simultaneously improving knowledge gain and recall abilities.*"[40] Strategies that support active learning include using a flipped classroom design, breaking up didactic approaches like lectures with a bulleted break or quick pause for a pop quiz, group work, or a mini project. This pause gives learners time to process, think, reflect, and apply what they are learning.

Barbi Honeycutt, PhD, is an educator with 22 years of experience advocating for professional development in academia. She notes,

> *When we're working with adult learners, we want to make sure that what we're sharing with them is very relevant and practical, because that's the best way to keep their attention. Instead of asking "What am I going to say?", try asking: "What are my learners going to do?" and then build out some activities that fit your context.*

CME/CE educators and writers who have to create content for busy health care professionals can especially benefit from implementing active learning strategies.

Strategies to Support Learning

CME/CE content is made for health professionals—people with incredibly full schedules, busy minds and lives, who often require a significant amount of buy-in to sit down and watch an educational video or attend a lecture. That means CME writers have the challenging job of engaging a somewhat distracted audience. CME/CE writers can keep their audiences in a receptive mode by creating experiential learning experiences in which participants take an active part in their education. That means we need to create content that lets learners test new ideas using context they already know and to apply what they have learned in a professional context or simulated environment.

Pro Tips to Reduce Cognitive Load[41]

Understanding learning theories can help us optimize content by reducing cognitive load and increasing retention. By identifying intrinsic and extrinsic loads, we can adjust the amount and manner of information we present to learners in our content, making it easier for them to process and retain relevant information and form strong neural connections. This process is based on the principle that cells that fire together, wire together. Repeated activation of neural networks is crucial for memory retention.

- **Stay on track:** Ensure that written content addresses the learning objectives
- **Edit ruthlessly:** Reduce distractions and eliminate extraneous information
- **Outline key points:** Highlight essential points for the learner
- **Build iteratively:** Sequence the presentation of ideas from simple to more complex
- **Parse it out:** Chunk complex ideas into bite-sized portions of text
- **Pair image with text:** Embed images, graphics, audio, or video clips to break up text where appropriate
- **Offer opportunities for retrieval practice:** Include questions to encourage long-term memory retrieval and help learners connect new information with prior knowledge
- **Promote active discovery:** Include exercises or activities such as matching, polling, or multiple-choice questions to help learners identify gaps between what they thought they knew and what they ought to

Strategies to Beat the Forgetting Curve

Insights from the learning sciences indicate incorporating certain tactics and types of difficulty into the learning process to support deep, durable learning.[42] These "desirable difficulties" require learners to exert more cognitive effort, which can lead to better encoding and retrieval of information.

Interleaving. Mixing different topics or types of problems within a single study session. This contrasts with blocking, where one topic is studied extensively before moving to the next.

Microlearning. Microlearning involves delivering short bursts of content that are media-rich and spaced out over time. This tactic is thought to boost interactivity and retention by reactivating memory, avoiding cognitive fatigue, and more efficiently moving new information from short- to long-term memory.[43] Studies have shown that microlearning in continuing education for health profession improves learners' procedural skills, knowledge retention, studying habits, and collaborative learning participation.[44]

Spaced repetition. Spaced repetition involves repeating material at defined intervals with different activities in between. This improves memory and retention.

Interactivity. A learning curve is a correlation between a learner's performance on a task and the number of attempts or time required to complete the task. Interactivity is one way to shorten the learning curve. Interactivity correlates with higher learning impact. The more actively learners engage with educational content, the more likely they are to retrieve and apply information in the appropriate context.[45] For instance, e-learning activities that boost interactivity include activities that require effortful and repeated recall, recognition, and retrieval tactics.

Experience. Experience is considered an important baseline for reflection. Put simply, we encounter a problem (a concrete learning event); we take stock of our options for addressing this problem (we reflect); and we actively experiment in designing solutions to the problem (sometimes called "knowing-in-action").[22] Experiential learning often includes activities that involve self-appraising current practice, identifying a problem in that practice, and problem-based learning as an individual or within in a team.

Competency-based learning. In competency-based education for health professionals, learners need to be able to develop expertise and progress from novice to mastery levels of competence. The trajectory toward mastery requires deliberate practice, a key ingredient in information processing and skills acquisition that involves effort, repetition, and feedback.[46]

Feedback. Constructive feedback helps us evaluate our progress and identify areas for improvement. Learning theories use feedback in different ways, such as to reinforce learning with positive or negative comments or action (behaviorism), to check understanding (cognitive theory), or to check how knowledge is being constructed (constructivism). Social and situational learning theories use feedback in the form of observation, such as watching yourself do something or watching others model actions or procedures. Examples of written feedback include expert or virtual patient commentary or notes about clinical outcomes that occurred because of decisions the learner made in the activity.

Deliberate practice. Deliberate practice is a common characteristic of virtual simulations or case- and vignette-based activities. Cases and vignettes are designed to mirror real-world challenges in health care and enable learners to practice reasoning, communication, and procedural skills. In online environments, patient cases are often highly interactive and are accompanied by feedback that offers insight into the consequences of learner choices, guides the learner toward an end goal, and allows room for failure and course corrections.[46-48]

Psychological safety. CME/CE content designers, planners, and faculty need to earn the trust of learners to ensure active learning. When learners feel like they belong and can express themselves without judgment during activities with interactive components, they are much more likely to engage with discussions, ask questions, and admit mistakes; all of which leads to better learning outcomes.[49] Psychological safety in content means incorporating openness, authenticity, and self-recognition into the material.

Peer-to-peer learning. Peer-to-peer learning involves creating opportunities for team members to learn from each other through collaboration and social learning and is increasingly part of an expanded format toolbox for delivering continuing education to health professionals. Peer-to-peer learning can involve conversations between HCPs, online interactive sessions with expert faculty, and using social media as a platform for distributing knowledge (e.g., Tweetorials).

STRATEGY	DESCRIPTION	EXAMPLES
Spaced repetition	Review informational increasing intervals to improve retention	Review after 1 day, 1 week, 1 month
Active learning	Engage learners to actively process and apply information	Group discussions, case studies, exercises, quizzes
Microlearning	Break down information into small, digestible pieces	Short videos, podcasts, infographics
Blended learning	Combine online, in-person, on-the-job activities	Online modules and in-person coaching/training
Practice and feedback	Provide opportunities to apply information and get feedback	Real-world scenarios, patient cases, written/verbal feedback

How to Beat the Forgetting Curve

How to Apply Adult Learning Principles in CME Writing

As a medical writer specializing in CME/CE, you are instrumental in crafting educational content that informs and engages health professionals. Our job as writers is to create as much clarity as possible in content to optimize learning and application of what is learned. You can do this by using adult learning principles to develop CME/CE content.

Five Tips for Effective CME Content

1. **Learner-centric.** Focused on the needs of the audience, not on the desires of the educator.
2. **Problem-oriented.** Each piece of learning content should aim to resolve a specific issue the learner is struggling with in clinical practice.

3. **Relevant to practice.** The content should make sense in the context of the learner's current experience or practice setting.
4. **Based on educational need.** Gaps in learning and practice should be identified before learning begins so the content can directly address specific needs.
5. **Aligned with anticipated outcomes.** Content should focus on the knowledge and skills directly tied to solving learner problems to get the anticipated outcomes.

Practical Applications of Adult Learning Principles in CME Content

Consider using these best practices to translate theory to practice:

Ensure content relevance. Consult the needs assessment to ensure the content addresses the current challenges and gaps in practice faced by learners.

Identify your audiences. Who are the learners? What are their needs? What experience or background do they bring to the educational activity? Review the anticipated outcomes. Identify the problem the content needs to address. What do learners need to know or be able to do when they have read the material?

Apply SMARTER goals to the content. Set clear, achievable learning objectives that align with anticipated outcomes. Keep the content specific; measurable; action-oriented; relevant to the learner, learning objectives, and anticipated outcomes; time-specific; evaluable; realistic.

Facilitate. As a writer, you might not see yourself as a facilitator. A facilitator acts as a guide in the learning process. The facilitator's job is to make it easy for learners to achieve an outcome, often by designing a process that helps learners reach a specific goal. The facilitator creates a safe and engaging environment that fosters connection, meaning, and purpose. In the CME/CE context, that means tuning into your audience's needs and designing interactive activities that blend seamlessly into the course content, allowing learners to explore the concepts they just discovered. Adopting a facilitation mindset can help you create meaningful content that goes beyond content delivery and supports active learning with interaction, dialogue, and exploration.

Lean on the learning objectives. Design content with learning objectives in mind and work backward. For example, when writing patient cases, think about the kind of clinical experience health professionals will have with a similar patient in a real-world clinical setting. You can optimize learning outcomes for patient cases by ensuring the content is authentic, tells a compelling story, uses real-world clinical data, promotes active discovery, and builds in formative feedback to learners.

Use real-world scenarios. Case studies, patient cases, and simulations based on real-world scenarios are excellent tools to demonstrate the practical application of knowledge. Storytelling can aid retention, as emotions help trigger memory.[45] Learners are presented with realistic patient scenarios and guided through the decision-making process based on available evidence and best practices. Either expert faculty or integrated online tools provide support and feedback throughout the learning process, presenting the best available clinical knowledge in an intelligently filtered format. Case- or story-based learning can nudge learners and trigger desired actions via prompts to help learners absorb information and foster retention, recall, and action.

Encourage reflective practice. Include an open-ended question to encourage learners to relate new knowledge to their past experiences.

Chunk content. Add dimension to content by breaking content into smaller chunks and incorporate interactive elements like polls, quizzes, and reflection exercises to enhance engagement and retention. You can also try using "ask then tell" techniques to encourage learners to think before diving into description or explanation.

Instructional Design

In my early days as a CME writer, I worked with instructional designers to develop educational content designed to increase awareness about racial and ethnic disparities in health care.[50] You might, too. Instructional design (ID) is the systematic process of creating learning experiences and materials to support the acquisition and application of knowledge and skills. It involves analyzing learning needs, designing effective training programs, developing instructional materials, implementing learning experiences, and evaluating the outcomes to ensure optimal learning results.

CME writer and instructional designer Mark Hagerty, MSOB, recommends cultivating an ID mindset to support CME content creation.

1. Involve as many senses as possible in the learning experience to improve retention and make it more engaging. Use visuals, audio, and interactions along with text.
2. Incorporate storytelling and narrative elements to tap into emotions and make content more relatable and memorable for learners. Build characters, conflicts, and resolutions.
3. Recognize that emotions play a crucial role in learning. Don't try to remove emotions from instructional content. Instead, acknowledge and leverage emotional responses appropriately.
4. Create opportunities for deliberate practice where learners can apply skills, not just acquire knowledge. Use scenarios, simulations, and interactive elements.
5. Focus on the humanity and real-world experiences in cases/examples to foster empathy and engagement with the content.
6. For writers, learn narrative writing techniques to infuse scenarios with elements like characters, obstacles, and emotional resonance.
7. Follow instructional design models like ADDIE (analysis, design, develop, implement, evaluate) as a framework for effective instruction.

See the Appendix for resources on educational and instructional design strategies.

Conclusion

In the CME/CE field, we cannot control how learners use the content we create. However, we can be more intentional and mindful of incorporating learning science strategies into CME/CE content. By doing so, we can promote positive learning outcomes and increase the effectiveness of CME/CE activities on clinician behavior.

Key Takeaways

- Motivation, self-direction, relevance, and self-efficacy are crucial in adult learning
- Apply adult learning principles when developing CME/CE content
- Incorporate active learning strategies into educational content
- Consider learners' motivation and self-efficacy when designing content
- Use a variety of learning theories to inform your approach

Crafting Effective CME

Chapter 7

Assessment and Evaluation

Change is the end result of all true learning.

— LEO BUSCAGLIA

Introduction

As a CME writer, it is essential to understand assessment and outcomes evaluation, including how outcomes are measured. While assessment focuses on the immediate, learner-level impact of CME activities, outcomes evaluation examines the broader, long-term impact of CME programs on health care providers, patients, and communities.[1] Both are important for understanding the effectiveness and value of continuing medical education. Assessing outcomes in CME helps to evaluate the effectiveness of educational interventions and ensure that health professionals acquire and retain the necessary knowledge and skills to provide high-quality patient care. Outcomes are important to both clinicians and the public to show that continuing education is meaningful, trustworthy, and credible.[2] Education providers also use outcomes results to identify ongoing areas of improvement and tailor educational content to meet specific needs.

Until the early 2000s, the effectiveness of CME was largely measured by how many health professionals attended an event and how satisfied they were with the location, accommodations, and educational content.[3] However, as we saw in Chapter 1, in response to increasing public scrutiny of CME, the field began to shift from a lecture-dominated education model that emphasized credit acquisition toward a new paradigm of learner-centered, practice-based change education. This shift was accompanied by recognition that the field needed to find better ways to demonstrate the effectiveness of CME in improving learner knowledge, skills, competence, and performance.[4]

ACCME further reinforced this shift by introducing new accreditation criteria in 2006 that emphasized assessing and measuring learners' knowledge, competence, performance, and patient outcomes, with assessment of change in competence required as a minimum.[5] Then, in 2009, Don Moore, Joe Green, and Harry Gallis published a seminal and much-quoted paper on how to assess desired results and learning outcomes.[6] Accordingly, CME has become increasingly invested in measuring learners' knowledge, competence, performance, and beginning with "end in mind." All activities in the accredited education space aim to achieve some kind of learning, mindset, or behavioral transformation.

This chapter reviews what outcomes are, why they are important, and how they are measured. When you understand assessment and outcomes frameworks, you can more effectively align content with the intended goals and objectives of the educational activity.

Moore's Outcomes Model

For any CME/CE activity, the central outcomes question is: What has changed as a result of the education activity or intervention?

In the early 2000s, Don Moore and colleagues synthesized research on CME effectiveness into a model designed to help education providers plan, deliver, and assess clinician learning, competence, and performance.[6] Moore's outcomes framework is widely used to measure and evaluate outcomes in CME and is recommended by a number of consensus papers and best-practice guidance.[7] The framework is designed to measure differences between desired standards and what is actually occurring in clinical practice or performance in a stepwise, unidirectional fashion, through distinct levels of outcome. As Chapter 5 outlined, desired standards are determined by current clinical evidence, guideline recommendations, professional competencies, performance and quality indicators, health policy, and patient expectations.

Brian McGowan PhD, one of the authors of the Outcomes Standardization Model, notes that Moore's framework is not a validated model but is, instead, a conceptual framework designed to evaluate outcomes on different levels, from participation and satisfaction; to learning, competence, and performance; to patient and community health. Patient and community level outcomes are the most highly sought outcomes levels but are also the most challenging to achieve. The ACCME reports that almost 100 percent of activities are designed to change competence.[8] Many education providers try to measure outcomes at many different levels in one activity as well as educational outcomes in a series of activities over time.

Evaluation using Moore's framework focuses on the following questions:

- Did learners learn what they needed to know? Do they know something new that they did not know or know how to do before (learning)?
- Can learners show that they can do something differently after the education (competence)? Are they able to put into practice what they learned in either a simulated environment or a clinical context?
- Are learners able to do something differently after the education (performance)? Has their practice or performance changed because of what they learned? For instance, have they achieved any objective standards (such as performance metrics), and have

any patients or community outcomes improved as a result of clinical learning?

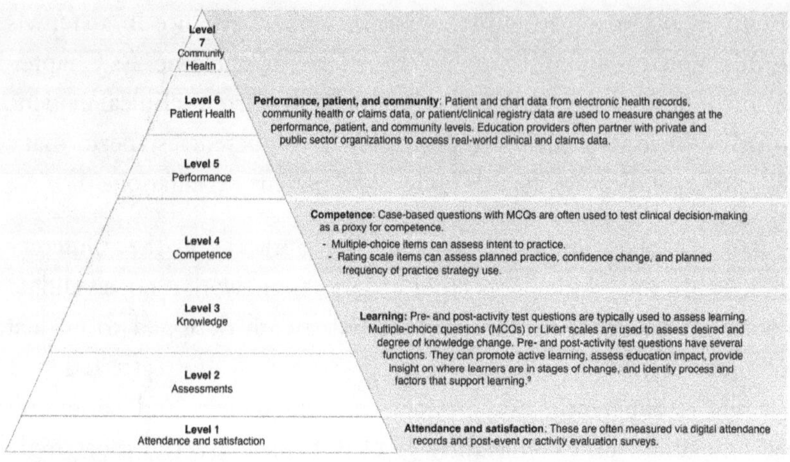

Level 7 Community Health
Level 6 Patient Health
Performance, patient, and community: Patient and chart data from electronic health records, community health or claims data, or patient/clinical registry data are used to measure changes at the performance, patient, and community levels. Education providers often partner with private and public sector organizations to access real-world clinical and claims data.
Level 5 Performance
Competence: Case-based questions with MCQs are often used to test clinical decision-making as a proxy for competence.
- Multiple-choice items can assess intent to practice.
- Rating scale items can assess planned practice, confidence change, and planned frequency of practice strategy use.
Level 4 Competence
Level 3 Knowledge
Learning: Pre- and post-activity test questions are typically used to assess learning. Multiple-choice questions (MCQs) or Likert scales are used to assess desired and degree of knowledge change. Pre- and post-activity test questions have several functions. They can promote active learning, assess education impact, provide insight on where learners are in stages of change, and identify process and factors that support learning.9
Level 2 Assessments
Level 1 Attendance and satisfaction
Attendance and satisfaction: These are often measured via digital attendance records and post-event or activity evaluation surveys.

Measuring Outcomes with Moore's Framework[1, 9, 10]

The Kirkpatrick Model

Like Moore's outcomes pyramid, the Kirkpatrick Model of Evaluation is a hierarchical model. Developed by Donald Kirkpatrick, PhD, in the 1950s, the Kirkpatrick model was initially designed to help managers with Human Resources training. In more recent years the model has been used to monitor the impact of workplace training on productivity, cost-effectiveness, and other business indicators.[11] The model has also been used to evaluate continuing education impact in the health professions[12] and is validated to evaluate education in a range of organizational settings. The updated New World Kirkpatrick Model includes affective aspects of participant reactions to learning.[13]

Kirkpatrick has four levels.

1. **Reaction.** How did learners react to what they learned? Was the activity relevant to their clinical practice? Was the activity engaging or valuable?

2. **Learning.** What did participants learn? Did learners gain knowledge or acquire skills as intended by the education?
3. **Behavior.** Did this new learning change behavior? Are learners taking what they learned into their workplace and applying it to clinical practice?
4. **Results.** What were the results of those changes? What impact has behavior change made on patient, community, or clinical outcomes?

While this model has only four levels versus the seven in Moore's framework, it has the advantage of allowing scrutiny of not only outcomes (Did the education produce the results we intended?), but also how an education activity's context impacts learning (How did the education work and for whom?).[12]

Kirkpatrick evaluation has been used to evaluate continuing education interventions with pharmacists to enhance opioid risk assessment, quality improvement, and the effectiveness of using standardized patients in CME.[14–16]

Self-Efficacy, Intent to Change, and Commitment to Change

Self-efficacy, intent to change, and commitment to change are all used as indicators of initiating and maintaining behavior changes resulting from exposure to CME activities.[17–20] These concepts originate with different learning theories, including Social Cognitive Theory, TTM, and the Theory of Planned Behavior. The relationships between these concepts are still being teased out in the field and are the focus of ongoing research.

Self-efficacy. Refers to an individual's belief or confidence in their ability to successfully perform a specific task or behavior. High self-efficacy can lead to a sense of competence and resilience, while low self-efficacy results in feelings of helplessness and avoidance of difficult tasks.

Intent to change. Represents an individual's readiness and willingness to initiate behavioral changes. Intent to change is a precursor to actual behavioral change, indicating the individual's motivation and commitment toward adopting new behaviors.

Commitment to change. Signifies an individual's dedication and resolve to implement and sustain behavioral changes over time. Commitment to change is considered crucial for maintaining behavior modifications.

Outcomes specialist Katie Lucero PhD, Chief Impact Officer at Medscape, notes that self-efficacy can be a significant predictor of behavior, sometimes even more so than knowledge or competence scores. Learners with high self-efficacy are more likely to engage deeply with the subject matter, employ effective learning strategies, and persevere through challenges. Furthermore, self-efficacy has been linked to higher post-learning confidence, which in turn predicts a greater likelihood of applying new knowledge and skills in real-world settings.

> *I found in looking at some data across different types of outcomes levels, if you want to think about Moore's levels, that self-efficacy is a really good way to measure impact of a program with a question type that is not so difficult to write and can be written in a way where it does collect reliable, valid information.*
>
> — KATIE LUCERO, *WRITE MEDICINE* PODCAST

Self-efficacy, intent to change, and commitment to change are often measured through self-assessment rating scale questions. Questions using a Likert scale will gauge an individual's confidence, intent, or commitment at a particular moment in performing specific tasks, such as using a screening tool, making a diagnosis, evaluating a patient using a particular algorithm, or selecting therapy according to patient characteristics.

For example, in a CME activity focusing on new therapies for managing Covid-19 symptoms, a question might ask: "How confident are you in your ability to treat a patient who has adverse outcomes from Covid-19?" Learners rate their confidence on a scale, providing a snapshot of their perceived ability to apply what they have learned. To effectively measure these concepts in CME assessment, the assessment questions need to be aligned with the learning objectives of the educational program. The questions should be specific and focus on key tasks or decisions that learners are expected to perform after completing the activity.

These concepts are valuable tools in CME assessment, but they have limitations. They provide a snapshot of an individual's perceived ability or intent to apply what they have learned. Self-reported data may be subject to bias, as learners may overestimate or underestimate their confidence and intent. As a result, self-efficacy is often used in conjunction with other assessment methods (such as knowledge tests, competency assessments, and performance evaluations) to provide a comprehensive picture of the impact of CME interventions.

Methods and Tools for Evaluating CME Activities

CME assessment and evaluation uses multiple quantitative and qualitative tools to collect and analyze outcomes data.

1. **Pre- and post-activity baseline assessments**
   - **Surveys and questionnaires.** Pre- and post-activity surveys gauge the knowledge, attitudes, and skills of participants before and after an education activity. This helps in measuring immediate learning outcomes and changes in perception.
   - **Tests and quizzes.** Employing tests before and after the program can quantitatively measure the gain in knowledge and understanding of the subject matter.
2. **Observational methods**

- **Direct observation.** Observers can assess decision-making, communication, and performance in simulations or real-world clinical settings to evaluate skill application.
- **Indirect observation.** Recording education participation sessions or simulations for later analysis can provide insights into decision-making, communication, and performance.

3. **Feedback from participants**
   - **Focus groups and interviews.** Conducting focus groups or interviews with participants after the activity provides qualitative data on their experiences, perceptions of the program's effectiveness, and suggestions for improvement.
   - **Participant reflections.** Encouraging participants to write reflective essays or journals can provide deep insights into their learning process and the application of skills in practice.

4. **Longitudinal tracking**
   - **Follow-up surveys.** Fielding surveys weeks or months after the activity can assess the long-term impact of the education on professional practice.

5. **Patient outcomes and satisfaction**
   - **Patient feedback.** Gathering feedback from patients on their care experience (e.g., via Hospital Consumer Assessment of Healthcare Providers and Systems Survey [HCAPS]) can provide direct insights into the effectiveness of care post-education.
   - **Health outcome metrics.** Analyzing health outcomes, such as reduced hospital readmission rates or improved management of chronic conditions, can link the education interventions to tangible patient benefits.

6. **Performance metrics in clinical settings**

- **Quality of care indicators.** Monitoring changes in quality-of-care indicators relevant to the education focus area, such as medication errors or time to treatment, can provide objective measures of the program's impact.

7. **Case studies and anecdotal evidence**
   - **Documenting specific instances.** Collecting and analyzing case studies where the education had a clear impact can provide compelling evidence of effectiveness.
   - **Anecdotal reports.** Gathering stories and testimonials from participants about how the training impacted their practice can be powerful, though subjective, indicators of success.
8. **Technological tools and data analytics**
   - **Learning management systems (LMS).** Using LMS data to track participant engagement, completion rates, and performance in online education.
   - **Data analytics.** Applying data analytics to evaluate large datasets, like hospital performance metrics, can reveal patterns and impacts not immediately apparent.

Crafting Test Questions

Test questions serve as tools to measure knowledge, skills, and learning outcomes in CME. They can be used before, during, and after educational activities to assess learners' understanding, engage them in the learning process, and provide valuable feedback. Most CME writers will tell you it is challenging to create effective test questions, and there are few opportunities for training in this specialized skill. CME as a field tends to favor multiple-choice questions (MCQs), which require a stem, one correct answer, and plausible distractors. Pitfalls in writing MCQs include vague stems, irrelevant distractors, and using "all of the above" or "none of the above" options.[21]

Outcomes expert Angelique Vinther, CHCP, notes that writing and validating test questions is truly a skill unto itself, and most of us are just scratching the surface in CME/CE. While the field of psychometrics studies writing and validating good test questions, it is valuable for CME professionals to have an understanding of different types of questions and how they are used to measure outcomes.

Types of Test Questions

1. Knowledge-based questions:

- Often in the form of MCQs, which can be effective[21]
- Measure recall and basic understanding of concepts
- Example: "Which of the following is a common symptom of Covid-19? a) Fever b) Rash c) Hair loss d) Muscle growth"

2. Engagement questions:
    - Used during educational activities to maintain learner engagement
    - Can guide remedial content and provide feedback
    - Often show what other learners have chosen and provide rationales for correct answers
    - Example: "What percentage of patients with Covid-19 experience fever as a symptom? a) 25 percent b) 50 percent c) 75 percent d) 100 percent"

3. Application/competence questions:
    - Designed to assess learners' ability to apply acquired knowledge
    - Gauge competence rather than simple recall
    - Example: "A 45-year-old patient presents with fever, cough, and difficulty breathing. Based on current guidelines, what is the most appropriate next step in management? a) Prescribe antibiotics b) Order a chest X-ray c) Administer a Covid-19 test d) Recommend over-the-counter cough suppressants"

Strategies for Writing Effective Test Questions

Angelique Vinther, recommends the following strategies for writing effective test questions:

1. Align questions with learning objectives.
2. Each question should measure only one task.
3. Ensure clarity and concision in question stems.
4. Develop plausible distractors for multiple-choice questions.
5. Avoid negatively phrased questions and "all of the above" or "none of the above" options.
6. Use real-world scenarios and case-based questions to assess application of knowledge.
7. Incorporate feedback and rationales for correct and incorrect answers.
8. Collaborate with subject matter experts to ensure accuracy and relevance.

The "NBME Item-Writing Guide" is a great resource that covers test item and vignette writing as well as best practices in creating MCQs. You can download the guide at: https://www.nbme.org/item-writing-guide.

Qualitative Data in CME/CE

Qualitative research methods are valuable tools for gathering insights about learning, behavioral change, and practice change in CME/CE. Unlike quantitative research, which analyzes numerical data using statistical techniques, qualitative analysis employs structured, interpretive steps to examine textual or image-based data. By focusing on the complexity of meanings that participants bring to their experiences and the context in which practice occurs, qualitative research provides additional nuance and depth to learner evaluations. This helps educators understand the norms, motivations, and values that shape how learners interact with educational activities and materials.[22]

Analyzing qualitative data involves an iterative process called coding, which breaks text into discrete units and groups those units according to their characteristics. This approach, known as grounded theory, builds insights derived from what learners say rather than making assumptions or judgments about what they should say. It is helpful to ask three questions when using a qualitative approach to outcomes data collection and analysis:

- *What is happening?*
- *What is important?*
- *What patterns are emerging?*

By analyzing qualitative data, educators can identify what matters to participants, detect obstacles to changing clinical performance, and explain why learning and/or performance improves (or doesn't).

Qualitative data analysis can be valuable across the CME/CE planning process; from the initial planning phase of identifying education needs and gaps, through the design phase of identifying barriers to and facilitators of learning; as well as during program implementation for formative evaluation, and in the final program evaluation for generating context-sensitive outcomes measures.

Outcomes Standardization Project

"Outcomes" is a term that has different meanings to different people. Although many education providers use Moore's framework to measure outcomes, there is not yet a common language for outcomes in CME/CE. Hence, providers take different approaches to outcomes measurement. As Emily Belcher and Wendy Cerenzia of CE Outcomes note,

> *There is now greater sophistication in abilities to gather, analyze, and report outcomes data; however, there is wide variation in the types and formats of outcomes data generated and reported.*[23]

As such, it remains challenging to effectively understand and communicate the value of CME/CE. The challenge isn't academic. The variety of approaches and methods used are combined with an absence of interpretation and insight. As a result, outcomes reports, which we will review in Chapter 8, are often filled with data but no context.

The Outcomes Standardization Project (OSP) is trying to change this. The OSP is a collaborative initiative developed in 2018 and is part of the ongoing professionalization of CME/CE.[24] The project seeks to create standardized outcomes terminology and approaches for measuring the impact of education activities. A standardized framework will allow providers and supporters to more effectively compare and aggregate outcomes data and insights. The OSP project group published a preliminary glossary in 2020 that is available at: https://outcomesince.org.[24]

By providing a unified framework for assessing the impact of educational interventions, the goal of the OSP is to support evidence-based analysis of educational needs and promote best practices in CME/CE.

Conclusion

It's always been difficult to measure the effectiveness of CME in building knowledge and changing clinical behavior, competence, and performance. There are so many variables that can confound the transfer of knowledge and skills from the education context to a clinical setting. And research tells us that gaining knowledge does not necessarily result in behavior change in health care or clinical practice.[25] Nonetheless, CME/CE is an important way to address competency gaps among practicing clinicians and facilitate quality improvement initiatives within clinics and hospitals.[26] To do this effectively, the field recognizes the need for a sophisticated approach to assessment and evaluation that captures not only outcomes but real-world context and process. By doing so, educational content can be tailored to highly specific learning objectives, built to ensure clinical authenticity by simulating real-world scenarios, and delivered via formats that are interactive and participatory.[27–31]

Key Takeaways

- Moore's Outcomes Framework is widely used in CME/CE
- Assessment can measure knowledge, competence, performance, and patient outcomes
- Both quantitative and qualitative data are valuable in evaluation
- Self-efficacy and commitment to change are important predictors of behavior change
- Learn to develop effective assessment questions

Chapter 8

Key Formats and Deliverables

Variety is the very spice of life/That gives it all its flavour.

— ENGLISH POET WILLIAM COWPER (1731–1800)

Introduction

While needs assessments are a common starting point for new-to-the-field CME/CE writers, you will increasingly work on many other formats and products, including live courses, symposia, or meetings; journal activities; and enduring text or image-based print or online materials, which form the bulk of activities that are produced in the accredited CME space. You might also be asked to write outcomes questions and develop outcomes reports.

Traditional formats like live presentations, webcast discussions, and print-based materials continue to be widely used in CME/CE. However, delivery platforms have evolved toward online, multimedia, and interactive formats, such as simulations, virtual patient cases, and educational games. Social media platforms are also being explored as a delivery medium. This chapter provides an overview of the different formats medical writers will encounter in CME/CE and reviews some of the research about their relative effectiveness.

Common CME deliverables

- Slide decks
- Patient cases
- White papers
- Outcomes reports
- Roundtable reports
- Needs assessments
- Evaluation questions
- Performance reports
- Case-based vignettes
- Pre/post-test questions
- Multiple choice questions
- Patient education materials
- Conference/poster abstracts
- Quality improvement reports
- Animation/podcast/video scripts

Paywalls and restricted content can make it difficult to access examples of CME/CE activities, but you can create free accounts for platforms like Medscape, the Annenberg Center for Health Sciences, the Academy for health care Learning, and Clinical Care Options that will allow you to explore various education formats and deliverables.

Format Effectiveness

Certain education formats have been shown to be more effective than others in supporting learning and clinical practice change. A meta-analysis of published outcomes studies in CME/CE concluded that there are three main characteristics of formats that are effective in learning and behavior change.[1]

1. **Interactivity.** Deliberate practice is a key ingredient in information processing and skills acquisition that involves effort, repetition, and feedback.
2. **Multimedia activities.** Audio, video, text, quizzes.
3. **Case-based activities.** Active problem-solving promotes critical thinking.

Formats vary in effectiveness depending on stage of learning and learner need.

Multimodal Learning

It is important to create educational content in various formats and delivery modalities that support the learning journey. Multimodal learning refers to the use of multiple modes or methodologies to teach a concept that engage various sensory systems simultaneously. This format involves organizing various educational elements (such as simulations, adaptive e-learning, virtual reality, gamification, and social media) in a way that guides learners through a process of learning.

Multimodal learning assumes that text and image do not simply represent information in different ways. When combined, multiple sources of information and different formats more effectively support information processing.[2] By engaging multiple senses, multimodal learning approaches keep learners more engaged and attentive, improve knowledge retention, and allow for greater flexibility in how health care professionals access and engage with CME content. They can also make a more inclusive and culturally sensitive learning environment that reaches a wider audience.

As a result, multimodal learning allows education providers to create content that appeals to a wide range of learners and makes education more accessible. As Allison Kickel, Bonum Education CEO notes, with multimodal content, learners can choose the format that best fits their schedule and learning preferences, whether that's watching a video, listening to a podcast, reading a printable monograph, or participating in an interactive simulation. Practical considerations, like the learner's professional context (e.g., academic vs. community oncologists) and personal constraints, should guide the selection of content delivery modes.

Insights on Multimodal Learning from Eve Wilson, PhD

Multimodal learning often combines multiple instructional practices, learning formats, and technologies, such as simulations, adaptive e-learning, virtual reality, gamification, and social media. For example, an all-day CME program might include an icebreaker learning experience in the morning, followed by a game, a didactic session, and a case exploration. The key to effective multimodal learning is structuring these components in a meaningful, logical sequence that builds upon each other, creating a coherent learning journey.

When developing multimodal CME activities, consider the potential for cognitive overload. Learners may struggle to process and retain information if they are exposed to too many different types of activities in a condensed timeframe. To mitigate this risk, mix innovative approaches with more traditional ones, such as didactic sessions that provide the "nuts and bolts" of a topic. Breaking complex subjects into digestible chunks and teaching them through various methods, such as case studies and didactics, can also help manage cognitive load. Additionally, incorporating breaks and opportunities for learners to interact with each other in a noneducational context can provide necessary rest and recovery time.

For writers working on multimodal CME projects, keeping track of the various components can be challenging. Content mapping is a useful tool for organizing and visualizing the relationships between different elements. A content map typically consists of a table with tactics listed in rows on the left and columns for learning objectives, key takeaway points, and assessment questions. This structure ensures that each tactic aligns with the learning objectives and key teaching points, and that everything has a clear purpose. Content maps can also be used during faculty calls to help organize content requests and assign tasks.

Universal Design for Learning

Multimodal learning shares similarities with universal design for learning (UDL). Both approaches aim to cater to diverse learning needs by offering multiple modes of representation, action, and engagement. UDL emphasizes creating inclusive learning environments through flexibility and customization to accommodate all learners.

Barbi Honeycutt, PhD, an educator with twenty-two years of experience advocating for professional development in academia, recommends offering choices in assignments, activities, and participation modes to allow learners to engage in the way they are most comfortable. She also suggests using a "plus one" approach to content modality by adding one more way for people to access and engage with content, such as providing a transcript for a podcast.

Ask yourself: What's the one more thing I can do? So, if you're doing a podcast, maybe you provide a transcript; that's the plus one, so someone can read it or they can listen.

Learn more about the UDL framework at: https://udlguidelines.cast.org/.

Online/Digitized Education

Although the research literature on the effectiveness of online learning in CME is dated, studies suggest its value. An analysis of more than 200 studies reported that online education is more effective than offline, when measuring behavioral changes and sustained gains in knowledge.[3] Similarly, an analysis of 600 CME programs reported that online CME is more effective than live or other CME activities for facilitating and reinforcing evidence-based decision-making -- due, in part, to its customizable, interactive, and measurable formats.[4]

Online education provides an especially effective critical link in building awareness among physicians about emerging agents and technologies prior to approval, as well as preparing them to integrate novel therapies and interventions to clinical practice postapproval.[1, 5–8] The Covid-19 pandemic necessitated a shift to virtual and online learning platforms to ensure the continuity of education while adhering to social distancing measures and restrictions on in-person gatherings. While clinician demand for online CME was growing before the pandemic, online CME increased considerably in 2020.[9–14]

It is likely that online platforms will remain central to education delivery. Digital learning can be designed to be more personalized for learners and direct them toward remedial and support resources based on their learning journey, needs, and outcomes.[15] Digital or online learning is also a valuable modality to engage and retain learners across a CME/CE activity, provide wider access to education materials, and deliver learning content in smaller sequences and segments to support microlearning and spaced repetition.[15–16]

For examples of online learning head on over to Medscape Education at: https://www.medscape.org/. You can create a free account and explore different activity types.

Gamification

Gamification represents a rapidly growing format and delivery modality in CME/CE. The effectiveness of gamification in adult learning is based on our need to connect, compete, and succeed. "Serious games" are the most applied form of gamification in CME/CE. Serious games are digital applications specifically designed for the purpose of educating health professionals.[17]

Gamification involves incorporating game elements and mechanics (such as points, badges, leaderboards, and challenges) into nongame contexts as a way to engage and motivate learners.[18] This approach aims to increase retention, motivation, and active participation by providing a sense of progress, competition, and achievement within the learning process.[19] Gamification transforms learners from passive recipients of information to active participants in creating knowledge and makes learning more enjoyable and interactive, especially in online learning environments.

CME/CE-focused games typically incorporate video segments and can be delivered via desktop and smartphone platforms. Top Derm is such an example. A recent narrative review of serious gaming/gamification suggests that this modality is at least as effective as controls in improving knowledge, skills, and satisfaction, and is superior in many cases.[19]

Wheel of Knowledge[20]

Gamification can be a powerful tool in promoting knowledge transfer and long-term retention in health professions education. In 2015, Array, a content engagement organization, and Vindico, a medical education prover, developed a game called Wheel of Knowledge. The game, led by faculty experts, involves learners answering questions from predetermined educational categories, earning points for participation and correct answers. The implementation of this gaming strategy demonstrated high levels of learner engagement (97 percent completion rate) and knowledge retention (92 percent knowledge scores at 30 days postlearning).

Simulation

My first experience of simulation was with an orange and a manikin. As a student nurse in Scotland in the 1980s, I practiced injection techniques by sticking needles into an orange and cardiopulmonary resuscitation (CPR) with CPR Annie (a manikin also known as Resuscitation Annie). Now there are many simulation modalities, including simulated scenarios, manikins, virtual patients, and other tools to provide learners with realistic and immersive learning experiences that mimic clinical situations.

Simulation-based education is used at all levels of training in health care, including CME/CE.[21] Simulation activities are designed to enhance clinical competence and enable health professionals to acquire diagnostic, surgical, and treatment administration skills in a risk-free environment that they can later apply to real-world medical scenarios.[22]

Simulation-based education provides the following:

1. Helps learners engage in deliberate practice, repeatedly testing their knowledge and exploring the implications of their decisions in a safe, controlled environment
2. Provides timely, specific, and nonevaluative feedback to encourage self-reflection and course correction
3. Allows learners to track their progress toward learning goals

Martin Warters, MA Ed Tech, CHSE, POPM, is a leader in digital design. He describes virtual patient simulation as an:

> *Amazing device that portrays a virtual representation of a real-life patient so you can do all the things that you would do in a real-life practice setting. You can order tests, make diagnosis, administer treatments, prescribe follow-up, and every step of the way you're getting targeted feedback on the appropriateness of the decisions you're making. So it's a great tool for reinforcement of learning, but it also operates as a catalyst of change. In a safe environment, you can make mistakes, you can experiment, you can try things out, and you're getting targeted feedback on whether it's a good thing or a bad thing, and the data behind the choices as well, to show why it is such a good or bad thing.*

Examples of Simulation-Based Education in the Health Professions

Simulation-based education in the health professions allows health care professionals to practice skills, improve decision-making, and enhance teamwork in a safe and controlled environment.

1. **Task training.** Simulation can be used to practice specific technical procedures, such as suturing, intubation, or catheter insertion. By repeatedly performing these tasks in a simulated setting, health care professionals can enhance their proficiency and confidence before applying these skills in real clinical settings.[23]
2. **Team training.** Simulation is valuable for training health care teams to work effectively in high-stress environments like the operating room or emergency department. Team-based simulations help improve communication, coordination, and decision-making among team members, leading to better patient outcomes and safety.[23]

3. **Therapy selection.** Virtual patient simulations are used to simulate clinical decision-making and improve evidence-based treatment selection.

◇◇

Virtual Patient Simulation in HIV[24]

Medscape Education developed a simulation activity with two HIV-positive virtual patients to help infectious disease (ID)/HIV specialists and HIV primary care providers develop appropriate patient care strategies. The activity consisted of two virtual patient cases in an immersive environment that allowed clinicians to assess the patient, review electronic health records, and make open-ended clinical decisions from an extensive database of diagnostic and treatment possibilities matching the scope and depth of clinical practice.

Core elements included:

- An electronic health record interface that updated in real-time as the learner progressed through the simulation
- Real-life clinical practice workflow
- Practice features such as a prescription pad, test orders, and realistic lab reports
- Third-party drug database to support prescribing options that mirror actual clinical practice.
- Clinical decision supported by a data-and-guideline-based decision engine

More than 22,800 clinicians who directly care for HIV-positive patients participated in the activity. After participation, physicians showed significant improvements in a variety of areas, including in baseline laboratory assessments, provision of preventive care, and initiation of antiretroviral therapy. Analysis of learner data uncovered significant gaps and educational needs in a variety of areas, including timely initiation of anti-retroviral therapy for HIV infection.

◇◇

Simulation has emerged as a powerful tool in health professions education, supporting learning through the principles of mastery learning, effective feedback, and a learner-centered approach. As health care education evolves, simulation will likely play an increasingly important role in developing clinical skills, expertise, and confidence among health professionals.

Escape Rooms

Escape rooms have emerged as an innovative learning modality in CME. Escape rooms are action-adventure games that use elements like time pressure, strategy, challenge, and rewards to create an engaging learning experience that encourages participants to apply their knowledge in a practical and interactive setting. Participants are locked into interactive live or virtual environments where they solve puzzles and challenges related to health care delivery and clinical content within a set time frame. The puzzles and challenges follow a storyline or theme and solving the puzzles ends the game.[25]

Effective educational escape rooms incorporate authentic clinical data, realistic documentation, and relatable patient stories to create a deeper connection with the learning material. By integrating elements of storytelling, escape rooms enable learners to apply their knowledge and skills in contextualized, memorable ways. The escape room experience for participants can be autonomous and self-paced or live with a moderator and can include single players or small groups to support interprofessional collaboration.[26]

Martha Johnson, MSN, RN, CEN of *BreakoutRN*, notes that escape rooms are valuable application exercises to help learners apply skills and knowledge they have previously learned. By incorporating principles of game design, escape rooms aim to enhance knowledge acquisition, critical-thinking skills, teamwork, and problem-solving abilities in a fun and stimulating environment. These application exercises are designed with clear learning objectives in mind. They offer valuable opportunities to hone skills, from math calculations to IV insertions and assessments, and foster professional behaviors such as teamwork, communication, leadership, and thriving under pressure and time constraints.

Pro Tip

Overall, escape rooms offer a dynamic and effective way to deliver educational content in CME by providing hands-on experiences that promote active participation, knowledge retention, and skill development among health care professionals. Games like escape rooms need scripts, patient cases, storylines, answers to player comments and questions, and consequences. As such, they represent a growing opportunity for writers to create content.

As educators continue to seek active learning strategies that bridge the gap between theory and practice, escape rooms offer a promising tool for enhancing student engagement, motivation, and the acquisition of both technical and nontechnical skills.

Journal Manuscripts

One of my earliest CME projects was helping an education provider develop a manuscript for publication in a peer-reviewed journal. The manuscript focused on results from an assessment of an education intervention designed to improve nurses' knowledge regarding pain management.[27] My job was to search and synthesize the literature to frame the story and develop manuscript structure.

As a published author myself in peer-reviewed journals, the project was straightforward. I was able to apply existing skills and help education providers get their work into the public domain. And since 2010, I have provided manuscript assistance as just described or been a coauthor on several publications for peer-reviewed journals.

You can, too.

CME providers have vast experience and productive insights to share. When clients tell me about the interesting, thought-provoking work they are doing in CME, I always ask, "Are you planning to write about your discovery, experience, or insights?" The answer is invariably "No." Here's why.

First, many people don't think of themselves as writers, or at least not as writers of something longer than a blog, an email, or a grocery list—say, like an article, a journal manuscript, or even a book. Sometimes that is because people don't think they have anything to say (they think it has been said before or that other people say it better), and sometimes it's because they simply don't know where to start.

Second, CME providers are particularly hesitant to publish their outcomes in peer-reviewed journals. This reluctance can be traced, at least in part, to myths associated with peer-reviewed publications—that they have little impact on behavior, are only of value within academia, and reach a limited audience, especially in a digital world.

But there are many reasons to publish. Publishing needs assessments, outcomes studies, case studies, best practices, and commentary on new educational methods advances the CME field by building credibility and reputation for CME providers and supporters. Publishing CME findings lays a foundation for evidence-based practice that optimizes the use of providers' internal data and shares trends over time. CME providers can also learn and improve their own practice by publishing articles on how their education intervention explicitly and implicitly impacted learners and that showcase the methodologies they have used to collect and analyze data. By publishing, providers can establish themselves as preferred providers, secure funding for educational grants, raise the bar for the CME enterprise, and, in so doing, increase participation in CME programs and activities. Publishing a manuscript is also a good way to wrap up a project, put it on the record, and communicate the value of CME to clinicians, providers, and supporters.

Manuscripts are a stellar deliverable opportunity for medical writers in CME. Peer-reviewed publications play a crucial role in disseminating knowledge about CME initiatives, sharing best practices, and contributing to the ongoing improvement of educational interventions in the health care sector. As CME increasingly advocates for scholarship in its shift toward professionalization, education providers are keen to find opportunities to publish in the scholarly literature. Two ways to do so include publishing findings from comprehensive needs assessments, and from education outcomes assessment and evaluation. There has been an increasing emphasis in the CME field over the last decade to publish and disseminate outcomes from educational activities and many journals accept education outcomes manuscripts.

Pro Tip

If you have written manuscripts based on clinical data outside the educational field, then writing education outcomes manuscripts is an opportunity to consider as a deliverable for CME clients. As the writer, you will typically be involved in not only drafting the content for a manuscript, but also potentially identifying appropriate journals.

Abstracts and Posters

Despite the dip in attendance at scientific meetings during the Covid-19 pandemic years, posters and presentations at scientific and professional meetings remain an important way for many clinicians to get access to CME. Writers can help education providers develop these posters and abstracts.

They can also help education providers develop posters and journal abstracts that showcase their work. Like manuscripts, these shorter formats provide a way for education providers to highlight and share valuable insights about both needs assessment and educational outcomes with the CME/CE community. Writers are often hired to help education providers shape the story of the outcome and to search and synthesize literature to support the discussion and conclusion of an abstract, poster, or manuscript.

Patient Cases

Interactive patient cases are core learning activities in CME. Cases provide learners with the unique opportunity to engage in clinical reasoning, problem-solving, and decision-making, within the context of real-world patient care scenarios.[28] Crafting these cases allows you, the writer, to build a narrative around a patient's lived experience that also reflects the complexity of patient care.

Patient case studies are invaluable tools in CME for several reasons:

1. **Real-world application.** Case studies demonstrate the practical application of theories, concepts, and clinical data, bridging the gap between theoretical knowledge and clinical practice.
2. **Skill development.** Learners can hone their analysis, evaluation, and decision-making skills by working through patient case studies, preparing them for similar situations in their own practice.
3. **Engagement and relevance.** Well-crafted case studies capture learners' interest by presenting relatable, authentic scenarios that mirror their professional experiences.

Patient case studies are an effective learning tool in CME because they can be used to demonstrate the real-world application of theories, concepts, and clinical data. Cases allow learners to hone the analysis and evaluation skills needed in the clinical setting and provide them with guidance on how to approach similar cases in their own practice.

Patient cases specifically support learning in CME by:

1. **Promoting active learning.** Case studies encourage learners to actively engage with the material, applying their knowledge and skills to solve problems and make decisions.
2. **Providing feedback.** Incorporating feedback mechanisms within case studies allows learners to receive guidance and reinforcement, enhancing the learning process.
3. **Facilitating self-directed learning.** Adult learners in health care settings often prefer self-directed learning, and case studies cater to this preference by allowing learners to explore scenarios at their own pace and depth.

Types of Patient Case Studies in CME

There are several types of patient case studies used in CME, each with its own structure and purpose:

1. **Case-based learning (CBL).** CBL case studies are inquiry-based and often feature a gradual unfolding of information over time, engaging learners in analysis, evaluation, and decision-making. These case studies may include branched learning with alternative outcomes based on learner decisions.
2. **Single patient journey.** Some case studies follow the journey of a single patient from initial symptoms to diagnosis, treatment, and aftercare, providing a comprehensive view of the patient experience.
3. **Multiple patient cases.** Other case studies feature several patient cases representing different points on the disease or treatment trajectory, offering learners a broader perspective on the topic.

Patient cases provide learners with authentic, engaging, and interactive learning experiences that foster active discovery and include targeted feedback. By understanding the importance of case studies, how they support learning, and the various types available, you can craft effective and impactful case studies that enhance the learning experience.

Videos and Podcasts

Videos (such as those included as components of serious games) and podcasts are increasingly valuable learning tools in CME that support enhanced learning benefits, flexibility and accessibility, and personalized learning. These tools provide a dynamic and interactive way to present information, catering to different learning preferences and enhancing knowledge retention.

Video

Video-based CME content has been around for a while, starting with the introduction of webinars as a content delivery vehicle. Many of my early content projects in CME involved developing webinar scripts and the accompanying slide decks, then editing the transcript and materials after recording to align with CME compliance.

Many education providers use video as a component for content delivery, which might include livestream, recorded video, or interactive slideshows with narration. Focused roundtable discussions among experts about a defined topic are also often recorded and delivered as video-based CME.

Videos can be viewed online or downloaded to devices like computers, smartphones, or tablets, allowing health professionals to engage with CME materials at their convenience, whether in clinical settings, during commutes, or at home. Educational videos foster engagement by presenting complex information in a visually appealing format that can include graphics, animations, demonstrations, and real-life scenarios that enhance understanding, critical thinking, and application of knowledge in clinical practice.

Podcasts

Podcasts offer learning opportunities in accessible, bite-sized chunks that health professionals can access on the go. Podcasts help create and reinforce communities of practice (see Chapter 6), provide just-in-time training, and fill knowledge gaps.[29] They are growing in popularity as a preferred method for busy clinicians across specialties to access asynchronous educational content, including in CME.[30] For instance, Annals on Call is an internal medicine podcast with thousands of CME credits claimed.[31]

Pro Tip

Video-, podcast-, or animation-based CME activities often need writing support to build out the content. Video and podcast scripts are tools to help a group of people have a focused discussion about a defined topic. The discussion might also include a moderator who defines the situation, establishes the tone of the discussion, ensures flow and coverage of the content, and develops a conclusion. An effective script prepares the moderator and provides support for the discussion, giving an appearance of a seamless conversation while ensuring that salient issues are objectively covered.

Activity Agenda

When you as a CME writer are developing a needs assessment, it is common to be tasked with creating an activity agenda for an educational program. The activity agenda is a crucial component of the grant proposal and outlines the key topics and content areas that the educational activity will focus on to address identified practice gaps and achieve the desired learning objectives and outcomes. The good news is that if you developed the needs assessment, you already have the content you need to create an activity agenda.

Steps to Create an Effective Activity Agenda

1. **Review the needs assessment.** This document serves as the foundation for the activity agenda. Carefully examine the identified practice gaps, learning objectives, and anticipated outcomes to ensure that the agenda aligns with these elements.
2. **Identify key topics.** Based on the needs assessment, determine the main topics that the educational content should cover to bridge the practice gaps and meet the learning objectives. These topics will form the headings and subheadings of your agenda outline.
3. **Organize the content.** Arrange the topics in a logical sequence that facilitates learning and builds upon the participants' existing knowledge. Consider the flow of information and how each topic relates to the others.
4. **Develop clear headings and subheadings.** Use descriptive and concise headings and subheadings to clearly communicate the focus of each section of the agenda. These should reflect the knowledge, skills, and attitudes that the education aims to address.
5. **Provide sufficient detail.** While you are not expected to design the complete educational activity, include enough detail under each heading to give the client a clear understanding of the proposed content. This might include specific subtopics, key points, or examples that will be covered.
6. **Align with the learning objectives.** Ensure that the content outlined in the agenda directly supports achievement of the stated learning objectives. Each topic should contribute to closing the identified practice gaps and improving patient outcomes.
7. **Consider the target audience.** Tailor the agenda to the needs and preferences of the intended audience, taking into account their existing knowledge, learning styles, and professional roles.

By following these steps and using the needs assessment as a guide, you can create effective activity agendas that provide a roadmap for the development of educational content.

Reporting Outcomes

Outcomes reports are pivotal in the feedback loop between education providers and supporters in CME. These reports showcase the impact of educational programs, provide valuable insights into achieved outcomes, share participant feedback, and identify areas for improvement in future initiatives. A compelling outcomes report describes how the program performed, whether the education reached the right (and enough) people, and whether the education contributed to learning. Outcomes data also tells providers if there are some persistent needs—areas where learners have performed poorly on post-activity assessment.

Outcomes reports are essential for several reasons, including to:

1. Demonstrate the effectiveness of educational interventions to supporters, showing how their funding has been put to meaningful use.
2. Identify areas of practice that require further education, helping providers tailor future activities to address persistent needs.
3. Document the successes and failures of designing and delivering educational activities, contributing to the knowledge base in CME/CE.
4. Help supporters make the case for continued funding within their organizations.

Outcomes Reports

Outcomes expert Angelique Vinther, CHCP, recommends including the following items in an outcomes report for grant supporters:

- Executive summary slide

- Program overview (formats, goals, focus, learning objectives)
- N values
- Collection and analysis methods
- Definitions of terms

To see examples of outcomes reports, head on over to the *Academic for Continued Healthcare Learning* at: https://www.achleducation.com/our-results.html. On the Outcomes page, click on any panel with Final Outcomes to see reports that include links to the need for education, the education design, and a table showing how the gaps, root causes, learning objectives, and expected results are linked. These reports also show the full wording of MCQs and open-ended assessment questions.

However, outcomes reports are challenging to develop. A recent study on outcomes reports in the field found that while outcomes reports improved since 2018, a significant minority are still of poor quality.[32] Common problems with outcomes reports include providing too much data without contextual interpretation (a "data dump") and lack of focus on how the educational activity impacted clinical practice. Here is where medical writers can flex their storytelling muscles! Outcomes reports beg for storytelling that reveals the meaning and relevance of outcomes data. *Effective Data Storytelling: How to Drive Change with Data, Narrative, and Visuals* by Brent Dykes is an invaluable resource for building outcomes reports.

Creating Effective Outcomes Reports

As a medical writer tasked with creating outcomes reports, you will need to consider several key aspects:

1. **Understand the purpose of an outcomes report.** Collaborate with the original creators of the educational activity to gain context about the intentions, objectives, and desired outcomes. In the process of the creation, administration, and evaluation of CME/CE activities, the initial premise gets obscured. By collaborating with the people who initiated the activity, you will get more context about the intentions of the activity as well as the objectives and desired outcomes it was meant to produce. Working from this foundation, you will be able to prepare an outcomes report that shows the effectiveness of the educational intervention.
2. **Familiarize yourself with outcome measures.** Be knowledgeable about different methods to assess effectiveness, such as knowledge tests, surveys, self-assessments, and performance evaluations. Chapter 7 is a good start.
3. **Develop awareness of statistical analysis.** Basic statistical concepts and methods are indispensable accessories in a medical writer's toolkit if you are working on outcomes reports. Some things that would serve you well to understand include measures of central tendency, variability, and significance testing. When you can interpret outcomes data using these measures, you will be able to present better insights and more comprehensive information in your outcomes reports.
4. **Be clear and concise.** In any data collection exercise, there is an abundance of information. CME/CE outcomes are no different. When writing outcomes reports, you should be able to present the results of the outcome measures clearly and concisely. Use tables, graphs, and other visual aids to present the data in a meaningful way that can be easily understood and digested. Provide a summary of the findings and their implications for future CME/CE activities.

Outcomes reports are a vital component of the CME/CE landscape, providing a powerful tool to effect change in clinician practice and patient health. By understanding the purpose of reports, familiarizing yourself with outcome measures, and presenting data clearly and concisely, you can deliver a powerful tool that contributes to the continuous improvement of CME programs.

White Papers

As a former academic, my exposure to white papers was mainly limited to that of government and policy, such as those produced by the RAND organization. White papers are also used as business to business (B2B) assets as part of the marketing and sales armamentarium. In 2006, Michael Stelzner of Social Media Examiner wrote the breakout book *Writing White Papers* that became the go-to guidebook for marketing copywriters and still represents the best overview of white paper process and structure. In CME, think of white papers as a hybrid deliverable that informs, educates, and markets. I have developed several white papers for clients on interprofessional education, simulation, outcomes evaluation, immuno-oncology, patient education, and more, and recommend these deliverables as a way to combine your creative and research insights.

A white paper is an authoritative document that presents information, expert analysis, and insights into a specific medical topic or solution to a health care-related issue. In CME, education providers use white papers to educate their peers, clinicians, and supporters or education funders about new research findings, best practices, or innovative approaches in education. Medical education companies are more likely to use white papers than other education providers such as medical schools or specialty medical societies. White papers serve as valuable tools for establishing authority, thought leadership, and sharing knowledge within the CME community. They are also a way to disseminate education outcomes without having to submit to a journal publication peer review process.

White papers typically use a funnel structure, starting with a big picture overview of a problem or challenge, then drawing the reader into a narrower picture that includes the solution to the problem. In CME, these deliverables tend to focus on informational and educational content and can be more technical than other types of content, providing detailed information supported by research, statistics, and expert opinions to promote a product, service, or methodology. If you have ever written marketing copy, then white papers are an opportunity for you to deploy your marketing chops in the education field.

Patient-Directed Education

The landscape of health care has undergone significant change in recent years, with patients transitioning from passive recipients of care to active participants in their own health management. This shift has been driven by legislative changes, such as the Patient Protection and Affordable Care Act, which encourages patient engagement, and technological advancements that have made health information more accessible.

In response to this evolution, the ACCME introduced new criteria that emphasize the importance of including patients as both planners and audiences for continuing education.[33] As a result, patient-facing education has become an increasingly important aspect of CME, presenting new opportunities for medical writers. Patient-directed medical education involves learning activities focused on building knowledge about disease states, awareness of evidence-based treatment options, and behaviors to support health-related self-efficacy.[34]

Continuing education providers develop patient-oriented education in three main ways:

1. **Standalone activities.** These are educational activities designed specifically for patients, aiming to empower them with knowledge and skills to manage their health more effectively. These activities may be delivered through various formats such as online interactive modules, question-and-answer sessions, or downloadable resources. Many education providers

engage patients for patient-directed CME through patient advocacy channels.

2. **Integrated curricula.** Patient education can also be incorporated as part of a larger educational curriculum, ensuring that both health care providers and patients receive consistent and complementary information. This integrated or tethered approach helps reinforce key messages and promote a shared understanding of disease and health management strategies. Examples of tethered education include activities to address health equity issues in breast cancer, disease-modifying therapies for managing patients with multiple sclerosis, and disease self-management in B-cell non-Hodgkin lymphomas.[34–36]
3. **Tools and resources for patient education.** CME providers develop resources that health professionals can use to educate their patients. These tools (such as flip charts, decision aids, and educational handouts) are designed to support meaningful conversations between providers and patients about specific therapeutic areas or disease states. By equipping health professionals with these resources, CME providers aim to enhance the quality and consistency of patient education delivered in clinical settings.

Pro Tip: Opportunities for Writers

The growing emphasis on patient-facing education in CME presents several opportunities for medical writers:

1. **Developing online patient educational activities.** Medical education companies, such as PlatformQ Health and MedIQ, are at the forefront of creating interactive online patient educational activities. Medical writers can develop engaging, patient-friendly content that is accessible, accurate, and actionable. Many US adults have limited literacy. A majority read

at an eighth-grade level, while 20 percent read at or below a fifth-grade level.[37] Regardless of literacy levels, patient-facing education requires clear, concise, and plain language that incorporates design features such as simple illustrations and graphics.

2. **Creating patient education tools for health care providers.** Organizations like the American Association of Nurse Practitioners develop educational tools (such as flip charts) that health care providers can use when discussing specific clinical issues with their patients. Medical writers with a strong understanding of patient communication and health literacy can play a key role in developing these resources, ensuring that the content is clear, concise, and effective in supporting patient-provider conversations.

As patient engagement continues to be a priority in health care, the role of patient-facing education in CME will likely expand. Medical writers who possess expertise in patient education and communication are well-positioned to contribute to this growing area, whether by developing standalone patient education activities or creating tools and resources for health care providers to use in clinical settings.

Social Media

Health professionals have used social media or digital channels for many years to network, share information (e.g., about guidelines and protocols), recruit for clinical trials, and learn from others via platforms like X (formerly known as Twitter™), Facebook™, Instagram™, Linkedin™, blogging platforms, WeChat, and Whatsapp™.[38–39] During the Covid-19 pandemic, social media use increased as a means of professional communication and education and gained traction within CME.[40]

CME providers use social media for multiple purposes, including audience generation, sharing faculty perspectives, quick clinical tips, animations or case simulations, hosting virtual meetings, polling, and click-throughs to educational programming or websites.[41]

Social media platforms help disseminate timely information and experiences during conferences and major medical meetings. Live tweeting or blogging during conferences with accompanying hashtags facilitates virtual attendance, which is appealing to learners with limited time or resources.[41] They also offer opportunities for interactive learning and engagement in CME, allowing clinicians to share opinions and engage in conversations with peers and experts. These interactions encompass both informal conversations and more structured CME activities, like journal clubs. For instance, ASEchoJC is a moderated cardiology journal club on X/Twitter that allow individuals worldwide to discuss clinical and scientific literature and offers CME credits.[41] Many journals now use social media as part of their content strategy and have their own X/Twitter journal clubs that offer CME credit.

Other social-media-based CME activities include tutorials on X/Twitter that include text, images, videos, and other resources in a series of 10 to 20 tweets that enable participants to learn about a specific topic from expert faculty and each other in real time. One such recent activity showed significant knowledge improvement across multiple-question items.[42]

Despite the growth of social-media-based CME and its capacity to support peer-to-peer learning and eliminate barriers to access, there is limited empirical research on its effectiveness. However, health professionals are active on social media for professional purposes, including CME activities.[43]

Monday Night IBD, Allison Kickel, CEO Bonum CE

Every week, an invited co-moderator presents a case vignette. The case is accompanied by a polling question, which opens a discussion for a live X/Twitter chat on management of the case. The idea behind the IBD cases is: those involved are trying to address management for a patient who falls outside guideline-recommended care. Then you crowdsource information for what best practices look like, and what different institutional barriers might present and how to get around them. It's a very active conversation.

A few days later, the spotlight shifts to the patient perspective. A patient advocate leads a discussion related to that prior Monday's case under the hashtag "patient experience." The discussion with the patient could be, for example: How was your biologic therapy managed when you were planning a family? These conversations attract the attention of clinical learners and yield valuable insights that go beyond scientific data and test results, and there are major takeaways. As one co-moderator aptly pointed out, "We're scientists. We'd love to order tests, we'd love to have data on hand. But we have to balance the burden of a colonoscopy and how regularly that's done with patient needs." We see a lot of really thoughtful commentary in the discussion.

Later in the week, a wrap-up ties together the clinician and patient conversations. This summary highlights the key takeaways and consensus achieved from both discussions. The weekend prior to the Monday case, a back-to-the-basics presentation for trainees equips them with the knowledge necessary to actively participate in the upcoming case discussion.

Legal/Ethical Concerns with Social-Media-Based CME

Concerns regarding the use of social media as an educational platform primarily revolve around ensuring the accuracy and integrity of educational content, managing interactions and engagement on social media to prevent the promotion of specific products or services, and safeguarding the privacy of participants. In response to these concerns, ACCME provides guidance on its website for CME providers on using social medial platforms to deliver CME. The CME Coalition published a social media compliance guide that shares information on social media use cases and recommendations for content creation.[44]

Visual Communication

Visual communication is an increasingly important strategy in CME/CE to enhance learning, improve engagement, and increase the efficiency of information delivery. Incorporating visual elements like tables, charts, illustrations, and infographics can improve the speed at which learners consume information, reduce cognitive load, increase engagement through interactivity, allow learners to navigate content at their own pace, and facilitate understanding of complex concepts. As the field of CME evolves, several trends in visual formats are emerging, including interactive infographics, gamification elements, visual decision aids for clinical practice, enhanced conference posters, and visual abstracts for publications.

The key to effective visual education is not being an artist, but being able to think visually. Infograph-Ed founders Karen Roy and Bhaval Shah encourage effective visual design through elements such as:

- Simplicity and clarity in presentation
- Layering and chunking of information
- Consistent use of icons, colors, and styles
- Cultural sensitivity in imagery
- Balance between text and visuals.

To develop visual thinking skills and create effective CME/CE materials, medical writers can practice translating text into visual concepts, study successful infographics and data visualizations (like Florence Nightingale's infographic on causes of death during wartime), experiment with visual note-taking techniques, and consider formal training in data visualization.[45] There are numerous tools and resources available for visualizing information, including built-in features in presentation software, online resources for color palettes and icons (e.g., https://coolors.co/), and data visualization books. See the Appendix for a list of visual communication resources.

Conclusion

The CME landscape is evolving, with a growing emphasis on interactive, multimodal, and case-based learning formats that cater to the diverse needs and preferences of health professionals. As CME providers increasingly leverage technology and innovative approaches to enhance the effectiveness and accessibility of educational content, medical writers have the opportunity to create content that supports the learning journey of health professionals from traditional formats like live presentations and print materials to emerging modalities such as gamification, simulation, escape rooms, and social-media-based activities.

Key Takeaways

- CME/CE can be delivered through various formats (live, online, print, etc.)
- Interactive and multimodal approaches are often most effective
- New technologies are expanding possibilities for CME/CE delivery
- Familiarize yourself with various CME/CE formats and their strength

Chapter 9

Competency and Craft

Writing is an exploration. You start from nothing and learn as you go.

— E. L. DOCTOROW

Introduction

Transitioning into the CME/CE field can make writers feel like they're starting from scratch. There are a lot of skills to master, especially for someone who does not come from a medical background. On the flip side, education providers struggle to find writers with the specialized knowledge and skills needed to excel in CME/CE. Competencies provide common ground to bridge this gap between CME/CE writers and clients.

This chapter explores the core competencies you need to become a better CME/CE writer, enhance your value in the CME/CE field, and manage expectations with clients and peers.

Understanding Competencies in CME/CE Writing

In Chapter 1, you read about the birth of competency-based education for the health professions and how various organizations set the knowledge, skill, and assessment menus for health professionals. CME/CE is a competency-based field with an emphasis on transforming what learners can do, as opposed to focusing only on what learners know.

But what about competencies for CME/CE writers? And what is the difference between competencies and skills?

What Are Competencies and Skills?

The idea of competency is rooted in adult learning and the idea of ability or behaviors that individuals can do or enact.[1] Competency can also be collective, based on the idea that knowledge is constructed through participation, as social learning theory insists (see Chapter 6). Though the terms "skills" and "competencies" are sometimes used interchangeably, they are closely linked but not the same thing. Competencies are a combination of knowledge, behaviors, attitudes, and skills that allow you to be successful in a task. Problem-solving is a competency. Skills, on the other hand, refer only to specific learned abilities or techniques required to complete a task that we can acquire through training and practice. It takes skill to identify and describe clinical and performance practice gaps. To become better CME/CE writers, we need to nurture the essential competencies clients are seeking while simultaneously honing the necessary skills.

Competence in the context of CME/CE writing combines knowledge, skills, attitudes, and behaviors that help us effectively create educational materials that meet the needs of health care learners. Competence encompasses a holistic understanding of the subject matter, audience needs, educational principles, and ethical considerations inherent in developing CME/CE content. Competencies in CME/CE writing involve a blend of technical expertise, critical thinking, communication skills, adaptability, and a commitment to lifelong learning and professional development. These competencies help CME/CE writers produce high-quality, evidence-based educational content that engages learners, promotes knowledge retention, and ultimately contributes to improving patient care outcomes.

Competency Guidelines: Educating the Educator

ACEHP has set out national learning competencies for CME/CE and CPD providers under the Educating the Educator curriculum.[3] Broadly split into core and specialized knowledge, the fundamental competency areas are health care and CPD landscape, adult learning, program planning and design, and accreditation. In addition, these areas are divided into the recommended knowledge, skills, and attitudes that CME/CE professionals (including CME/CE writers) can develop to design and deliver content successfully. This curriculum is a great start for anyone working in the CME/CE field, especially as it offers guidance on the core knowledge needed to create CME/CE content. The curriculum also provides the foundation for the Certified Healthcare CPD Professional (CHCP) credential.

However, these competencies do not explicitly address the needs of writers tasked with creating the content for educational activities in CME/CE. Competencies and skills also include being able to tailor CME/CE content for health professionals according to specialty and professional designation and combine text, images, and storytelling techniques in multiple ways to create different formats and deliverables.

Research on CME/CE Writer Competencies

Medical writers Don Harting and Haifa Kassis recently conducted research to identify the knowledge, skills, and attitudes that CME/CE writers need to excel and the deliverables that they should be able to develop. These researchers consulted with a panel of experts (including me) using the Delphi method to determine relevant and essential standards and competencies for CME/CE writers.

Preliminary consensus-based findings from this research emphasize skills and competencies ranging from general medical writing (e.g., literature search and synthesis, analyzing information) to CME/CE-specific competencies such as crafting actionable learning objectives, identifying and describing clinical practice gaps, and interviewing and collaborating with clinical experts.

Essential Competencies and Skills for CME/CE Writers

We can expect these competencies to evolve and for more specific guidelines to emerge in the future. The curriculum I create for my courses is aligned with this consensus framework and is designed to fill a critical training gap for CME/CE writers.

So, what competencies and skills do you need to be successful as a CME/CE writer?

Writing Skills

It goes without saying that being able to write with clarity, concision, and accuracy is a non-negotiable foundational skill. The stakes are high in CME/CE and your writing needs to be accurate, trustworthy, and inspire confidence in your readers. If you feel shaky here, write more. There are no shortcuts to improving your writing chops. Deliberate and continued practice is the only way to make progress. See the Appendix for writing guides.

Technical Skills

Proficiency in reference management software and other tools is essential for managing sources, citations, and evidence. You will need to be able to adapt to the software applications your clients use to efficiently handle references and documentation (e.g., EndNote, Mendeley, and Zotero).

Terminology

If you trained as a health professional or have a background in science, you are probably familiar with medical concepts and terminology. If not, the American Medical Writers Association offers resources on terminology, and the Appendix in this book provides a list of books that describe medical terms. You'll also need basic knowledge of statistics to help interpret clinical trials and research studies. Look no further than Tom Lang's *How to Report Statistics in Medicine* for support there.

Research and Evidence Gathering

As a CME/CE writer, you need to be able to research the peer-reviewed literature efficiently to identify relevant, high-quality sources to support needs assessments and educational content creation. Refining your search strategy techniques can make a real difference in discovering quality material. Although peer-reviewed journals and clinical trial data are the starting point for evidence-based content, the gray literature, internal data from education providers, and insights from the social and behavioral sciences also offer a treasure trove for CME/CE writers to explore. You will need to be able to interpret data for insights and understand the implications of analysis. Consider attending workshops or courses to deepen your understanding of statistics, trial methodology, and reporting standards.

Communication and Collaboration

Effective communication with clients, health professionals, education faculty, and other stakeholders is key. This includes the ability to educate clients about best practices and negotiate content that adheres to ethical standards while meeting educational objectives. Beyond refining the nuts and bolts of your writing proficiency, it is crucial to cultivate client-facing skills that will set you apart from other writers. We will explore how to do so in Chapter 10.

Adult Learning Principles

Being familiar with the adult learning principles we explored in Chapter 6 is a core ACEHP competency. You will need to be able to identify clinical practice and performance gaps and learner needs, and craft or create content aligned to learning objectives.

Continuous Learning

The field of medical education is continuously evolving, requiring writers to stay updated on new therapeutic areas, treatment guidelines, and educational technologies. Be prepared to learn and integrate new information and technologies into your work, like digital learning, data visualization, or patient-centered education.

Assessment and Outcomes Frameworks

Measuring change in learning, behavior, and practice is the heartbeat of CME/CE. Get to know the common assessment and outcomes frameworks used in CME/CE and how to use them to describe anticipated outcomes.

Ethical and Professional Integrity

Chapter 3 explored the regulatory oversight that ACCME and other accreditation bodies provide to ensure that educational content is fair, balanced, and free from commercial influence. In order to be effective, this oversight needs to be applied. Writers are vital to this application and in maintaining standards of integrity and independence to ensure content validity.

We often grapple with questions that lack clear-cut answers. What kinds of sources are permissible to support content? How should evidence be presented, and at what level of detail? What is the best way to navigate fair and balanced content when financial support for CME/CE activities often comes from parties with vested commercial interests in the therapeutic area being discussed? You will thus need to be familiar with accreditation and regulatory requirements like ACCME Standards,[4–5] as well as other accreditation criteria from organizations such as the American Nurses Credentialing Center (ANCC), the Accreditation Council for Pharmacy Education (ACPE), the PhRMA Code, and the American Medical Association.

Six Essential Skills

CME/CE writer Rhona Fraser, BVMS, emphasizes the following six skills as essential in effective CME/CE writing:

1. **Attention to detail.** Precision in medical content creation is paramount. This involves ensuring accuracy, adherence to standards, and presenting content suitable for diverse professional audiences. Meticulous records, careful observations, and precision serve CME/CE writing well. The stakes are high when education guides clinical practice.
2. **Critical thinking.** Evaluating relevance and accuracy underpins quality content. Assessing data impartially to spotlight bias is essential for producing unbiased, evidence-based content. Writers must evaluate information rigorously, discerning validity and significance in medical data.
3. **Problem-solving.** Navigating ever-changing medical landscapes requires resourcefulness. Embrace questioning, analyzing, and creative thinking. The dynamic nature of the medical field requires a proactive approach to address evolving challenges and find effective solutions in content creation.
4. **Communication.** Syncing with teams and learners depends on clear messaging. Hone your skills in explaining complexity both scientifically and conversationally. Both verbal and written communication skills are crucial. This includes

clear expression, negotiation, and building effective professional relationships.

5. **Organization.** Become a juggler who remains cool under pressure. Anticipate obstacles early when multiple timelines and tasks compete. Managing multiple projects, deadlines, and information efficiently is key. Anticipating potential issues and addressing them proactively is part of effective project management.
6. **Adaptability.** Switching specialties as assignments evolve builds agility. Adjust writing style and ramp up subject mastery in stride. Flexibility in adapting to changing project scopes, priorities, and therapeutic areas is highly valued. This includes the ability to handle varied writing styles and formats.

◇◇

Plain Language

Effective writing for health professionals is more important than ever. CME/CE is full of complex medical terminology and data-heavy information. This can make absorbing and acting on the content difficult, especially when health professionals are doing so much of their learning online or on their phones. That is why plain language principles are so important for medical education writers and designers.

Plain language is a communication approach that focuses on presenting information in a clear, concise, and easily understandable manner to make complex concepts accessible to the targeted audience. We can use plain language principles in CME/CE writing to enhance comprehension, engagement, and knowledge retention among learners.[6] As Robert Bonk notes in *Writing for Today's Healthcare Audiences*, and as we explored in Chapter 6, health professionals want to apply information as soon as possible. Thus, the content we create must be usable and applicable. By using simple language, numbered steps, companion graphics, defining technical terms, and organizing information logically, CME/CE writers can effectively convey key concepts, guidelines, and best practices to health care professionals in a way that is easily digestible and actionable.

Embrace Simplicity

It is easy, as medical writers, to get drawn into a deep rabbit hole of scientific complexity as a way to exhibit our own authority. But we don't relinquish our authority by writing with simplicity; instead, simplicity enhances understanding and empathy. Ahaha Leibtag, president and owner of Aha Media Group, LLC, is an expert on plain language and health care communication. She advocates for using clear, concise language and structuring digital content in a way that accommodates the reader's cognitive processes—through chunking text, using short sentences and bullet points, and providing ample white space. Adding these elements can make it easier for readers to engage with and explore your content, rather than facing an overwhelming wall of text. By embracing simplicity you will reduce reader stress, promote better comprehension, improve learning outcomes, and empower health care professionals to more effectively apply new knowledge and skills in their clinical practice.

Skills in using textual, visual, and numerical data to communicate clinical data and research implications from bench to bedside and beyond, with precision, nuance, and care, is more indispensable than ever. If you need to brush up on these skills, AMWA, the European Medical Writers Association, and many other organizations offer plenty of options. The Appendix also lists plain language resources.

Cultural Competence

The CME/CE community is increasingly engaging with diversity, equity, and inclusion (DEI) issues, including disparities in care and social determinants of health.[7] As writers, we need to be as up to date about these concerns as we are with therapeutic agents and disease states. We need to consider linguistic, cultural, and identity differences to create inclusive materials that engage diverse audiences. We can do this through the framework of cultural competence.

Almost 20 years ago the Commonwealth Fund defined cultural competence as "the ability of providers and organizations to effectively deliver health care services that meet the social, cultural, and linguistic needs of patients."[8] To this end, accreditation bodies expect CME/CE providers to integrate cultural competence into education for the intended learner audience, be they physicians, pharmacists, or nurse practitioners.

The California Medical Association, which accredits CME/CE organizations in California, has also developed standards to ensure the inclusion of cultural and linguistic competency statements in accredited CME/CE, as well as content that addresses, implicitly or explicitly, topics like communication skills, health care disparities, biases/stereotyping, cross-cultural pharmacological issues, and sociocultural factors that affect health beliefs and behaviors. ACCME is also working to ensure that diversity, equity, and inclusion are incorporated into all aspects of accredited education.

Intersectionality and Equity

Intersectionality and equity are closely linked concepts in health care. On the one hand, intersectionality, which is rooted in 1970s Black feminist activism and scholarship, serves as a tool to understand how different systems of social, economic, and political oppression play out in the lives of individuals and reinforce structural inequality. On the other, equity emphasizes the fair distribution of resources and opportunities. These concepts can be applied to improve health care and reduce disparities in access to care, treatment outcomes, and health care outcomes among different populations. CME/CE can give form to intersectionality by asking the right questions, bringing the right people to the table, and listening.

◇◇

Broadening Representation

A primary way to integrate cultural competence standards to CME/CE is by broadening representation within educational content, such as in patient cases. Sapana Panday, MPH, is a medical education specialist with over two decades of experience. She argues that diversity goes beyond racial diversity and includes gender, sexual orientation, body types, neurodiversity, and age diversity. Sapana suggests simple steps to broaden representation and DEI content in CME/CE.

1. Diversify the social, cultural, and linguistic characteristics of patient cases by using diverse names and describing different marital statuses and relationships.
2. Include images that represent people with disabilities, as well as Black, Indigenous, and additional people of color, and people in LGBTQIA+ communities.
3. Educate ourselves on cultural norms related to communication, decision-making, family dynamics, spirituality, and other factors affecting health and health care.

So how do we build inclusion, equity, and cultural respect across identities and cultures into CME/CE content?

Use Inclusive Terms

Move beyond the gender binary and use preferred names to demonstrate respect and validate lived experience. At the very least, model safety by adding your pronouns to meeting introductions, your email signature, and Zoom profile. ReadySet has a brilliant resource on diversity, equity, inclusion, and accessibility: https://www.thereadyset.co/

Incorporate Alternative Wording into Images

You will find great resources on content accessibility at the National Center on Disability and Journalism and on digital accessibility from Harvard University and Digital.gov.

Avoid Discriminatory or Stigmatizing Language

Embrace intersectionality. Acknowledge history, oppression, and systemic bias, and ask the people you are working with about their preferences for identity- or person-first language. There are several updated resources on inclusive language, cultural competence, and cultural humility specific to medical writing.

◇◇

Health Equity Series Case Study

Targeted, thoughtful CME/CE activities can transcend traditional education, drive systemic change, and ultimately enhance patient outcomes by addressing the root causes of health disparities. A combination of employee grassroots activity and Californian legislation allowed Heather Clemons to pursue a unique, health equity-focused CME/CE and quality improvement process at Sharp Healthcare. Its CME/CE-accredited Health Equity Series focused on topics such as food insecurity, weight stigma, and the unique health care needs of diverse communities, including Asians and Pacific Islanders. This series, part of a larger DEI initiative at Sharp, offered health professionals a platform to deepen their understanding of the social determinants of health and their impact on patient care. Heather and her colleagues used formats like breakfast forums to discuss the results of community health needs assessments to educate its staff on crucial public health issues and catalyze actionable changes within its system. These changes included integrating food insecurity screening into EMRs and establishing connections with social services to address patients' needs directly. Listen to our conversation on diversity, inclusion, and health equity on the Write Medicine podcast.

◇◇

Audience

Who is Your Audience?

It's easy to lose track of the audiences for whom you are creating content. Sometimes you might not even know that much about your audiences beyond their specialty, designation, and workplace setting. How many of us really invest in a more thorough investigation of learner audiences by exploring their roles and responsibilities and the challenges they face, or even create personas for our learners? Understanding our audiences is paramount in creating effective CME/CE content. By adopting an audience-focused mindset you will be better able to understand your readers' emotions and convey the right tone in your writing. After all, it's easiest to write content that resonates with your audience when you have a deep understanding of their pressing needs and issues. When you know who you are writing for, you can more effectively shape the content's direction, language, and complexity.

A thorough needs assessments is indispensable here, as is gathering data on the target audience's knowledge gaps, interests, and educational needs.

Learn as much as you can about your audience. To define the audience for your content, you'll need to identify the specific group of health professionals who will engage with the educational material and consider factors such as their specialties, levels of expertise, learning preferences, and practice settings. If you are unsure about what different health professionals do, review Chapter 1 for a primer on the roles and responsibilities of clinicians. Medical or clinical memoirs, like Jay Baruch's *Tornado of Life: A Doctor's Journey Through Constraints* *and Creativity in the ER*, are also a great way to learn about the messy, challenging experience of working as a health professional.

Conduct audience research. Before you begin writing, outlining, or even researching your next project, take the time to understand the people on the receiving end of your content. Peek into the background challenges and trends that form the context of clinical care and learning for your audience.

- What are their most pressing worries?
- What kind of learning experiences work best for them?
- What skills do they need to walk away with at the end of the day?
- What are the learner's daily tasks, challenges, motivations, and mindset?

Recognize context. Find a window that lets you peek into the background challenges and trends that form the context of clinical care and learning for your audience. Explore additional demographics for your target audience such as their roles, responsibilities, and typical workflow. Workflow is often a major friction point for health professionals and is worth having some background on.

Leverage expert insights. When possible, consult with health care professionals directly involved in the topic area. Their firsthand experiences and challenges provide invaluable insights that enrich your writing and ensure it addresses the real needs of the audience. Open-ended questions are a good fit here. You can generate a lot of contextual information from one or two focused interviews with your target audience.

Edit for your audience. CME/CE writer Michelle Rizzo edits her work from the perspective of her readers. If something would not make sense to a nonexpert on the subject, it has to go, as painful as it is to get rid of words you put on paper. While all the research you may have done helped you write about the topic in a concise way, it is important to remember that the audience has not done the same due diligence. "The reader has not gone through your thought process. The reader has not gone through your research level," Michelle reminds us.

At the end of the day, Michelle says creating engaging CME/CE content is about tuning into your audience's perspective and pulling them into the story with thoughtfully placed facts, without overwhelming them with irrelevant details. It's a balance that even seasoned CME/CE writers will need to strive for every time they sit down to work on a new project.

Additional Audience Analysis

Social listening can help you learn about your audience's emotions, mindsets, and what they care about. X/Twitter is a common listening space and has an advanced search feature you can use to create custom searches based on keywords and hashtags associated with the therapies, medical terms, or clinical care issues you are interested in exploring. You can specify relevant filters such as language, location, and date range to narrow the results down to tweets from different types of clinicians or specific regions and pay attention to their opinions, insights, recommendations, or concerns. Look for patterns or recurring themes in their discussions.

Sentiment analysis allows you to analyze free-text natural language—the words and symbols used in a message—in positive, negative, or neutral terms.[10] Again, X/Twitter is commonly used for sentiment analysis of health care tweets, and there are several open-source or commercial tools that support sentiment analysis of health care social media content, like TextBlob. As you can imagine, this is a space in which AI-powered tools are rapidly emerging. But be cautious, because they are not all appropriate for analysis in the health care space.

Writing for More Than One Audience

Very often, CME/CE writers are asked to create content that will be taught by others—such as faculty members and subject matter experts. That means your job becomes twofold. This unique situation requires you to consider both the needs of the audience and the presenter, ensuring that the content is not only informative and relevant, but also easy to deliver and understand. When writing for both the audience and the presenter, it is essential to maintain open communication with the faculty throughout the process. This collaboration helps ensure that everyone is on the same page regarding the content, tone, and objectives of the presentation. By keeping faculty in the loop, you can avoid unnecessary revisions and build a strong working relationship based on trust and mutual understanding. Being in alignment with your presenters can eliminate a lot of back and forth down the road and create goodwill. This will also help you maintain a consistent style and tone of voice.

Keeping your audience at the forefront of your mind is essential for creating effective and impactful CME/CE content. By understanding the demographics, needs, and preferences of your target audience, and maintaining open communication with faculty presenters, you can develop materials that not only inform and educate but also inspire and empower your learners to improve their practice and patient outcomes.

◇◇

These tactics will help you get to know your audience so that you can help health professionals process, synthesize, and apply new information effectively in the relevant context.

Empathy and Connection

While data is clearly important in clinical decision-making and can provide important insights and consistency, data alone in CME/CE content cannot always account for the complexity of individual cases and patient experiences. If CME/CE content doesn't connect with learners—health professionals—they are not going to feel supported in their work and they are certainly not going to receive and act on the learning that the content serves.

We need to have empathy to create a connection with learners.

There is growing research on the importance of empathy and connection as guiding principles in adult learning that support inclusivity and accessibility.[12] In fact, human-centered design puts empathy at the heart of the learning experience. CAST (formally known as the Center for Applied Special Technology) created Universal Design for Learning guidelines to optimize learning for all people based on scientific insights into how we learn.[13] These guidelines point out how to use multiple means of engagement, representation, action, and expression in designing learning experiences that are accessible, inclusive, and participatory.

We all know that health professionals are extremely busy and their in-the-moment learning capacity is affected by many factors, including specialty, proficiency level, and workplace setting. For many people, text-only content is not the most effective way to learn. Text-only content can be especially challenging for health professionals who already have a busy schedule yet find themselves adopting the role of learner in between various complex responsibilities. And yet, much of current CME/CE content is text-based.

Our goal in CME/CE is to help learners process, synthesize, and apply new information effectively in the relevant context. We can do that by helping learners connect to the content we create. Consider some of these empathy-enhancing tips when working on your next CME/CE project.

Look for the human element in CME/CE content. Behind every clinical study are stories of clinicians and patients, so consider the points of view of your protagonists and the audience's needs. What is the real story behind the facts and the concepts? Ask yourself what is on the line and why your audience should care.

Identify opportunities for narrative. How can you make your audience connect with the protagonists in your content, whether patients in a case study or characters in a scenario? What challenges do these characters need to overcome?

Engage the senses. How can your audience experience the content in a variety of ways?

- Is there room for audio/visual elements, interactive activities, or quizzes?
- Are there opportunities for reflection and self-assessment in the content?
- How could you use design principles and writing techniques (e.g., cues and prompts) to ensure information is accessible to different categories of learners, such as novices versus experts?
- Can you guide goal-setting for learners by offering examples of how they can apply new knowledge to the clinical context?

Find factors that motivate. Identify the factors that motivate learners to participate in educational content. Self-Determination Theory can be a helpful framework here.[14] Self-Determination Theory emphasizes that adult learners need to feel autonomous, competent, and related (or connected) to what they are learning as well as the people they are learning with.

Acknowledge everyday emotions in patient care. Acknowledging that a patient may be afraid, upset, or very distracted, and describing how a health professional can respond to these emotions can infuse enough humanity for the content to be more relatable.[11]

Emotions as a Resource in CME/CE Medical Writing

Mark Hagerty, MSOB, is an instructional designer and CME/CE content developer. He observes that sometimes emotions are seen as superfluous or even dangerous in CME/CE content. After all, we assume that health professionals must act cool and collected, even as those around them are losing composure. However, denying the emotional experiences of health professionals can have a detrimental effect on learning. Mark explains,

> *Saying that we need to cut out the emotional content is like saying "I need to shut off half of you as a human being in order to teach this," and it just doesn't fit in the real world later on.*

He emphasizes that acknowledging the presence of emotions like frustration, anxiety, and fear in health professionals and providing examples of how characters deal with them in real time only adds to the learning experience.

In addition to narrative elements, Mark recommends creating CME/CE content that invites learners to experience the concepts, not just read about them. This can be as simple as adding visual elements, like images and infographics, as well as subtitled videos or audio clips throughout the education activity. For in-person or more involved online content, this approach could also include hands-on practical exercises. These tactics center empathy in learning experiences and foster connection by being inclusive.

Perspective

To ensure that content is targeted correctly, immerse yourself in audience perspectives and their unique challenges. By focusing on the patient experience and incorporating their stories into your writing, you can create more engaging and impactful content that ultimately leads to improved patient outcomes.

How do you infuse the patient perspective into your content creation?

Michelle Rizzo is a trained journalist who turned her curiosity and lifelong interest in medicine into a thriving career as a CME/CE writer. Michelle currently works as an associate medical director and senior writer at a boutique CME/CE content company, where she often finds herself writing and researching about rare diseases. She recommends using patient stories to introduce content rather than overwhelming readers with data from the outset. "You have to pull the reader in. Otherwise, they're not going to care," she says. By learning about the daily challenges and experiences of patients living with a specific condition, you can craft a more compelling narrative that resonates with your audience.

This approach is particularly valuable when writing needs assessments, which, while necessarily supported by facts and figures, sometimes run the risk of being dry. But this approach works for other content too. Focusing on perspective is also an excellent way to bring empathy and humanity into CME/CE writing, which starts by looking at the human element and diving into the real-world conflict and hazards.

Storytelling

By creating CME/CE content that acknowledges the human experiences of patients and health professionals, we may help learners retain core concepts. Time and again, research shows that people learn best from stories and shared metanarratives.[15] As writers, we can create educational content that recognizes the human aspects of clinical practice, including real-world conflict and hazards, and use authentic scenarios that are relevant to their clinical practice.

Use Storytelling to Connect with Learners

Storytelling is a powerful tool for capturing attention, conveying information, and inspiring action. Eleanor Steele, also known as Medcomms Mentor, recently shared storytelling techniques and frameworks on the Write Medicine podcast to craft compelling stories tailored to clinical audiences and that are optimized for logical flow and audience engagement.

Set the scene. Provide context and background information to orient your audience.

1. **Introduce a problem or unmet need.** Highlight the challenge or knowledge gap that your content aims to address.
2. **Present a solution or response.** Explain how the information or skills covered in your content can help overcome the problem.
3. **Share results and outcomes.** Demonstrate the impact of applying the solution, using real-world examples or case studies.
4. **Offer a resolution.** Summarize key takeaways and provide a call to action for implementing the learning in practice.

Here are some tips to optimize storytelling in CME/CE content:

Don't be afraid to over-research. Time constraints are always a concern, but if you are writing about a topic you're not familiar with, strive to learn as much as you can before putting pen to paper or fingers to the keyboard. Follow your natural curiosity as much as possible in order to write CME/CE content that addresses the right challenges. And if you are a CME/CE writer without a medical/science degree or clinical expertise, reading extensively before writing is your ticket to creating stronger content.

Incorporate patient stories. Start your content with patient stories to humanize the data and statistics. These narratives make the information more relatable and compelling, reminding health care professionals of the real-world impact of their knowledge and decisions.

Use accessible language. While it is essential to maintain scientific accuracy, strive for clarity and simplicity in your language. Avoid jargon and technical terms that might alienate readers not specialized in a particular area.

Reflect on personal experience. Consider your own experiences as a patient or a caregiver. This perspective can infuse your writing with genuine empathy, making the content more engaging and impactful.

Focus on the why. Always keep the audience's interests and needs at the forefront. Think about the questions they might have and use the content to answer these questions. This approach ensures the content is relevant and engaging.

Apply conflict and resolution. Every good story shows a struggle, the journey to a better outcome, and the final result. CME/CE case studies, needs assessments, and other education deliverables are no different. Turning health professionals into protagonists of their learning also makes them more invested in the content and more likely to complete the educational activities in a timely manner. Adding narrative elements into your content doesn't just add interest or some entertainment value—it helps learners retain information and move more deliberately toward an anticipated learning or behavioral outcome.

Review and reflect. After completing a writing project, take time to review your work critically. Consider what worked well, what could be improved, and how the story could be told more effectively. Use this reflection to continually refine your storytelling skills.

Seek feedback. Whenever possible, seek feedback from peers, mentors, or members of your target audience. Constructive criticism is invaluable for honing your storytelling abilities and ensuring your content resonates with readers.

Interviewing Experts

Cultivating interview skills is a crucial competency for CME/CE writers. As part of research for CME/CE content creation, we often need to interview subject matter experts (SMEs) or expert faculty to gather detailed information and specialized knowledge. Interviews with SMEs offer an invaluable opportunity to clarify complex medical concepts, obtain up-to-date insights on advancements in health care, and ensure that the information being communicated is both accurate and aligned with current clinical practice.

However, interviewing SMEs presents a unique set of challenges, particularly when working with busy health professionals who may have limited time or availability. You might have only 10 to 20 minutes to get quality information to support your content. Additionally, it can be daunting to navigate the clinical language and terminology used by experts in various specialties. Here are some tips to help you crush your SME interview:

Understand why you are doing the interview. Clarify your client or team's needs and motivations for getting interview material. Interviews are great for all phases of education planning (i.e., needs assessments, content development, outcomes evaluation) as well as for identifying gaps and acquiring patient perspective. By digging into what your client needs, you can tailor your interviews to capture meaningful insights.

Do your homework. Familiarize yourself with key concepts and terminology before the interview. Develop a basic understanding of the disease state, therapy, and standard of care before the interview. This information creates a baseline that will help you ask more targeted questions.

Research your SMEs. I like to read about the person I am scheduled to interview ahead of our conversation. This gives me a sense of their positions on various topics, their publication record, and other interviews they might have done.

Structure and conduct interviews strategically. A successful interview is all about strategic planning and pacing. Create an interview guide to keep you on track, ensure topic coverage, and establish a logical question sequence. Begin with broad, open-ended, easy-win questions to establish rapport with your interviewee and gradually navigate toward more specific and sensitive questions. Use open-ended questions to encourage thoughtful, in-depth responses. Formulate questions that dig deep, but respect the expert's time. Your client/team might provide questions; that's fine, but they are not always great questions. Feel free to suggest alternatives. Also tell your client/team that you will follow up or probe a bit more if the SME shares information that seems relevant but not necessarily part of your explicit agenda.

Listen actively. It is crucial to actively listen to your interviewee. I read an article in *Rolling Stone* once about the friendship between Pete Townsend of The Who and Eddie Vedder of Pearl Jam. Townsend commented that he was drawn to Vedder because the latter "really listened" to him. That got me thinking, what does it mean to really listen, and how can we listen better?

- In interviews, open-ended questions elicit more meaningful responses while also building rapport and trust with interviewees.
- Show you are interested in the information the interviewee is sharing with you and you will extract valuable insights.
- Offer feedback to ensure you have understood main points—either at the time or later, via email.

Doorknob Phenomenon

SMEs, interviewees, and patients always seem to say things or ask questions as they are exiting the interview or clinical encounter. UX researchers, qualitative researchers, health professionals, and writers have all likely encountered the "Oh, by the way," interview experience.

That moment when you have turned off recording, or when the interviewee is about to leave an interview, hand on the doorknob, and suddenly has something else to share. In the United States, this phenomenon is actually known as the "doorknob phenomenon."

You can reduce the potential for doorknob phenomenon in your interviews.

1. Ask, "anything else?"
2. Embrace silence as an interviewing technique.
3. Leave your recording device on until the interviewee has exited the room or virtual space.

The ability to conduct effective interviews is not just about asking the right questions. It's about active listening, adapting to the flow of conversation, and translating specialized knowledge into content that resonates with the intended audience and is grounded in real-world clinical practice and patient care.

Finding Focus

Crafting effective CME/CE content requires a clear, well-defined focus. A strong focus helps guide the writing process, ensures clarity for the reader, and ultimately leads to more impactful learning outcomes.

Ben Riggs, a writing coach and specialist communications expert at Kettering Health in Ohio, says that the focus statement lies at the heart of focused writing. A focus statement is a single sentence that encapsulates the main idea your content needs to convey. A well-crafted focus statement:

1. Creates clarity for the reader by providing clear direction and purpose
2. Helps the writer identify what information to include or exclude

3. Organizes ideas and outlines, ensuring a logical flow of information
4. Builds confidence for the writer by providing a roadmap for the content
5. Provides backbone and structure, making the writing process more efficient

If you are like me, at some point in the CME/CE writing process you will probably struggle to find focus for your content. This lack of focus can manifest in various ways, such as:

- Feeling stuck or overwhelmed by the writing task
- Cramming an outline with every piece of information related to the topic
- Struggling to find the perfect opening line or introduction

These challenges can lead to frustration, wasted time, and, ultimately, less effective content.

To help overcome these challenges and find focus in your writing, Ben suggests the following strategies:

1. Craft a focus statement as a single sentence that includes an action verb. This helps ensure your content has a clear purpose and direction.
2. Test your focus by examining your beginning and ending. Do these sections introduce and revisit the same central point? If not, you may need to refine your focus.
3. Identify the most important idea from your research, write some "burner ledes (temporary introductions)," and select what is most helpful for your reader. This process can help you distill your main message.
4. Consistently ask yourself, "What is this about?" throughout the writing process. This simple question can help you stay on track and maintain focus.

5. Refine your focus statement until there is no ambiguity or obscurity. A clear and concise focus statement will guide your writing and ensure clarity for your reader.

The Benefits of Focus

By implementing these strategies and achieving a clear focus in your writing, you'll experience numerous benefits, including:

- Increased clarity and confidence in your writing
- More efficient and effective writing process
- Greater engagement and understanding from your readers
- More impactful learning outcomes for your CME/CE audience

Ultimately, focus helps you answer the crucial questions, "What do I want to say?" and "Have I said it?" By keeping these questions at the forefront of your mind and using the strategies outlined above, you can ensure your CME/CE content is focused, engaging, and effective in achieving its educational goals.

Generative AI

I'm guessing you are well aware of the phenomenon of generative artificial intelligence (gen-AI) in medical writing that exploded onto the scene in 2022. Exemplified by chatbots, such as ChatGPT, Claude, and Perplexity, gen-AI demonstrates uncanny language proficiency and is rapidly transforming the landscape of medical writing, including the development of CME/CE content. This technology uses vast datasets to produce content based on patterns in the data it has been trained on.

It is fair to say that gen-AI is a polarizing topic. While some of us are excited about the capabilities of AI tools, others see it as a harbinger of doom for all content creators, including CME/CE writers. In reality, the truth is likely somewhere in the middle. AI can take some of the more mundane aspects of content creation out of human hands. For instance, the application of gen-AI in CME/CE writing spans from brainstorming ideas to conducting literature reviews and generating initial drafts. But this technology comes with limitations that require a sharp, skilled editorial eye to correct.[16] As a CME/CE writer, you will need to understand both the promise and limitations of this technology and the long-term risks of outsourcing critical thinking.[17]

◇◇

Use Cases for AI in CME/CE

The incorporation of gen-AI into the CME/CE content development process offers the potential for significant efficiency gains. By automating the initial stages of content creation (such as drafting, summarizing research, and generating content outlines) AI can help writers focus on higher-level tasks that require human expertise (such as critical analysis, interpretation of data, and tailoring content to specific learning objectives and audience needs).

CME/CE Writing

- Rephrasing convoluted text
- Summarizing literature reviews
- Checking grammar and punctuation
- Developing creative titles and taglines
- Outlining knowledge gaps and practice problems
- Proposing story arcs and cases to illustrate themes
- Flagging overweight paragraphs or dense sections
- Extracting key statistics and passages from journal articles

Grants and Needs Assessments

AI has the potential to transform CME/CE grant and proposal writing. Instead of spending hours poring over journals and searching for relevant articles, CME/CE writers could use AI tools to streamline data collection, identify relevant information, and highlight gaps, thus freeing time to focus on deeper analysis and presentation. Tools like Graphi.ai and ScholarAI cater specifically to medical and science writers' needs for comprehensive, citable content.

Chatbots

AI chatbots offer another innovative application in CME/CE, by simulating patient scenarios for interactive learner practice. Chatbots blend elements of standardized patient encounters, simulations, and interactive cases, enhancing skill development in real time. While chatbots can provide valuable performance data and personalized feedback to improve learning outcomes, accuracy and evidence-based support remain paramount.

Challenges in Using AI for Developing Content

As with any tool, gen-AI has risks. Over-reliance could dull the sharpness of your writing, and without direct reference links, sources can slip through the cracks. AI-generated content typically lacks depth, context, and nuance, compared to content created by experienced CME/CE writers. Gen-AI output lacks context and likely offers one-sided perspectives, reminding us that human writers are who truly uphold the integrity of CME/CE content. The risk of perpetuating biases and inaccuracies is also a significant concern, given that AI models can only replicate patterns in the data they have been trained on. And you will need to navigate ethical considerations regarding copyright, data privacy, and informed consent to avoid legal risks and reputational damage.

Reproducing Bias

Bias is a serious ethical concern with gen-AI, which is trained on speech, text, and images it scrapes from real-world content that is already in the public domain. Much of this content is structured by an existing inbuilt text and image bias that obscures heterogeneity in terms of gender, race/ethnicity, and other characteristics. Researchers like Timnit Gebru, founder and executive director of the Distributed Artificial Intelligence Research Institute, note that the data that large language models like ChatGPT encode are more likely to represent the perspectives of people who already occupy considerable internet real estate, compared with women and people of color, who spend less time and have less access to determining online content. So, the idea-starters and writing prompts that initially seem appealing as efficiency levers might already be culturally and racially biased, or at least lack cultural sensitivity and specificity. Unless medical writers are intentionally using ChatGPT and other AI tools through an equity and inequality framework, we will unwittingly reproduce bias.

Getting Started with Gen-AI: Clarify Your Process

Writers who understand their own writing process will have an easier time discerning where gen-AI can assist. If you lack a consistent workflow, ask the AI to help map one out as an initial experiment. While generative tools cannot (yet) produce complete CME/CE narratives from scratch, they excel at discrete tasks like summarizing articles, improving readability, expanding outlines, and suggesting new perspectives.

1. Provide clear, specific prompts to AI tools to ensure the generated content is as relevant and accurate as possible.[18] You'll find links to CME/CE-targeted prompt cheat sheets in the Appendix.
2. Use AI-generated content as a starting point, not a final product, and use your expertise to refine and validate the information.
3. Remain vigilant about biases and inaccuracies in AI-generated content and commit to rigorous fact-checking and source verification.
4. Adhere to ethical guidelines and best practices in using AI tools, particularly concerning copyright, data privacy, and the representation of diverse perspectives.

The key is targeting where in your process gen-AI can provide a boost while you retain creative control.

Navigating Legal and Ethical Gray Areas

Using third-party gen-AI raises copyright, privacy, and ethical concerns due to how these systems process and reproduce vast swaths of text. Here are tips for reducing risk:

1. Avoid feeding confidential text into public chatbots.
2. Review content closely before submission. Tools often lack nuance around diversity and social issues.
3. Disclose AI involvement to clients and secure advanced permission. Transparency builds trust.
4. Do not publish verbatim AI-generated text as your own without significant modification.

When used judiciously as a collaborator, gen-AI can enhance efficiency and creativity—acting as a proficient research assistant, collating ideas, structuring thoughts, and crafting initial outlines with prompted instruction. Treat gen-AI as an interactive muse as opposed to a ghostwriter. Lead with your expertise and perspective. The successful integration of AI into CME/CE writing processes requires a balanced approach that utilizes AI's strengths while compensating for its limitations with human expertise and oversight to safeguard quality, originality, and ethical integrity.

Research

Not all those who wander are lost.

— J.R.R. TOLKIEN, *THE FELLOWSHIP OF THE RING*

Research is a critical skill for CME/CE writers. Your ability to dive deeply into a topic, unearth key insights, and synthesize information into compelling educational content is what will set you apart from other writers. But a key concern I often hear from CME/CE writers is how to rein in this tendency to burrow into the rabbit hole when researching.

Here's an example: You are working on a project about hypertension prevention for an education piece on new antihypertension therapies. You begin reading about hypertension prevention and notice references to multilevel public and community health interventions that are based in barbershops and hair salons; before you know it, you're reading about pharmacists who check Black men's blood pressure and provide health information and prescriptions in barber shops to help patients lower their systolic blood pressure.[19] Then you're reading about awesome lifestyle and community changes that multilevel education and health promotion interventions can create and wondering where drugs fit into this picture at all.

Rabbit holes run deep. They can pull us further away from the task at hand; then we have to find our way back in the dark with no map. And if we go down the rabbit hole far enough, we lose precious work time and perhaps even forget the intention behind our initial reading. Like you, I am up against the rabbit hole challenge too. But I see rabbit holes as the modus operandi of the thinker, the synthesizer, the connector, the collector of curiosities, all of which encompass the mindset needed for strong CME/CE writing. It's what allows us to unearth quotable gems about the lived experience of a rare disease for a needs assessment and to structure interactive patient cases with authentic details, color, and flavor.

Being a Collector of Curiosities

The early phase of research is about permitting yourself to be a collector of curiosities. To wander and wonder. To dive deep into the scientific literature, explore tangential areas, and make connections between ideas. This early stage in the research process feeds the hunger of the inquiring mind and nourishes your creativity. Embrace it.

Setting Up Your Project Infrastructure

Establish an organizational system and process to ensure your research remains productive and efficient.

1. Create a project checklist, including scope of work, client materials, learning objectives, outline, timeline, and space for keywords, quotes, or sources. Evernote, Notion, Click Up, Asana, and other apps have extensive functionality that allow you to set alerts and sync with Google, Outlook, and other calendars.
2. To make it easy to store, retrieve, and synthesize project materials and the information they will generate, create a storage folder with subfolders for materials, PDFs, and draft versions of your work. I set up a folder in Dropbox or Google drive with the client's name and create at least three subfolders labeled materials, PDFs, and progression (or drafts).

Conducting Preliminary Reading

1. Once you have a checklist and folder system prepared, and before you start reading preliminary material, make a separate checklist of reading material and PDFs that the client has provided.
2. Pull any client-provided references into a reference manager (e.g., EndNote, Zotero, Mendeley).

3. Read this preliminary material quickly to get the gist of the topic and create keywords and key phrases to support a wider literature and materials search.
4. Identify gaps in your materials, based on questions that pop up as you read that you don't yet have answers to.
5. Stop searching for new material when you reach topic saturation. You are seeing the same arguments or interpretations from new sources.

Reading Strategies

There are different types of reading. In the early stages of a project, I am rarely deep reading. In this early phase, I would say I read quickly—and I do read a lot. This is the phase where I build in some buffer time to allow following interesting paths and diversions, and, yes, falling into the rabbit hole. But I am skimming and scanning, not doing any deep reading.

1. **Skim.** Look for headings and topics. Try to get the gist of a paper and sort it into a yes, no, or maybe pile. This feels a bit like cleaning out your closet. What's essential? What's interesting/related, but not necessarily essential? And what's on the periphery of the topics?
2. **Scan.** Take a deep dive into materials in the essential bucket first. Look for keywords and phrases, perhaps quotes or other text or numeric nuggets that jump out at you, and orient ideas—themes and connections with the client brief.
3. **Dive deep.** Identify the materials that will require a deeper read. Deep reading is often slower reading. Deep reading requires thinking, comprehension, and

integration of ideas and concepts into the client brief and what you already know about the topic at hand.

Note-taking

Take structured notes, highlight and tag ideas, and start connecting concepts. When I'm at the stage of skimming and scanning, I will make notes, draft out lines of thinking, and paraphrase content. I begin to connect topics and ideas in my head and on the page, either with colored highlights or tags or some other system of synthesis that helps connect the dots. If you already have an outline, map readings/keywords to sections; if you are creating outline, build topic headings from your preliminary reading.

- Paraphrase, outline thoughts, and retain context and connections.
- Notes are only as valuable as their context. Use a note-taking system that suits your style (e.g., in an outline, an app) and allows you to connect ideas and concepts.
- Allow time to process, think, and integrate notes with what you know.
- Return to sources if new questions arise during drafting.

Writing

I write slowly, and I am very slow to integrate the process of reading and writing. I also need time away from reading and note-taking in order to process, think, and integrate. In this writing phase, new questions sometimes pop up and prompt a return to the literature or to existing sources for answers. This type of search usually takes less time than the initial search, and at this point I am skimming and scanning again, versus deep reading. Writing is not a linear process for me (maybe it isn't for you, either) and I like to move things around as I write.

Ultimately, research for CME/CE writing is both an art and a science. It requires rigor and process, but also space for imagination. Your job is to embrace the winding path of discovery, knowing that it will lead you to creative insights that enrich your work—and expand your wonder. Wandering through the research rabbit hole isn't something to resist; it is an essential part of the continuing education you provide for your audience and for yourself.

Writing Ethics

By now you will be aware of writing ethics in CME/CE. Chapter 3 detailed considerations for creating content with integrity. But like everything these days, CME/CE content is increasingly created at speed. Turnaround times for content deliverables can be tight. Staff turnover can mean that your client is less familiar than you are with ACCME *Standards for Integrity and Independence in Accredited Continuing Education*.[4]

There is no room for shortcuts. Remember, you are an important brick in the firewall between industry and education. So supercharge your ethical compass and make sure you follow ACCME guidance as well as tips in this book for developing ethical, trustworthy CME/CE content.

As Eve Wilson, PhD, notes: Whether you are developing content from scratch or reviewing materials that faculty share with you, your job is to ensure content validity and that the content is fair and balanced.[20]

Guidelines for Ensuring Content Validity and Fair Balance in CME/CE Writing20

Source Selection

- Prioritize peer-reviewed clinical and scientific articles from high-impact factor journals.
- Consider peer-reviewed abstracts for upcoming medical meetings as acceptable references.
- Use judgment when including non-peer-reviewed posters or textbooks. They do not always present the most current information.

- Include guidelines or special reports from government sources or medical societies.
- Avoid using UpToDate as an original source, despite its comprehensiveness.

Sources to Avoid

- Blogs, Wikipedia, or other non-scholarly websites
- Other CME/CE programs
- Websites or press releases from ineligible companies
- Outdated or obsolete references

Fair and Balanced Content Checklist

- Include a variety of perspectives, when appropriate, to avoid bias.
- Present alternative treatments or management options, if applicable.
- Discuss the limitations, risks, and benefits of diagnostic and treatment options.
- Avoid exaggerating the significance of study findings or their application to patient care.
- Use generic names for drugs and devices unless necessary for clarity.
- Use references judiciously to support key clinical recommendations.
- Clearly distinguish between evidence-based information and expert opinion.
- Provide a balanced view of controversial topics, acknowledging any areas of uncertainty.

Reflect

As you embark on your journey as a CME/CE writer, it is vital to develop the necessary knowledge, competencies, and skills to excel in this field. You probably have more of these than you are aware. In fact, I recommend that you conduct a comprehensive skills inventory as a first step in skills identification.

Pause here to reflect on your current skills and competencies. Ask yourself: What are my current skills and areas of specialist knowledge and expertise? Don't overthink it. Just allow whatever bubbles to the surface of your consciousness. Reflect on your past work and accomplishments in various fields. Pinpoint your strengths, proficiencies, and unique attributes and make a note of them, because these skills are points on a compass to help chart your path in CME/CE. Another way to discover your own skill gaps is to immerse yourself in the work of other CME/CE writers. Make it a habit to read needs assessments, webinar slides, patient case studies, and other forms of CME/CE content just as much as you would read clinical studies.

Why is this question about skills and competencies important?

Because every single person who finds themselves at the gate to the CME/CE field has a unique set of skills and competencies they can draw on. Maybe you have specialist knowledge in a particular disease state or therapeutic area, or experience in publications, grant writing for academics or nonprofits, or website content for patients and consumer health. Or perhaps you have written test questions in the education system. Or you have a clinical background, so you are familiar with the context of health care.

My point is, we all have skills and competencies that we can draw on and modify. It is common for new-to-the-field CME/CE writers to be daunted by the breadth and depth of this community. But it is important to recognize the expertise and skills that you bring from your professional life to date and explore how they might translate to what education providers need from writers. Being clear about your skills and services will help you get your foot in the door.

Key Takeaways

- CME/CE writing requires a specific set of competencies and skills
- Cultural competence and plain language are increasingly important in creating CME/CE content
- Understanding your audience is crucial for effective writing
- Conduct thorough audience analysis for each project
- Commit to ongoing professional development

Thriving in the CME Ecosystem

Chapter 10

Building Your Business

Do not go where the path may lead, go instead where there is no path and leave a trail.

— RALPH WALDO EMERSON

Introduction

This chapter digs more deeply into how to grow a network and market your freelance CME/CE writing business. As a freelance CME/CE writer, at the time of writing (2024) you represent 38 percent of the workforce in the United States.[1] Nearly half (47%) of freelancers provide knowledge services.

Like you.

Although these numbers are not directly translatable to the world of medical writing, much less the specialized world of CME/CE writing, the general trend toward freelance work and freelance medical writing appears to be upward. It also appears that professionals from academia, clinical research, and health care are flocking to freelance medical writing in pursuit of freedom and flexibility.

What does this mean for you? You will have to create a specialty niche within CME/CE that helps you shine and differentiate yourself from your competitors. You will also have to cultivate business building skills, because breaking into the field and establishing yourself as a medical writer who specializes in CME/CE isn't just about the writing.

The writing is important, for sure. But really, that is the baseline competency. If you want to propel your success, build your authority, and fill your pipeline with prospects and returning clients, you need to build competencies in:

- Planning
- Marketing
- Prospecting
- Prioritizing
- Setting goals
- Tracking metrics
- Building relationships
- Establishing parameters
- Researching new opportunities

This chapter guides you on how to effectively niche down, create a strong portfolio, network, and build relationships in the CME/CE writing field. Let's dig in.

Identity

There's a thread you follow. It goes among things that change. But it doesn't change.

— WILLIAM STAFFORD, FROM *THE WAY IT IS.*

When we are making the transition into building a specialist freelance medical writing business, it's easy to forget that we already have a considerable well of experience and expertise to draw from. We go looking for something external and forget that we already have most of what we need to be successful. As William Stafford describes in his poem, The Way It Is, we follow a thread.

If you are not yet sure what your thread is, pause right now and take inventory of your skills, interests, and passions—your thread. I teach this thread-following approach in WriteCME Pro, my professional development membership for CME/CE writers, because it is foundational for building a specialist CME/CE writing business.

Why is it foundational to find and follow your thread?

Because who you are matters. Clients want to work with you because of your unique qualities and competencies. But you need to know who you are (your thread) in order to make it matter. Once we know that, we can refine our process of taking notice of what is going on around us and internally get better at cultivating insights for ourselves, our businesses, and our clients.

Nourish Your Niche

Finding and following your thread is also foundational for enriching your niche. While it's natural to explore different avenues initially, a niching strategy will help you build a foundation for your writing business that you can layer later on when you have honed your craft and have systems in place to support your business. Finding a clear-cut sweet spot within CME/CE will make it easier for you to promote your unique value, carve out a distinct position in the market, and build a thriving CME/CE writing business.

Wait, I hear you say, isn't CME/CE itself a niche? Yes, absolutely. But you can niche even further and establish yourself as an expert in very specific areas within the CME/CE field.

A niche is simply a specialized segment or service offering within the broader field of medical writing. A niche can be directed toward serving particular client or project types, therapeutic areas, disease states, and more. Niches are not carved in stone and evolve over time.

As you walk the CME/CE writing path, you might discover pockets of interest and specialty areas that stimulate you intellectually. Or you might find education provider types whose mission aligns with your values—for instance, medical associations or societies—or learner groups that you are motivated to serve, such as nurse practitioners or physician assistants. Concentrating on a few specialties also allows you to build expert knowledge and conserve your intellectual energy.

Here's How I Niched Down Within CME/CE

As I shared in Chapter 1, I have a professional background as a nurse, an academic, and as a qualitative researcher. Over the last two decades I have personally cultivated niches in developing white papers and educational outcomes manuscripts (project-based), working with medical specialty societies (client-based), and conducting qualitative evaluations of CME/CE programs (skill-based).

After four years of writing needs assessments, monographs, and patient cases, educating myself on the CME/CE/CPD field, and regularly attending the annual ACEHP conference, I began to hear education providers talk about their desire (and the scholarly need) to publish education outcomes. I also heard providers talk about the importance of qualitative data and the challenges associated with collecting and analyzing this type of data.

As my awareness of these needs grew, I began to build my visibility in the field as a source of authority on both manuscript development and qualitative research. I started asking clients about their plans for publication and whether they had considered using qualitative data for either needs assessments or outcomes evaluation. I wrote blogs on developing manuscripts and presented workshops and sessions at the ACEHP conference on qualitative research (with Wendy Turrell, DrPH).

Slowly, I built a specialist niche in helping education providers publish manuscripts based on their needs assessment and outcomes data and became a qualitative research partner for many providers. Over the years, not only have both revenue streams been the highest generating for my business, but they have helped me establish a robust publication track record that further consolidates my authority, and generates repeat business with clients I know, like, and trust. You can do this for your business too.

Pros and Cons of Nourishing a Niche

Clients prefer specialists. In practice, clients tend to favor specialists over generalists, especially when it comes to therapeutic areas or disease states. They believe that your deeper understanding of specific areas will result in more focused and efficient project handling. In part, this is because many providers do not know therapeutic areas that well and rely on writers with clinical or specialist expertise to fill in the gaps about important clinical trials or clinical practice. You can position yourself as strategic thought partner by cultivating expertise in particular therapeutic areas or disease states.

Streamline your client acquisition. Cultivating a specialty niche often leads to repeat business and more opportunities with existing clients. Repeat business is good because it reduces the burden on you to constantly hunt for new clients.

Build your authority. Your deep niche knowledge and skills enhance your credibility with clients, lead to a stronger reputation, and attract better projects.

Increase your revenue potential. As a specialist CME/CE writer you will generally command higher fees than generalists. Specialization also reduces the time you spend on research per project and indirectly boosts your revenue.

Targeted marketing. A clear niche will simplify your marketing efforts, enabling you to be more targeted and ensuring your messaging resonates more deeply with potential clients.

Selective engagement. You can be more deliberate in selecting the clients and projects you take on so that they align with your personal and professional interests and goals. Hopefully, you will feel greater satisfaction and work-life balance.

Of course, niches have downsides too. Variety narrows, boredom can set in, and skills may stagnate over time. Personally, I have found that hopping between disparate gigs often proves more taxing long-term. In the end, aligning niche services with my personal values and business goals has paid off.

How to Find a Nourishing Niche

Here is a simple exercise to help you identify a specialist niche within CME/CE:

1. Reflect on your background, interests, and expertise gained from projects thus far. What skills or experience could address an unmet need?
2. Make a list of your competencies—research, instructional design, data analysis, and so on. Do any align with trends or challenges facing CME/CE providers?
3. Now list your most financially rewarding project types and favorite activities. See any overlap with the previous?
4. Finally, brainstorm specialist services only you can provide. Examples might include:
    - Instructional design
    - Therapeutic or clinical expertise
    - Outcomes publications
    - Qualitative data analysis

- Assessment measurement
- Write and evaluate cases
- Virtual simulation developer

Building a niche takes time, perseverance, and adaptability. By following these steps, you can identify a unique niche within the CME/CE field that draws on your strengths, meets market needs, and helps you establish a strong portfolio. You do not have to scrabble to find a niche that works for you. Rather, niches are refined out of your existing skills, talents, and interests. Chances are you already work in a specialized area, like consumer health or patient education. Perhaps particular deliverables form a core component of your revenue. Thus, start from where you are, what you enjoy, and what generates revenue for your business. Remember that success doesn't come from pursuing every opportunity. It comes from intentional focus on opportunities that align with your skills, energy, and values. In the end, a niche does not have to be narrow. It just needs to be focused.

Build a Portfolio

Your portfolio needs to reflect your niche. One of the most common questions I get from new CME/CE writers is, "How do I get clients when I don't have samples?"

The answer is surprisingly simple. Create your own!

Creating samples that directly address the needs and pain points of potential CME/CE clients or employers is helpful. An extensive portfolio isn't necessary, so focus on developing samples that align with topics you are interested in within CME/CE. It bears repeating that when you understand your skill set, you can use this understanding to build a portfolio that showcases your capabilities.

Here are some suggestions on how to build your starter portfolio:

1. If you already possess writing samples, adapt and rework them to address the specific needs and pain points of potential CME/CE

clients or employers. Or share the samples and explain the skills or competencies that they demonstrate.

2. If you have written a needs assessment or two, and you want to move into writing education activity content, terrific! The problem is that your work will likely be proprietary, so you can't share it with prospective clients. But you could seek permission from clients to share relevant excerpts from your work without disclosing sensitive information. Use the excerpts to highlight your contributions.
3. Create fresh samples and showcase them on your website. Your website serves as a digital storefront, providing potential clients with an understanding of your capabilities and areas of expertise. So, use it to display your writing. Create a blog or a portfolio section, and make sure your website navigation is clean, accessible, and points visitors to your writing right away.

However you develop your portfolio, highlight your ability to write clearly, meet deadlines, and be easy to work with. While your portfolio doesn't need to be extensive, it should demonstrate your reliability and professionalism.

Networking

Once you establish that network and you prove yourself to be a decent person or demonstrate that you're coming at it for the right reasons, people will just go out of their way to help you.

— ANNE JACOBSON, MSPHARM, CHCP

Every medical writer I have interviewed on the Write Medicine podcast says the same thing: Networking is core to building a freelance medical writing business. The field of CME/CE is no exception. In fact, building relationships is the magic key that opens doors to great clients and projects in the CME/CE writing field. This is a very small, highly specialized field. That is why networking is so important. In some ways, it is a little easier to network in this field because it's smaller and more contained than, say, the regulatory field.

What is networking and how can you start? And who should you network with? One of my business coaches, Ilise Benun of Marketing Mentor, calls networking "making business friends." And who doesn't want more friends? Networking is all about connection and brings you into contact with people you might want to work with and projects that interest you. By networking, you get to create your own inventory of what is going on in the field, see who's doing interesting work, and decide where you want to focus your energy and talents. You can start the networking process with a conversation online or in person. Then, keep the conversation going.

The magic of networking is based on what Mark Granovetter calls the strength of weak ties.[2] Incidentally, in my early days as a freelance writer, I wrote starter essays for EBSCO. One of these was on weak ties and networks. Weak ties are more valuable than strong ties, like close friends and family, for accessing new information and opportunities, particularly in the context of connecting with clients and job seeking.[3] Weak ties give us access to valuable contacts outside of our immediate social circle and expose us to new ideas and connections. As a result, cultivating a network of weak ties, rather than relying solely on strong ties, can be a powerful strategy for professional growth and accessing new resources.

Networking Strategies

Volunteer. Volunteering your energy and expertise is a terrific way to build a network. Over the years, I have volunteered in different capacities with ACEHP and have consistently submitted abstracts and presented several sessions at the annual conference. This kind of volunteering raises your visibility within the organization and showcases your field expertise within your community of practice.

Connect with people you already know. Search for alumni who are now medical writers and take them for virtual coffee. Ask about their journey into medical writing. People enjoy recounting their path.

Let genuine curiosity drive your informational outreach. Simply listen and learn from other medical writers' experiences without expecting jobs or referrals.

Build a networking habit. Add new contacts steadily without expecting instant benefits. Join LinkedIn groups to learn insider CME/CE terminology and trends. Respond to posts thoughtfully.

Informational Interviews. Approach interviews with curiosity. Learn from others' experiences without expecting immediate job opportunities.

Quality over quantity. Build authentic connections rather than forcing relationships.

Where to Network?

Social media platforms like LinkedIn and X/Twitter are invaluable for networking as a means to connect with prospects and clients. I have been using LinkedIn since 2007. It has been an invaluable platform for making connections, identifying field trends, and consolidating relationships. LinkedIn is the only social media platform I use, but there is always something to learn.

I urge you to consider attending industry events, such as the Alliance for Continuing Education in the Health Professions annual meeting. This is a veritable goldmine for networking, learning, and finding new opportunities because this is where your client market hangs out.

While a broad network matters, when you are building your CME/CE writing business, it makes sense to network with people who touch CME/CE in some way. Target medical society education directors, medical affairs teams, grant specialists, and fellow writers. You never know when they will need a writer or know someone who needs does.

Chapter 1 provides a list of people with roles that should be on your networking list.

Direct messages.

I am a big fan of Josh Spector who teaches creators how to optimize and monetize newsletters. That's not my goal, but I subscribe to his newsletter and am in his membership because he shares a lot of valuable information about how to create stellar content (which is one of my goals). In a 2023 tweet, he shared how to DM someone on X/Twitter.[4] I think his advice applies to LinkedIn, which is where most CME/CE clients hang out.

Here is my take on what Josh advises:

1. Use DMs to **strengthen connections** with people you have already connected with on a social media platform.
    - People you follow (or maybe they follow you)
    - People whose posts you have interacted with (or they have reacted to yours)
    - People who have posted something you find interesting and want to explore further
2. DM **after** two to three post interactions to ask what they are working on right now. Just be curious here.
3. If you know someone they would benefit from knowing or following, offer to connect them. I have done this type of "matchmaking" myself. You feel good. Your prospect feels good. It's a feel-good win-win.
4. Alternatively, share a resource or idea relevant to their goals. Content works great here—yours or someone else's.

- Be a resource here. This is a great opportunity to showcase your expertise and the work you have done if it aligns with the goals of the person you're connecting with.

5. Close by offering to help if you have the expertise and bandwidth.

If you stay curious, generous, and position yourself as a resource, you will find it easier to connect with prospective clients and build a nourishing network.

Stay Connected

Most CME/CE projects originate from previous partnerships. Once you complete an activity, stay connected with relevant contacts as a source for future collaborations. Here are three simple ideas to help you keep in touch with current, past, and potential clients:

Quarterly check-in email. Highlight some recent projects you have worked on, give updates on services, and provide your availability for new projects (what you're looking to tackle next and how much time you have).

Thank you notes. A quick thank-you email after a discovery call is the perfect opportunity to sum up your conversation and reiterate interest.

Thoughtful follow-ups. Don't fear the follow-up! Create a check-in schedule for cold pitches two weeks, a month, and two months after an initial email. Map out a schedule for client outreach emails, response, and follow-up.

Should You Have a Newsletter?

Building an email newsletter that you send consistently to clients and colleagues can also help you maintain an ongoing conversation with your network and deepen your connections with practitioners in the field. Writing a newsletter doesn't have to be an onerous task. Your newsletter can be monthly or quarterly, and simply share information you think your clients might be interested in and that showcases your latest projects. When I started my first newsletter in 2012, I noticed that clients often contacted me just after I sent out an issue. They had a project that required a writer and I was top of mind because I had just landed in their inbox. Your newsletter just makes it easier for your clients to find help when they need it.

Expanding your network is not just about networking; it's like curating a scrapbook of connections. Remember that establishing relationships and securing projects in the CME/CE field takes time. In fact, the timeline from initial conversations to signed contracts can range from six months to two years -- and that sales cycle might even be a little longer when the market is less stable. That is why maintaining consistent marketing efforts is crucial. Even if clients don't have an immediate need, staying top-of-mind ensures they will reach out when the time is right.

Marketing

Over the years, I have primarily directed my marketing efforts to the annual ACEHP conference. This strategy has allowed me to network directly and consistently with my client market. At the conference, I spend a lot of energy and time speaking to members and building relationships with prospective and ongoing clients in this field. As a longtime CME/CE freelance medical writer I have also long followed the guidance of experts like Ilise Benun, Lori De Milto, MJ, and Pauliina Rasi, all of whom I recommend as sources of invaluable and gracious marketing wisdom to help you promote your services, attract clients, and book your freelance medical writing business solid.

Cultivate Relationships for Business Growth

That brings me to additional competencies that are vital to growing your CME/CE writing niche or business. In CME/CE writing, building strong client and peer relationships is about more than delivering high-quality content; it's about creating trust, demonstrating reliability, and fostering communication that can lead to long-term collaborations. I've lost count of the number of clients who have shared with me that they too often work with writers who fail to meet deadlines or disappear off the grid in the middle of a project. For real. Do not be that writer. Know that being reliable and easy to work with is just as crucial as strong writing skills and can lay the foundation for a sustainable career in CME/CE writing.

I have worked with fifty-one clients over the last two decades. Ten of those clients have worked with me since 2010 and bring in my largest revenue year on year. Why? Because we've built solid working relationships and I have positioned myself as a strategic partner who writes and provides additional services (in my case, white papers, outcomes manuscripts, and qualitative research).

Education providers value writers who not only possess excellent writing skills but also exhibit dependability, trustworthiness, and strong collaboration abilities. These qualities often carry more weight than writing prowess alone. They go a very long way toward ensuring that you win repeat business from clients that know, like, and trust you, and that you know, like, and trust in return.

Strategies for Building Strong Client Relationships

Building relationships takes time. My strategy for building relationships involves conversation, generosity, and persistence. I've charted my own relationship-building metrics over the years and can see it takes between six months and two years from the first point of contact to landing a contract. I am OK with that because I want to be intentional about who I work with and the kind of work that I do.

Understand client needs. Each client has unique needs and working styles. As we saw in Chapter 1, the CME/CE landscape is broad and fluid. Recognizing the diverse needs of education providers is crucial. While some may only require basic writing services, others seek more comprehensive contributions, involving strategic thinking and in-depth analysis. Adapt your approach accordingly, without compromising your professional standards.

Active listening and empathy. Pay attention to what the client is really saying. Understanding their goals, challenges, and expectations can help you tailor your approach to meet their specific needs. Empathy goes a long way in understanding the pressures and constraints your client might be facing.

Consistent communication. Keep the lines of communication open. Providing regular updates, being responsive to queries, and proactively addressing potential issues can build trust and demonstrate your commitment to the project's success.

Delivering on promises. One of the fastest ways to build trust is by delivering what you've promised, whether by meeting deadlines, adhering to project guidelines, or maintaining the quality of your work. Consistently meeting your commitments reinforces your reliability. I'm always shocked when clients tell me that writers have bailed on them midway through projects.

Feedback and adaptation. Encourage and be receptive to feedback and, most importantly, use it to improve your services. This not only improves the project at hand but also shows that you value the client's opinion and are willing to adapt to their needs. Some clients do not provide much feedback, even when you ask them. But if they keep giving you business, and the business works for your goals, that's good feedback.

Building a partnership. View your relationship with clients as a partnership rather than a transaction. Understand their long-term goals and how you can contribute to their success. This perspective can transform onetime projects into ongoing collaborations.

Personalization. Treat each client as unique. Personalizing your approach based on the client's preferences, company culture, and communication style can make a significant difference in how your services are perceived and valued.

Professional development. Continuously improving your skills and staying updated with industry trends not only enhances the quality of your work but also demonstrates your dedication to providing the best service possible.

Focus on building long-term relationships, rather than treating each project as a one-off transaction. I have said it before and I will keep saying it: This approach leads to repeat business and quality referrals. Part of building a strong relationship is educating clients about the CME/CE writing process, especially when they lack experience or have unrealistic expectations. This is especially important when the field is in flux (see Chapter 1).

Negotiating

Building relationships is one thing. Negotiating project parameters and pricing is another.

I'll confess: Pricing, negotiation, and scheduling are the three parts of running a business that I really do not enjoy. Pricing can seem arbitrary and subjective, and negotiation can be energy draining.

I have realized over the years and through conversations with other experienced CME/CE writers that knowing your worth forms the foundation for your pricing and negotiation strategy.

Negotiation in medical writing, especially in the CME/CE landscape, isn't just about agreeing on a price. It involves understanding the scope of work, the complexity of the project, and the expectations of both the writer and the client. This process is vital for ensuring fair compensation and setting clear boundaries. Mastering transparent rate negotiations and pricing will help you sustain your profitability over the long-term.

Components of Effective Negotiation

Here is what I have learned from seasoned writers, like Christine Welniak of Upside Communications:

Get clear on scope at project initiation. Ensure that you understand the project's scope, objectives, and expected outcomes at the outset. This clarity will help you set realistic expectations and lay the foundation for effective negotiation. Proactively request background documents (e.g., past proposals, activity outlines, needs assessments, and outcomes reports) to grasp the client's vision and the alignment of this project with past projects. Ask as many questions as you can at the start of a project to ensure you understand the client's needs. No question is too stupid.

Develop a detailed scope of work. Clearly define what is expected in a project. I develop a written scope of work for every project I undertake, based on conversations with the client and materials they share to help me understand their needs. I include sections on the project goal; the terms of engagement (what is expected of me and the client); the timeline; anticipated deliverables, fees, terms and conditions; and a partial list of my past clients and projects.

Be direct and adaptable. When discussing project fees or timelines, be transparent. Express concerns about the workload versus compensation and suggest adjustments if necessary. Inform them of your requirements (like net 30 payment terms) and pair directness with adaptability. Work to understand the client's budget constraints and be ready to offer alternative solutions that can accommodate both parties.

Establish your non-negotiables. Identify aspects of your service that are non-negotiable, such as payment terms, ethical considerations, or project timelines. When you know your deal-breakers, you will feel comfortable being more assertive about your expertise, be able to clearly communicate boundaries upfront (preventing misunderstandings later in the project), and resist pressure to take on additional responsibilities without appropriate compensation.

Prepare for varied responses. Not all clients are open to negotiation. Be prepared for this and have a clear idea of your non-negotiables, like payment terms or provisions for scope creep. It's not unusual to find that communication will go dark when you share your estimated project rate or fee with a new prospect that breaches their internal price ceiling. This is not necessarily a bad thing!

Christine Welniak offers this advice:

> *Sometimes the client will come back, sometimes they won't. There is a knee-jerk reaction to lower your fee or rethink your non-negotiables. Don't do it. It will lead to resentment. Accepting that not all clients are right for you is an important aspect of having a sustainable business.*

Understand who is involved. It is vital to understand and clarify the roles of everyone involved in the project, including faculty, scientific directors, and project managers. Misunderstandings here can lead to scope creep and additional unpaid work. For instance, you might build two rounds of revision into your estimate, then find out that there are three reviewers, each of whom shares extensive feedback in separate documents. Now your tasks include not only revising content but also collating and consolidating reviewer feedback. See Chapter 1 to refresh your memory on key stakeholders in CME/CE.

Be vigilant about reviewing your contract. Always scrutinize contracts before signing. Review the payment schedule, kill fee, scope of work, and additional terms.

Navigating CME/CE Projects

Christine Welniak is a highly experienced CME/CE and regulatory writer who runs Upside Communications. She says that to successfully navigate medical writing projects you need to strategically position yourself as a valued partner, not as an interchangeable commodity. You can do this in several ways. For instance, while it's important to be flexible to accommodate client needs, it is equally vital to set and maintain boundaries. This could relate to project scope, timelines, or specific tasks you are willing or not willing to take on. You can also position yourself as a valued partner by sharing nuanced suggestions for project deliverables and processes grounded in your expertise versus just describing tasks and line items in your scope of work. And you can do this by being a problem-solver. Proactively offer solutions to challenges that arise during a project to solidify your reputation as a reliable and strategic partner.

Positioning and viewing yourself as a partner is never more important than when project roles or boundaries break down. Say your point person leaves the company, or the client doesn't deliver the materials you need to move the project to the next stage, or the client asks for an accelerated timeline or additional project tasks. At this point, Christine counsels, you need to clearly yet tactfully reestablish boundaries with your client while ensuring quality.

- When dealing with difficult situations like role breakdowns or project derailments, approach the problem with a calm, clinical tone. You don't have to defend yourself.
- Do not hesitate to push back respectfully when needed, especially when you're being asked to go beyond your contracted responsibilities.
- Use phrases like "That's beyond the scope of our agreed work; let's discuss a new arrangement" to reestablish boundaries.

The negotiation process is intricate, involving not just financial aspects but also a clear understanding of project expectations and role responsibilities. Despite the best laid negotiation and pricing plans, we all hit bumps in the negotiation road including weak project managers, scope creep, and unrealistic deadlines. Tailor your negotiation approach in these scenarios toward problem-solving and effective communication.

Christine recommends these strategies to troubleshoot derailment and keep the project on the road:

- If faced with unrealistic timelines, unavailable faculty, or scope creep, politely reinforce your process needs and constraints.
- Negotiate milestones tied to deliverables, not go-live dates. Push back on unreasonable payment terms.
- Calculate rates based on hours, effort, and cost of living increases rather than accepting dated project fees. Justify with full transparency.
- Stand firm on non-negotiables like net 30 payment deadlines that impact cash flow while staying solution-focused.
- List your specialized skills beyond writing ability when pitching a rate.
- Align fees to value-added services and experience.
- Develop a script bank for your responses to role ambiguity, scope issues, and schedule changes.
- Include the percentage cost of your business expenses in your hourly rate calculations.
- Practice tactful money talk with trusted colleagues. Your anxiety will thank you for it.

Negotiation and positioning in medical writing are not just about setting rates; they are about understanding your value, communicating it effectively to your network, colleagues, and clients, and aligning your services with the needs of your clients. Adopting a partnership mindset and approach will help you maintain the delicate balance of asserting your worth, while also being receptive to the client's constraints and expectations.

Pricing

Do you hate talking about money? You're not alone.

One of the first questions a proactive client will ask (if not the first question) is often about your pricing. But do not feel you have to share your pricing in the first conversation, and resist the temptation to blurt out a price for a project.

That doesn't mean you delay or avoid the money conversation. In fact, quite the opposite. Ilise Benun of Marketing Mentor recommends that you actually initiate the money question early in your conversations with a prospective client or new project. Otherwise, you run the risk of spending time researching or thinking about the project, only to find out they have no budget. Instead, Ilise recommends you say, "Let's make sure we can come to terms financially before we get too deep into the details."

Here are some other tips to support the money conversation about new projects with prospects and clients:

Establish your pricing foundation. Pricing anxiety plagues many writers, especially when we compare rates or receive vague requests that lack critical details. However, no standard prices exist. Your fees as a freelance CME/CE writer depend on your individual business needs, market dynamics, and project variables. By calculating the baseline revenue you need to run your business, you will start to grow your pricing power.[5]

Start with the basics. Ilise Benun recommends you set your goals before your prices.[6] Since no rate checklist applies universally, first get clear on your must-earn income. Tally your personal, family, and business expenses to determine your annual/monthly financial floor. Use this "money anchor" to qualify all the estimates you develop for prospective clients and reduce uncertainty about how much you need to make on a given project.

Austin Church suggests you identify your survival number and your dream rate.[5] At the root of these suggestions are questions like: What do you want the money you make to do for you? Your business? Your family?

Set your rates. With your baseline number defined, consider the contributions you will need to make on the project. To estimate the project fee accurately, you will need to consider factors like the complexity of the subject matter; turnaround time; time for research, drafting, creating tables or graphics; and rounds of revision. Use this information to develop a transparent pricing structure that clearly outlines your rates for each project and what these rates encompass.

Track your metrics. Regularly log your hours, earnings, client traits, and profitability. These metrics will help you calibrate and fine-tune your estimates. Over time, those metrics illuminate ideal projects and partners, too.

Research broader ecosystems. Review compensation surveys, crowdsourced data, and client conversations to get context on industry rates. Include information about geographic norms, topic expertise, efficiency, and more. Then review market rates for CME/CE writing services and see where your experience and expertise position you within that market.

How do you find the market rate? In CME/CE writing, that is not always easy. Freelance writers do not necessarily share their rates with other writers, unless they know them well (another reason to build a trusted network). Clients don't share their rates because they want to keep them as low as possible. Thus, you will need to be creative in your rate research.

- Start with the AMWA annual compensation survey to get an overview of medical writing salaries and freelance rates in general. About 20 percent of respondents to the 2019 survey said they worked in CME/CE. $77,000 was the median income for those who reported CME/CE as their higher source of income, with a median hourly rate of $110 for those who reported writing as their principal type of work.

- Don Harting and colleagues have conducted several annual surveys on fees needs assessments. Results from a 2019 survey and a 5-year trend analysis showed a median fee per needs assessment for freelance work of $1,500, with a range from $50 to $10,000 (n=33) and average fees of about $2,000 for needs assessments developed from scratch.[7-8] These rates will vary by word count, number of references, turnaround time, and other factors. More experienced writers can command fees on the higher end of the range.
- Laurie Lewis, author of *What to Charge*, recommends refining market rate data by region, industry segment, and special skill combinations.[9] For instance, reported AMWA survey rates for CME/CE are much lower than rates reported for regulatory or scientific publication writing. Within CME/CE, rates are also likely to vary by geography (e.g., lower in the United Kingdome and Europe than in the United States), and region (e.g., higher on the US West Coast than in the Midwest). Remember you can increase these rates by strategically positioning yourself as a partner who can problem-solve, be creative, and offer a menu of services that meets the unique needs of your client.
- There are other ways to research going rates for CME/CE. You can ask clients with whom you have a strong relationship about rates for particular project types, as Ilise Benun of Marketing Mentor suggests. You can search the internet for rate sheets too. Some CME/CE writers post their rates on their websites. You could even ask ChatGPT to find rates for you.

Pricing TL;DR

1. Set your money anchor.
2. Find out what the going rate is (as much as that is possible).

3. Experiment with different pricing models (e.g., hourly, project, per diem).
4. Track your hours, tasks, clients, and projects so that you have data on which to base your decisions.
5. Recognize that money is an emotional topic. How do you feel about it, and how does this affect your approach to pricing?
6. Evaluate your pricing after each project.
7. For every project you scope/estimate, what is the bottom line that will allow you to do the work with relish, even when you hit bumps in the road?

Many resources include exercises to help you calculate your internal bottom hourly line. Start with the rate calculator in *The Path of the Freelancer* by Jason Scott Montoya.

Insurance

Do you need insurance for your freelance medical writing business? This question alone demands its own book. You should consider several insurance options to protect yourself and their business.

- Professional Liability Insurance (Errors and Omissions Insurance) is crucial for covering legal fees and potential settlements related to claims of negligence or errors in your work.
- General Liability Insurance covers bodily injury, property damage, and personal injury claims that might occur while conducting business.
- Virginia Chachati, PharmD, of Write Clinic, identifies Cyber Liability Insurance as an essential to protect against data breaches and cyberattacks, especially given the increasing reliance on digital tools.
- Health insurance is vital for freelancers who don't have employer-provided coverage, with options including individual plans

through the Affordable Care Act marketplace or membership-based health plans.

- Income Protection Insurance (Disability Insurance) provides financial support if you are unable to work due to illness or injury.

These insurance types can help you manage risks and maintain financial stability for your business. Search the AMWA blog to learn more about different types of insurance.

Project Management

You are building relationships and negotiating rates. Next, when you win the contract, you will need to manage the project. There are at least two ways to think about project management.

First, consider the tools and resources you need to manage your own projects. Tools that help you track time, tasks, costs, revisions, feedback, and all the other moving parts.

Second, sooner or later you will work with education providers who do not have a strategic approach to managing the grant and content development process or have any well-honed project management processes in place. Perhaps they are relatively new to the field, are based outside the United States, or have a lot of internal new hires. Industry churn will result in a situation where staff do not necessarily have a clear overview of what the CME/CE grant process or education planning looks like, or appreciate all the components that go into a needs assessment. They are less likely to know all the different pieces of information that you need to know as the writer to develop the content for the project you are working on.

How Project Management Deficits Affect You

In these situations, you are likely to run into challenges like tight deadlines, no or poor-quality templates, and indeterminate editorial direction that will affect your ability to deliver quality work. You might also have to educate new-to-market or boutique providers about realistic revision cycle expectations, including how many rounds of revisions to anticipate, who will be involved in the revision process, or how revision comments will be collated and communicated to the writer.

As a result of their own limited exposure to accredited CME/CE, some clients will ask you as the writer to develop strategy for the needs assessment (as in, "We'd like you to write a needs assessment on lung cancer. No, we don't have particular gaps in mind. We're hoping you can find those for us."). Writers also report instances where providers are ambiguous about the scope of work, lack a documented process for content development, or do not share relevant materials with writers at project startup.

Typical scenarios with process deficits include when the provider:

1. Asks the writer to develop concise gap statements from a very long laundry list of need statements
2. Hires a writer to develop a needs assessment on a disease state without any strategic direction
3. Does not review draft work in a timely fashion
4. Adds last-minute requests that the writer feels obliged to meet

Here's what you need to be prepared for these challenges:

Poor content direction. Ask for a clear brief about the project and for foundational materials at project startup, such as key guidelines, clinical data, and templates. Make sure you understand the target audience and activity format. Your client should provide a documented agreement or scope of work that details the project parameters and tasks, timeline, remuneration, payment schedule, and revision cycles. If they do not share this information voluntarily, ask for a kickoff call so that you can get the information you need. You need to know the grant and needs assessment process well enough to be able to say with confidence, "Well, no, actually. You have to give me the following information to kick-start the project."

Revisions. While there is no industry standard here, experienced writers typically offer two rounds of revision, one major and one minor. When expectations around revision cycles are mismatched, both parties are likely to feel frustrated. Clear communication about revision expectations is key.

Communicate often. Suggest regular check-ins, maintain feedback loops, and promptly address emergent concerns. Successful partnerships depend on clear communication, setting expectations upfront, and developing trust over time.

Managing Projects with Confidence

Christine Welniak of Upside Communications recommends the following tactics for managing projects with confidence:

- Know the roles and responsibilities of all stakeholders (faculty, scientific director, project manager). Get clarity upfront.
- Be aware of common breakdowns—faculty not providing an appropriate case study or adhering to guidelines, weak scientific direction, scope creep from project manager.
- Document outstanding items and unanswered questions. Follow up in writing.
- Escalate issues early before they threaten project timelines.
- Gently educate faculty on CME/CE requirements if needed. Loop in the scientific director as necessary.
- Use phrases to reestablish boundaries, e.g., "Please check my availability," "That's beyond the scope," "I'd rather the timeline didn't assume weekend work."

- Stand your ground respectfully using a detached, clinical tone.

◇◇

Remember, you are a professional with skills and knowledge. Avoid taking on roles outside your scope, and make sure you are prepped and prepared before you jump into a project. You will feel empowered, and your clients will feel they are in a safe pair of hands.

Optimizing Client Communication in a Virtual World

As freelance writers, we rely heavily on virtual platforms to connect with clients, discuss projects, and collaborate on deliverables. However, the rapid shift to remote work during the pandemic has led to a phenomenon known as Zoom fatigue—a sense of weariness and energy depletion from constant online meetings.

To maintain professionalism and effectiveness in client communication, consider these tips:

1. Leverage Body Language

When meeting with clients via video, try standing up to speak. Eleanor Handley, a communications expert in New York, says this simple change in posture can improve your breath efficiency, allowing you to communicate more clearly and effectively. Standing also encourages natural gesticulation, which can help emphasize key points and keep your client engaged.

2. Choose the Right Medium

Not every client interaction requires a video call. In fact, the myriad visual cues in a video meeting can sometimes be distracting and overwhelming, making it harder to listen actively and contribute meaningfully. For certain discussions, a good old-fashioned phone call or even an email exchange might be more appropriate and efficient.

Consider the goals of the meeting and choose the communication medium accordingly.

3. Prepare and Practice

Before any client meeting, whether via phone or video, take a few minutes to practice your key points out loud. This simple exercise helps build muscle memory, making you sound more polished and professional when it's time to deliver. It also allows you to test the clarity and conciseness of your message. Remember, in the virtual world, succinct communication is often most effective.

4. Set Clear Expectations

When working remotely, it is crucial to establish clear expectations with your clients from the outset. This includes agreeing on communication channels, response times, and project milestones. By setting these parameters early, you can avoid misunderstandings and ensure a smooth, productive working relationship.

5. Maintain Professional Boundaries

While the informal nature of virtual communication can be tempting, it is important to maintain professional boundaries with your clients. This means being mindful of your background during video calls, keeping your language professional in all written communication, and respecting agreed-upon working hours. A little personal rapport is fine, but remember that ultimately you are there to provide a professional service.

These strategies can help you optimize your virtual interactions with clients and foster clear communication, productive collaboration, and strong professional relationships in the new world of remote work.

Measuring Success

If you are a solopreneur or freelancer, it's tempting to gauge success with dollar signs.

But success can be measured and celebrated in all sorts of ways.

- The books we read
- The skills we mastered
- The knots we untangled
- The clients who returned
- The relationships we nurtured
- The fresh faces in our network
- The clarity we discovered in chaos
- The wise financial decisions we made
- The progress we made in our business strategy
- The time we took for hobbies, family, and relaxation
- The growth from wrangling uncertainty and stress
- The changes we made to our work habits that amplified our output
- The bridges we built within our professional network and local community

What's your version of success, and how are you celebrating it?

Make Your Business Sustainable

Forecasts for the medical writing industry continue to predict growth in market size. Grand View Research reports that the medical writing market was valued at $3.8 billion in 2022 and continues to grow, driven by factors such as an increase in CRO outsourcing, clinical studies, and the ever-expanding search by consumers for health-related information.[10]

What do you need as a freelance CME/CE writer to ensure that you not only launch and grow your business but also guarantee its sustainability?

While autonomy and control over the nature and timing of work are primary benefits associated with long-term freelance medical writing, including CME/CE writing, challenges abound too, including the challenge of sustaining a business over the long-term. There is not a lot of robust research on how freelance writers do this, never mind freelance medical writers and the hyper-niche area of CME/CE writing. A 2020 study on the career trajectories of freelancers that use online platforms offers some clues about challenges, including the stress associated with long-term income uncertainty, fluctuations in demand, the labor required to be your own boss, and the effort to build and maintain an online/social media presence as well as manage clients. Limited social support and connections are also reported as challenging.[11]

Anne Jacobson, MSPharm, CHCP, is an established, highly experienced freelance CME/CE writer who spoke with me on the Write Medicine podcast in 2022. Anne recommends the following strategies to counter these and other challenges and ensure sustainability for your freelance CME/CE writing business:

Craftsman mindset. Most of us in CME/CE did not start with a pre-existing passion for medical writing or medical education. Instead, we discovered an interest while on the road to or from other things. Success requires us to cultivate our rare and valuable skills. Cal Newport's concept of the craftsman mindset is helpful here. Having a craftsman mindset means continuously striving for excellence, seeking to improve your skills, and staying up to date with the latest advancements in the field. Routinely reflect and reassess your goals and aspirations so you can stay in charge of the next phase and shape of your business.

Respect writing as a craft. CME/CE writing expertise is a serious craft that demands time and effort to develop. Invest your energy on producing high-quality, clean, well-edited content, and be open to learning and improving over time. Trust the 10,000-hour rule. Proficiency emerges from practice and patience more than raw talent.

Professional development. As an independent writer, you need to cultivate internal motivation to stay focused and productive. Being self-motivated also means taking initiative and seeking out opportunities for growth and development. So, embrace training and continuing professional development opportunities, participation in conferences run by ACEHP and AMWA, and consider CHCP certification to help you understand and keep up to date with the CME/CE field. Veteran writers reap benefits from professional development, too. Presenting at meetings or judging awards enhances a personal brand, and serving on steering committees also influences standards and rules.

Autonomy and choosing projects. With experience and skill, you can gain more control over your work, be poised to select projects that are personally and professionally meaningful, and work with clients who value and respect your contributions.

Community engagement. There is immense value in being part of a professional community for sharing knowledge and learning from others. While medical writers often operate independently, involvement in wider communities pays dividends. Identify and join relevant professional associations like AMWA, ACEHP, and specialty groups on LinkedIn or WriteCME Pro. These spaces share job leads and pricing insights, problem-solve ethical dilemmas, and provide empathy paired with advice.

Mentorship. Mentoring is a two-way relationship that provides social connection and can help you reflect on your own practices and continue to grow in your field. Consider finding a mentor who can nurture your talent and provide a fresh perspective on your work. In turn, consider mentoring others and cultivating intrinsic rewards for yourself.

Well-being. CME/CE professionals typically have a deep sense of purpose in the work we do to educate health care professionals. However, it is essential to balance professional demands with personal well-being and take care of your physical and mental health for long-term success in the field.

How to Ask for and Use Feedback to Build Your Business

Feedback is as important in building your business as it is in adult learning. Ideally, you want feedback from clients about particular projects and about the overall quality and direction of your work. You also want feedback from other business owners about your strategy and direction.

Client Feedback

Many clients will have a well-designed process for giving feedback during the life cycle of a project, although they vary widely in what this process looks like. In CME/CE projects, a common feedback process is reviewing comments that the project or program manager you are working with has collated into a master Word or Google document. The project manager might also gloss specific comments in an email to give you some direction when prioritizing feedback. I treat feedback on a project much as I would treat reviewer comments on a manuscript submitted to a journal. I work through the comments, address queries point-by-point, and document the rationale for any changes and recommendations I make.

Case Study: Every Writer Needs an Editor

It's hard to receive feedback about your writing because we hear feedback as criticism. I do too. I once submitted a manuscript that I was invited to write for a peer-reviewed journal. The commissioning editor liked the article, but one of the peer reviewers knocked it back with some brutal comments about style and content.

Ouch. I felt bruised. My ego was hurt.

I had work to do. First, to acknowledge my bruised ego, and second, to release my ego. For me, letting go of ego usually involves movement and meditation, which eventually allows me to see criticism as a learning opportunity. So I worked with an editor who reviewed my goals before I turned the manuscript over for additional feedback. The editor's feedback was qualitatively distinct and much more conducive to learning. She offered suggestions, guidance, and direction toward articles that provided more context and rationale for the writing choices I had made.

Here is an example of effective feedback: "What you have done here is a barrier to reader understanding. Let me show you another way that I think you'll find helpful." This feedback was helpful to me because it was offered as an invitation to grow rather than a slap for being stupid, so it opened my heart and brain to learning.

Ego gets in the way for everyone. And we all hit plateaus or develop blind spots. In 2011, Atul Gawande shared his experience in the *New Yorker* of hiring a surgical mentor, someone he knew and trusted, to observe him in the operating room.[12] Gawande felt he had hit a technique plateau and wanted tips on how to improve (because medicine inculcates perfectionism). The mentor identified small issues with surgical draping and the way the position of Gawande's elbow interrupted his kinetics and compromised his precision. Over time, Gawande's already small complication rate decreased further.

Being observed, having someone on your team to provide feedback, and taking time to review, think about, and work on that feedback are hallmarks of performance improvement and growth. It pays, as a writer, to work on ego release (and believe me, this is a practice that requires consistency). And it pays to work with an editor. I needed one. You will too.

Getting Overall Client Feedback

Getting feedback from clients can be easier said than done. Over the years, I have tried offboarding evaluation surveys and quick postproject interviews, calls, or emails. People are busy. I have found that if clients value your work and like what you do, they will offer repeat business and keep sending payments. Perhaps that's all the feedback you need to know that what you are doing works for your client.

Jonathan Agnew, PhD, is a freelance medical writer based in Canada. Here is how he thinks about feedback:

> *It's really what the client thinks. If they like it, they will pay you, and that's the definition of success. Better yet, they come back for repeat business. Then you've absolutely succeeded. And if you have that, I learned to get over the need to have feedback from clients. If they're coming back to me regularly for business, I'm doing a fine job; otherwise, they wouldn't be coming back. My definition of quality is that I'm getting paid for what I do. It clarifies it enormously.*

Peer Feedback

As you build your network, you will make and cement connections with other freelance business owners with whom you can exchange feedback about business challenges. This type of feedback is essential for growth and professional development. As hard as it can be to receive feedback, recognize that not everyone feels comfortable giving it. But there are strategies you can use, and encourage your peers to use, to help each other share feedback. Here are two suggested by Jason Evanish, CEO of Get Lighthouse, Inc.:

Five-word review. Ask for a five-word review (e.g., two to three positive, two to three negative). Set aside 45 minutes to discuss. Review the meaning of each word. Rinse and repeat with peers as necessary.

Feed forward. All feedback is future-facing and involves no judgment or criticism. Focus on an area you would like to improve and ask for two positive suggestions that will help you improve in the future. Rinse and repeat with peers as necessary.

Conclusion

Building a thriving CME/CE writing business requires a multifaceted approach that extends beyond excellent writing skills. By identifying and nourishing your niche, cultivating a strong portfolio, networking strategically, and building genuine relationships with clients and peers, you can establish yourself as a valued partner in the CME/CE industry. Embrace the power of negotiation, refine your pricing strategy, and develop effective project management skills to navigate the challenges of this dynamic field. Remember that success is measured not only by financial gains but also by professional growth, personal satisfaction, and the positive impact you make through your work. By staying adaptable, investing in your craft, and maintaining a commitment to lifelong learning, you can create a sustainable and rewarding CME/CE writing business.

Key Takeaways

- Niche specialization can lead to more success in CME/CE writing
- Actively network and build relationships in the field
- Understanding the business side of freelancing is essential
- Learn to market your services effectively

- Develop skills in negotiation, pricing, and project management

Chapter 11

Personal and Professional Well-Being

Taking care of myself doesn't mean "me first." It means "me, too."

—L. R. KNOST

Introduction

Freelance medical writers face unique challenges that can impact their overall well-being, such as fluctuating workloads, pressure to maintain multiple client relationships, and the need to continuously adapt to diverse project requirements. So, building a specialized freelance CME writing business requires not only honing one's craft but also cultivating a strong foundation of personal and professional well-being.

This chapter explores the importance of addressing personal and business well-being and provides practical strategies for maintaining physical health, nurturing mental well-being, establishing healthy work habits, and aligning your business with your values. These strategies are as relevant and valuable if you work from home as a traditional employee.

Mental Health

How do you look after your physical well-being and mental health when you are building a specialized freelance CME writing business? Is this question even on your radar? If not, it should be. The Covid-19 pandemic has made it a little easier for us to talk about mental health and topics like burnout and boundaries.

While freelance surveys, such as those conducted by Fiverr, Upwork, and the Freelancers Union, suggest that freelancing beats burnout and that freelancers see better general health and well-being than employees in a post-Covid world, other surveys focusing specifically on the mental health of freelancers report a muddier picture.[1]

The United Kingdom–based Leapers Annual Survey asked 691 freelancers in the United Kingdom, Europe, and the United States a series of questions about their work and mental health in 2022.[2] The responses are revealing.

- 35 percent of those new to freelancing think more frequently about their mental health since becoming self-employed
- 95 percent of freelancers work between 4 and 10 hours per day, with 20 percent working 8 to 10
- 75 percent took less than 28 days off in the last 12 months

The survey found that moving into freelance work is good for your mental health initially, but the longer people have been freelancing, the more likely they are to report a decline in mental health. Sleep and exercise are areas that have the least balance in the lives of freelancers.

Scroll through LinkedIn and you will find plenty of discussion in the freelance medical writing world about the stresses and mental health challenges associated with running a freelance writing business. As freelancers, we face fluctuating workloads, pressure to maintain multiple client relationships, and the need to continuously adapt to diverse project requirements. If we are not careful, these conditions can contribute to chronic exhaustion, pessimism, self-doubt, and physical or mental health conditions.

Burnout

According to the American Psychological Association (APA) and the World Health Organization,[3] occupational burnout results from chronic workplace stress that has not been successfully managed. The 2023 APA Work in America Survey paints a picture that confirmed the prevalence of workplace burnout and stress across various professional groups.[4] The report does not specifically call out freelance writers, but we would do well to recognize the signs of workplace burnout and stress:

- Feelings of energy depletion or exhaustion
- Increased mental distance from one's job or feelings of negativism/cynicism
- Reduced professional efficacy

Causes of burnout for entrepreneurs include obsessive passion, social isolation, financial uncertainty, and overworking.[1–2] Whether you see yourself as an entrepreneur or not, it pays to develop coping mechanisms and to engage in prosocial behaviors to counter these negative, burnout-causing behaviors.

Pro Tip

Strategies to avoid burnout include deciding on an optimal number of clients, choosing clients carefully, setting clear expectations with clients, managing time effectively, and prioritizing vacations. When timelines and turnaround times for grant submissions and activity launch dates are tight, you might find yourself very squeezed for time, energy, and cognitive load. Review Chapter 10 for strategies to manage your business.

In 2022, U.S. Surgeon General Vivek Murthy, MD, released the office's first-ever *Surgeon General's Framework for Workplace Mental Health and Well-Being.*[5] The Five Essentials for Workplace Mental Health and Well-Being are as valuable to folks who work from home as to those who schlep into an office on a daily basis.

1. Protection from harm (including security and safety)
2. Connection and community (including social support and belonging)
3. Work-life harmony (including autonomy and flexibility)
4. Mattering at work (including dignity and meaning)
5. Opportunity for growth (including learning and accomplishment)

In summary, while specific data on the prevalence of burnout and business collapse among freelance medical writers is not available, the general issue of burnout in the freelancing community is well-recognized and can be mitigated through effective strategies and awareness.

Growth Mindset

Not having a growth mindset is like navigating without a compass. You'll move, but not necessarily forward.

Recently, I scheduled a livestream Write Medicine podcast episode. It didn't go well. We had tech issues connecting LinkedIn streaming to the podcast recording platform and could not actually go live. I was disappointed, to say the least. I had a moment of thinking, "Why am I doing this? Who am I doing it for? And why bother?" I had to take some time that day to answer those questions for myself.

For the record, I try new things because I'm curious and like to challenge myself. I wanted to offer a unique listening experience and foster genuine connections with you, the listener. And I wanted to try something different because standing still is not even part of my vocabulary.

Practicing Nonattachment

The livestream experience for me was a reminder to practice nonattachment. In Patanjali's eight limbs of yoga (of which I am also a longtime practitioner), the Sanskrit word for "nonattachment" is *aparigraha*. It means letting go of the outcome, which Stephen Cope in *The Great Work of Your Life* calls one of the keys to a path of action.

Living a growth mindset means we have to let go of the outcome.

I had a conversation with my podcast manager, and we decided to send an email out to listeners and newsletter subscribers. The response from listeners and readers was overwhelmingly encouraging—and reassuring.

Cultivating a growth mindset and practicing nonattachment will work for your business too. As Audrie Tornow, managing partner at Excalibur Medical Education, said in our very first Write Medicine podcast episode on "Creativity and Failure in CME/CE":

> *People think that demonstrating failure means you aren't a trusted partner, that you aren't a successful business. That's definitely a perception that's valid, but I think there's so much to be learned by saying, "I tried this, here was the idea. And it didn't work." And it might be that next partner that says, "Actually, if you had just done this..." They might be the missing piece.*

A growth mindset is not a one-and-done thing. It requires ongoing effort and practice. Living a growth mindset is about embodying curiosity and pushing yourself out of your comfort zone, even when things don't go according to plan. It is about having the resilience to negotiate obstacles and seek out new opportunities for growth.

Five Steps to Cultivating a Growth Mindset

Here are five steps you can take right now to cultivate a growth mindset and build a foundation for your professional development. A mnemonic device for this could be CASAD. Think of this as a spin on the word casa, which means "house" in Spanish. Your growth mindset principles are the foundation, or the "house," of your personal and professional development.

1. **Celebrate small wins.** Focusing only on significant achievements can be discouraging. Celebrating small victories can fuel motivation and reinforce a growth mindset.
   - **Action step:** Keep a "wins journal." At the end of each day, jot down at least one thing you accomplished or learned, no matter how minor it seems.
2. **Acknowledge and reframe limiting beliefs.** Often, the barriers that hinder our growth are the beliefs we hold about ourselves. Recognizing and challenging these beliefs can pave the way for a more expansive mindset.
   - **Action step:** Dedicate a few minutes each day to self-reflection. Write down any limiting thoughts you notice, then actively reframe them into positive affirmations or growth-oriented beliefs.
3. **Shift from a fixed perspective.** Holding onto fixed beliefs about talents and intelligence limits growth. Embracing the idea that abilities can be developed fosters a love for learning and resilience in the face of challenges.
   - **Action step:** When faced with a difficult task, rather than thinking "I can't do this," reframe it to "I can't do this *yet*." This subtle shift in wording can greatly impact your mindset over time.
4. **Accept constructive criticism.** The overwhelmingly positive feedback from our listeners and subscribers reminded us of the importance of community and how valuable feedback can be. Feedback, when taken constructively, can be a roadmap for personal and professional growth. Embrace it as an opportunity to evolve.

- **Action step:** Actively seek feedback. Whether from a mentor, colleague, or customer, getting an external perspective can offer insights you had not previously considered. The next time someone offers feedback, resist the urge to get defensive. Instead, thank them, reflect on their words, and determine how you can use the information to improve.

5. **Detach from the outcome.** Practicing nonattachment to the outcome ensures we aren't disheartened by failures. Being invested in the **process** versus the result fosters a healthier mindset.

   - **Action step:** Incorporate a daily mindfulness or meditation routine. This will help you stay present and avoid becoming overly attached to outcomes.

Cultivating a growth mindset is a continuous journey. It's not about how often you stumble but how many times you get back up, having learned something new each time.

Embrace the journey, with all its the failures and the lessons they bring.

Managing Overwhelm

So many of us who find our way into medical writing are driven folks. Type As. Overachievers. Uberlearners. Perfectionists. We are chasing validation. Visibility. Valor, even. We want to be seen, praised, score the prize, and get the snaps and back pats.

Many people transition into CME writing from different fields, such as health care or academia. In your role as a clinician, researcher, or academic, you probably thrived on the drive toward knowledge, peer recognition, or financial rewards. There's nothing wrong with any of this. Drive is movement. Forward movement, toward goals that are often as important to others as to ourselves. After all, we work in a capitalist society, and capitalism is premised not just on the physical labor of workers, but also our cognitive and emotional labor.

However, these same motivating factors may not hold equal weight or meaning in your new career path. What drives us early in our careers might not always be the healthy or rational thing -- or even the right thing for us at this point in our lives. I'm here to tell you that surrendering to the drive to achieve can lead you to overwhelm and overdo. I hear again and again from medical writers with full schedules that they never feel they can say no because they worry about where the next gig is coming from. They accept whatever work comes their way, then find they have a more than full schedule, without buffer, and end up feeling exhausted and overextended. I know this all too well from my own experience, because in earlier days of my freelance business I continued working through bereavement and sickness.

Therefore, take time to dig into what drives you and commit to building your business without running yourself into the ground. Develop what independent CME writer Anne Jacobson, MSPharm, CHCP, refers to as a craftsman mindset.

Unearth your true motivations. The first step in avoiding burnout is to understand your driving forces. Take time to reassess what truly motivates you now. Is it the autonomy of freelancing? The impact of conveying complex medical information to a broader audience? Once you align your work with your true drivers, you will find it easier to manage your commitments.

Time-blocking. Cal Newport tells us in *Deep Work: Rules for Focused Success in a Distracted World* that much of the time we work on autopilot and let trivial matters creep into our workday. Time-blocking is his remedy to help you stay focused and avoid overcommitting yourself. Allocate specific time blocks for different tasks or projects and stick to them. I would add, consider time-blocking a part of each day or week dedicated solely to self-care or unexpected tasks. Whether it is a 30-minute walk, reading a chapter from a book, or spending time with family, this buffer will provide you with the mental space to recharge.

- **The Pomodoro technique.** Use Pomodoro technique to break your day into focused intervals followed by a short break. This not only increases productivity but also ensures you are giving yourself regular short breaks to relax and recharge.

Create buffer in your schedule. The allure of freelance work lies in its flexibility, but that flexibility can quickly evaporate if you're juggling too many projects simultaneously. One practical approach to avoid feeling overwhelmed is to create buffer slots or days in your schedule.

- **Avoid back-to-back deadlines.** Space out your project commitments so that you have adequate time for revisions, client communications, and unplanned life events. This will give you a safety net in case things don't go as planned.

Be selective with clients and projects. Saying "yes" to every opportunity that comes your way might seem like a good problem to have, but it can lead to a pileup of projects that leave you feeling overextended. Here are a few strategies to intentionally decide which clients and projects to take on:

- **Create an ideal client profile.** Define what an ideal client looks like for you. Do they value evidence-based content? Are they open to long-term collaborations? By understanding what you're looking for, you can quickly assess new opportunities and decide if they align with your goals.
- **Set a project minimum.** Consider establishing a project minimum—a set rate or scope below which you will not accept a job. This can help you filter out less-rewarding opportunities and focus on projects that are worth your time and effort.
- **Review and reflect.** Regularly review your workload and assess how each project aligns with your career and personal goals. If a project is draining your energy without providing sufficient rewards, it might be time to part ways and focus on more fulfilling opportunities.

As you build your CME writing business, the stakes can feel high. I have learned that it's crucial to strike a balance between your professional ambitions and your personal well-being. After all, a stressed and overworked writer is unlikely to produce their best work. You can avoid overwhelm by being self-aware, strategic, and, most important, kind to yourself. With the right approach, you can manage your workload efficiently without burning the candle at both ends and sacrificing the quality of your well-being.

The Antidote to Productivity

While we are talking about (over)achievement, let's also unpack productivity. Madelaine Dore writes in her wonderful book *I Didn't Do the Thing Today*, "When we conflate productivity with worthiness, what we do is never enough."[7]

Talk about a smack on the side of the head—in a gentle, nonviolent kind of way. For most of my life I have been productive. In pursuit of production. Full-tilt Miss Productivity. Hell, no. Full-tilt Dr. Productivity. In fact, my first paid job was at age 13, delivering tubs of cream to bougie neighborhoods (as well as promotional items, like a 1977 Queen's Silver Jubilee tea towel). I've been working ever since and for a long time embraced the idea that work is at the center of who we are. Maybe you can relate.

It is hard to avoid thinking about productivity because it's a regular topic of discussion on social media platforms, especially LinkedIn. Morning routine! Apps! Strategies!

But as Dore sees it, productivity is on a pedestal. It has become the weathervane for worth. And because of this, we are set up to fail. We will endlessly feel the pressure to do more, be more, achieve more, chase tools to help us do more with less, and optimize our resources—until something knocks productivity off the pedestal and we are forced to reevaluate the sources of our worth. That something could be a pandemic, menopause, an illness. Or exhaustion.

The antidote to productivity is fecundity and rest.

To be fecund is to be capable of growth. And to grow, we need light, rest, movement, nourishment, connection. As the Scottish-born naturalist John Muir describes it in *The Yosemite*: "Everybody needs beauty as well as bread, places to play in and pray in, where Nature may heal and cheer and give strength to body and soul alike."

Rest can be transformative too. Tricia Hersey founded the Nap Ministry to reclaim rest as a fundamental human right and a revolutionary act against the oppressive nature of grind culture.[8] Rest can be a means to resist societal pressures that prioritize productivity over well-being. Hersey encourages us to view rest as a vital practice that nurtures the mind, body, and spirit. Rest is not laziness. It is a form of self-care, healing, and empowerment.

Creating potent content about medicine and health care requires a unique and gentle medicine of its own. Dear reader, what are you doing to nourish fecundity? To ensure that you stay grounded, cultivate growth, and have the capacity to meet client or stakeholder demands without conflating productivity as worthiness?

Equanimity

For most of us as CME/CPD professionals, the demands of everyday life are fast, furious, and full-on. In the year's wheel of perpetual activity, many of us are constantly on high alert and have forgotten how to relax. Most of us feel stressed much of the time.

Stress is an almost inevitable part of life. It arises as our body's way of responding to any change that requires an adjustment, triggering a physiological reaction that prepares us to face immediate challenges. This can lead to a state of constant alertness that, if not properly managed, may cause various health issues. Stress, while sometimes motivating, can have detrimental effects on our physical and mental health if sustained, leading to symptoms like fatigue, headaches, and depression.

But we can learn to recognize stressors, the physical manifestations of stress within our bodies, and how to activate the parasympathetic nervous system (PNS) to restore balance. The PNS helps calm the body, encouraging a state of rest and digestion that counterbalances the fight-or-flight response initiated by the sympathetic nervous system. There are many practical techniques that focus on breath, touch, movement, and visualization to promote relaxation and help you return to a state of calmness and presence.

Mindfulness is such a technique. Mindfulness involves focusing on the present moment, observing thoughts and sensations without judgment, and being fully engaged in the current experience.9 Mindfulness can help us increase self-awareness, reduce stress, enhance emotional regulation, and promote a sense of calmness and clarity. This practice can be cultivated through techniques like meditation, breathing exercises, and paying attention to sensations in everyday activities. Mindfulness is not about emptying the mind, but rather about being present and accepting one's thoughts and feelings without attachment or criticism.

Here are two short practices to help you navigate the pressures of everyday life with equanimity:

1. The Bell of Mindfulness

See this bell? It's the bell of mindfulness.

It represents a little micro-practice to help you stay present.

In our culture of busyness, scattered thoughts and multitasking reign supreme.

Email. Texts. Social media. Phones.

All these demands intrude in our days and consciousness in ways that pull us away from the present, scatter our thoughts, and increase stress.

You know what I'm talking about.

So whenever you hear a bell—any kind of bell—take three slow breaths in and out through your nose.

Let the bell and your breath anchor you in the present moment.

This way equanimity lies.

2. Brain Shifts

Neurons are the social connectors that keep your brain informed about what is going on in your body.[10] Sometimes—probably a lot—those neurons are in overdrive.

- Constant chatter inside your head?
- Can't slow down?
- Feeling restless?

Your neurons are busy.

But when you shift what's going on in your body, you send a message to those neurons and your brain shifts too. These practices can change your physiology and strengthen your nervous system:

- Progressive muscle relaxation
- Deep belly breathing
- Guided visualization
- Restorative yoga
- Binaural beats

- Body scan
- Humming

When your nervous system is strong, you will have a locked-in tool to reduce the internal chatter and handle stress. The brain is an incredibly complex organ, but by using physical reset practices, we can help it function more effectively and efficiently.

Discipline

The Moon and Sixpence by W. Somerset Maugham is one of my favorite novels. Maugham—who started out as a medical student but ditched medicine for full-time writing—was pretty prolific. By the time he was 30 he had written ten novels and as many plays.

I don't know about you, but I am a little fatigued even contemplating that level of creativity. But the creativity stakes are high for creating content in continuing education for health professionals. Health professionals rely on accurate, engaging, and timely information to support their clinical practice. And clients and employers require reliable content delivered in timelines that can be short, to say the least.

Thus, the pressure for content creators in CME/CE can be daunting sometimes. But when we find ourselves waiting for that perfect wave of inspiration, take a leaf out of Maugham's book. He is said to have observed: "I write only when inspiration strikes. Fortunately, it strikes every morning at nine o'clock sharp."

For me, this is a gentle reminder that discipline trumps fleeting bursts of creativity! Consistency and routine can be our greatest allies. When we sit down to write, even if the muse feels absent, our dedication sends a signal to our brains that it is time to create. More often than not, inspiration follows. As Billy Oppenheimer has observed in his SIX at 6 newsletter, discipline and focus go together. The price of making things easier on yourself in the future is often discipline in the present.

When you make discipline part of your freelance business, it empowers rather than restricts you and helps you align your work with your freelance aspirations. For CME writers who are focused on evidence-based, trustworthy content, discipline can be the cornerstone of a sustainable and life-affirming business. Consistency in producing high-quality work, time management, and a commitment to continuous learning can all be fostered through discipline. By integrating disciplined practices into your routine, you can not only improve your productivity but also maintain a work-life balance that nourishes both your professional and personal lives.

Why Is Discipline Necessary?

Time management. Unlike a traditional nine-to-five employee (a diminishing category of worker), as a freelance CME writer you must allocate time for client meetings, research, writing, and looking after your business (e.g., bookkeeping, accounting, marketing). When you develop time discipline, you are building a habit that will help you meet deadlines and juggle your responsibilities effectively, leaving you space to say yes to the unanticipated fun stuff.

Quality control. For niches like CME writing, in which evidence-based information is vital, a disciplined approach to research and fact-checking is non-negotiable. Put systems in place that help you find, sort, store, and retrieve information quickly and efficiently. Use Notion, Google Sheets, Evernote, or ClickUp as support systems.

Client relationships. Discipline helps with setting boundaries, managing expectations, and maintaining professional decorum, all of which are essential for long-term client retention (see Chapter 10). By the way, if you need support and strategies to help you review and reset client relationships, consider joining WriteCME Pro, a professional development membership for medical writers who are growing their CME/CE writing businesses.

Self-care. Irony alert! Freelance CME/CE writers often overlook their personal well-being. A disciplined mindset ensures you carve out time for yourself, reduce the potential for injury, and prevent burnout.

Financial stability. Finally, discipline extends to financial management. As income may be irregular, disciplined budgeting and saving are key to surviving dry spells that do sometimes occur.

The next time you're seeking motivation, remember it's OK if it feels elusive. Set your "nine o'clock" and let your commitment open the door to creativity.

Imposter Syndrome

Most CME writers experience a sense of not belonging at some point or another. I know I have.

We doubt ourselves. Undervalue our contributions. Or feel trapped in a cycle of pursuing perfectionism. These experiences might be accompanied by fears of failure, inadequacy, and losing control.

These feelings might tell you that you are an imposter. You're not.

I am not a fan of the imposter syndrome concept. It's a way for capitalism to keep you hustling. As the Australian scholar and critic Rebecca Harkins-Cross says,

> *Capitalism needs us all to feel like impostors, because feeling like an impostor ensures we'll strive for endless progress: work harder, make more money, try to be better than our former selves and the people around us.*[11]

When you ask yourself the question, "Who am I to [fill in the blank]?" that question doesn't come from imposter syndrome. That question comes from pursuing perfectionism in a culture that makes us all chase perfectionism.

In recent years, the term "imposter syndrome" has gained significant attention, particularly among white, college-educated individuals posting on social media platforms like LinkedIn. While imposter syndrome is a legitimate behavioral health phenomenon, the overuse of this term diminishes its impact and mischaracterizes what may be better described as healthy self-doubt or performance anxiety.

Defining Imposter Syndrome

Psychologists Pauline Rose Clance and Suzanne Imes first coined the term in the late 1970s to describe high-achieving, college-educated white women who doubted their accomplishments and had a persistent fear of being exposed as a "fraud."[12] The concept has since been expanded to include men and individuals from diverse backgrounds and is disproportionately associated with academics and health professionals. Imposter syndrome includes pervasive feelings of self-doubt, anxiety, depression, and apprehension of being exposed as a fraud in one's work, despite objective evidence of success.[13] There is no widespread clinical definition for imposter syndrome, which is also known as imposter phenomenon. It's also challenging to gauge the prevalence of imposter syndrome, although it tends to be linked to women more than men, and to other marginalized groups.

Imposter syndrome has its critics. First, the concept medicalizes self-doubt, which is a normal part of the process of showing up, trying, and experimenting. Second, imposter syndrome overshadows structural inequalities. In a *Harvard Business Review* essay, Ruchika Tulshyan and Jodi-Ann Burey argued that focusing solely on individual feelings of fraudulence can detract attention from systemic issues that contribute to inequality in education and professional environments and systems designed to disenfranchise anyone who is not white and male.[14]

Similarly, in her 2023 commencement speech at Smith College, Reshma Saujani argues that imposter syndrome is not a personal problem that individuals need to solve, but rather a systemic issue rooted in structural inequality and a tool used to hold women back.[15] Some people experience self-doubt because they face actual prejudice or bias, not because they have imposter syndrome. Saujani notes that discomfort and anxiety are natural human reactions when facing unearned privileges and systems not built for everyone. Self-doubt can also be a response to crossing a threshold—from one social class, professional identify, or intellectual status to another.[11] Anthropologist Mary Douglas described this feeling as an expression of *matter out of place*. Third, the more frequently the term is used as a socially acceptable way to express insecurity, the less potent it becomes for describing the very real and debilitating self-doubt some individuals face.

Instead of pathologizing self-doubt as imposter syndrome, we can reframe it as a normal part of the process of growth and development. By recognizing that feelings of self-doubt and feeling like you don't belong are part of the journey, we can practice acceptance and nonattachment to these feelings. By rejecting the internalization of imposter syndrome as an expression of personal failing, we can more intentionally move toward our goals. We will also have, as Saujani notes, more energy and resources to address systemic issues like sexism, racism, classism, homophobia, and transphobia.

The antidotes to imposter syndrome are community, connection, and self-awareness. In moments when you feel when you feel self-doubt, inadequacy, or a sense of being an outsider, try these steps to reconnect with yourself and reestablish your inner compass:

1. **Pause.** Stop in your tracks and take a moment for yourself.
2. **Breathe.** Slow your breath. Watch your thoughts. Let them pass.
3. **Notice.** Notice how your body feels. Be curious and practice nonattachment—no need to get caught up in stories about what any of your feelings mean.

4. **Reassess.** Evaluate the situation and why you doubt yourself.
5. **Respond.** Be intentional with your response to your feelings or the situation in front of you.

How do you practice curiosity when faced with self-doubt or a feeling you don't belong?

Self-Care

Did I see you cringe when you saw the term "self-care" here? I get it. The wellness industry has co-opted this term and turned a healthy (in my view) concern for well-being into capitalist coin. But as medical education writer and health coach Reggie Wilson notes, it is pretty ironic that medical writers, working in a field that promotes health, also ignore their own health.

Working on a keyboard can trigger discomfort or pain in our wrists, hands, arms, elbows, shoulders, back, and neck. As a writer, you are at risk of developing musculoskeletal conditions resulting from trauma in the form of repetitive strain injury (RSI).[16] Given that we often perform the same actions repeatedly (e.g., clicking the mouse, typing on a keyboard) while maintaining a relatively static posture, we open ourselves up to RSI due to exertion and overuse of a limited set of muscles.

Additionally, we do not always maintain optimal posture or technique, take sufficient breaks, or invite sufficient movement into our day. The result? Pain that is often localized and limited to the upper body, particularly concentrated in the hands and arms, neck and shoulders, and back. Other symptoms can include fatigue, weakness, numbness, tingling, lack of control or coordination, and hypersensitivity.

Yes, we spend long hours sitting or standing at a desk and doing keyboard work. But the aches and pains that often accompany this work don't have to be a constant companion. You can take a proactive approach to self-care. By implementing preventive measures, you can reduce the likelihood of developing musculoskeletal conditions and maintain optimal physical health.

Some proactive strategies include:

1. **Ergonomics.** Invest in an ergonomically designed workspace that promotes proper alignment and reduces strain on your body. Consider factors such as desk and chair height, back and wrist support, and screen position.
2. **Take regular breaks.** Incorporate frequent breaks into your work schedule to prevent muscle fatigue and overexertion. Use this time to stretch, take a short walk, hydrate, or engage in brief exercises.
3. **Build strength and flexibility.** Combat the effects of prolonged sitting or standing by engaging in regular exercise to build strength and improve joint flexibility and mobility. Incorporate stretching into your daily routine to maintain flexibility.
4. **Get adequate rest.** As Tricia Hersey says in *Nap Ministry*, rest is resistance! Prioritize sufficient sleep and allow your body to recuperate from intense work sessions. Rest is essential for preventing pain and promoting overall well-being.

Simple Exercises to Alleviate Tension

I know, as both a writer and as a yoga teacher, how incorporating simple exercises into your daily self-care routine can help alleviate tension, improve functionality, and prevent pain. Try the following exercises, which can be performed even while seated at your desk:

1. **Seated cow-cat stretch.** With a long spine and relaxed shoulders, place your hands on your knees. Inhale and lift your sternum, drawing your hands up your thighs toward your groin. Exhale, tucking your chin and rounding your back. Repeat in rhythm with your breath.
2. **Neck stretches.** Tilt your head to draw your right ear to your right shoulder. Gently move your chin forward and back, holding the position to stretch tender areas. Repeat on the left side.

3. **Wrist circles.** Bend your elbows and make gentle fists. Move your fists in circles to relax your wrists, switching directions after a few breaths.
4. **Forearm stretches.** Extend your arms to the sides, making fists. Draw your fists down toward the ground and hold for 30 seconds to a minute. Release the fists and press the backs of your hands against your rib cage, holding for another 30 seconds to a minute.
5. **Starfish hands.** Rest your hands on your thighs, palms facing up. Exhale and curl your fingers into fists. Inhale and extend your fingers out into a starfish. Repeat for several breaths, focusing on the flow of air in and out of your body.

By incorporating these preventive measures and simple exercises into your daily routine, you can maintain your physical health, reduce the risk of injuries, and continue producing high-quality work as a CME writer. Self-care is not a luxury but an essential component of a building a sustainable CME writing niche.

Conclusion

As a freelance CME/CE writer you face unique challenges, such as fluctuating workloads, the pressure to maintain multiple client relationships, and the need to adapt to diverse project requirements. By cultivating a growth mindset, managing overwhelm, embracing discipline, and reframing imposter syndrome, you can foster resilience and maintain a healthy perspective in the face of these challenges. Additionally, incorporating self-care practices like ergonomics, regular breaks, exercise, and simple tension-relieving exercises can help prevent physical strain and injuries associated with prolonged writing and computer use. Your well-being is not a luxury. It is an essential foundation for producing high-quality work and building a sustainable CME/CE writing business.

Key Takeaways

- Freelance CME/CE writing can lead to burnout if not managed well
- Develop strategies to prevent burnout and manage stress
- Prioritize work-life balance and personal well-being
- Embrace a growth mindset and continuous learning
- Incorporate self-care practices into your routine

Conclusion

Ready, Steady, CME!

What you do makes a difference, and you have to decide what kind of difference you want to make.

—JANE GOODALL

In 1968, my kindergarten teacher wrote this in my report card: "*Alex is not, nor does she have to be, number one.*"

Oof.

That statement has pretty much defined my path in life. I focused a lot of my energy on the first part of that sentence—Alex is not number one—and it served me well for a while. The idea that I was not number one was a motivator and defined how I approached my professional life. I worked hard to establish and achieve goals. The idea also laid a strong foundation for lifelong learning.

But over time, I have realized that the second part of the sentence is actually more important: "*I don't have to be number one.*"

I do not have to be the best medical writer, the best CME writer, the best teacher, the best anything. As Avram Alpert argues in *The Good-Enough Life*, I need to be *good enough*. Good enough to complete the project efficiently and effectively. Good enough to meet client expectations and sometimes exceed them.

Good enough has served me for two decades and allowed me to grow and sustain my CME writing business with an annual revenue in the multi-six figures.

Maybe you are (or need to be) number one. That's OK; you do you! But be reassured that you do not have to be the best writer in the world to grow and sustain a rewarding and meaningful CME writing business. You can do that by learning about accreditation and ethics, developing robust skills and field-related competencies, strategically establishing a network, and investing your focus and energy in good (enough) work.

Key Takeaways

- Focus on being "good enough" rather than perfect
- Continuously improve your skills and knowledge
- Balance professional growth with personal well-being
- Remember that success in CME/CE writing is a journey, not a destination

References

Introduction

1. Pink D. Free Agent Nation: *The Future of Working for Yourself.* Business Plus. 2002.
2. Arizton. US continuing medical education market-industry outook and forecast 2023–2028. https://www.arizton.com/market-reports/us-continuing-medical-education-market. Accessed April 5, 2024.
3. Accreditation Council for Continuing Medical Education (ACCME®). *ACCME Data Report. Renewal and Growth in Accredited Continuing Education*—2022. https://www.accme.org/sites/default/files/2023-07/2022%20ACCME%20Annual%20Data%20Report%201003_20230713.pdf. Accessed April 5, 2024.
4. U.S. Bureau of Labor Statistics. *Occupational Outlook Handbook.* https://www.bls.gov/ooh/health care/home.htm. Accessed April 5, 2024.
5. Association of American Medical Colleges. *The Complexities of Physician Supply and Demand: Projections from 2021 to 2036*. 2024. https://www.aamc.org/media/75236/download?attachment. Accessed April 5, 2024.

6. Dov Bruch J, Roy V, Grogan CM. The financialization of health in the United States. *New Engl J Med.* 2024;390:178–182
7. Bain & Company. *Global Private Equity Report 2024.* https://www.bain.com/insights/topics/global-private-equity-report/. Accessed April 5, 2024.
8. Capstone Partners. *Online & Continuing Medical Education Industry Update. May 2021.* https://www.capstonepartners.com/wp-content/uploads/2021/05/Capstone-Partners-Online-Continuing-Medical-Education-MA-Coverage-Report_May-2021.pdf. Accessed April 5, 2024.

Chapter 1: Understanding CME/CE

1. Nissen S. Reforming the continuing medical education system. *JAMA.* 2015;313(18):1813–1814.
2. Accreditation Council for Continuing Medical Education. CME Content: Definition and Examples. https://www.accme.org/accreditation-rules/policies/cme-content-definition-and-examples. Accessed April 5, 2024.
3. Aparacio A, Chaudhry HJ, Staz M, Cain F, Mayo WS, et al. Supporting physician lifelong learning through effective continuing medical education and professional development. *J Med Reg.* 2016;102(1):7–15.
4. Riddick FA. The Code of Medical Ethics of the American Medical Association. *Ochsner J.* 2003;5(2):6–10
5. Cronin-Golomb LM, Bauer PJ. Self-motivated and directed learning across the lifespan. *Acta Psych.* 2023;232:103816.
6. Duffy TP. The Flexner Report—100 years later. *Yale J Biol med.* 2011;84(3):269–276.
7. Flexner A. Medical education in the United States and Canada. A report to the Carnegie Foundation for the advancement of teaching. The Carnegie Foundation for the Advancement of Teaching, Bulletin Number Four, 1910. https://www.scielosp.

org/article/ssm/content/raw/?resource_ssm_path=/media/assets/bwho/v80n7/a12v80n7.pdf. Accessed April 5, 2024.

8. Laws T. How Should We Respond to Racist Legacies in Health Professions Education Originating in the Flexner Report? *AMA J Ethics*. 2021;23(3): E271-275.

9. Mayo Clinic School of Continuous Professional Development. *96th Annual Clinical Reviews*. https://ce.mayo.edu/family-medicine/content/96th-annual-clinical-reviews.

10. Partin S, Kuschner HI, Kollmer Horton ME. A tale of Congress, continuing medical education, and the history of medicine. *Proc (Bayl Univ Med Cent)*. 2014;27(2):156–160.

11. Josseran L, Chaperon J. History of continuing medical education in the United States. *Presse med*. 2001;17(30):493–497.

12. Accreditation Council for Continuing Medical Education. History. https://www.accme.org/history. Accessed April 5, 2024.

13. Fox R, Bennett NL. Learning and change: Implications for continuing medical education. *BMJ*. 1998;306:466–468.

14. Stein AM. History of Continuing Nursing Education in the United States. *J Cont Ed Nurs*. 1998;29(6):245–252.

15. National League for Nursing. Historical timeline. https://www.nln.org/docs/default-source/default-document-library/nln-2023-historical-timeline.pdf?sfvrsn=7d5127ba_3. Accessed April 5, 2024.

16. American Medical Association. The Lifecycle of Licensure, Certification, and Maintenance of Certification in Selected Health Professions. https://www.aapa.org/wp-content/uploads/2017/02/The-Lifecycle-of-Licensure_2.7.16n.pdf Accessed April 5, 2024.

17. The Joint Commission. Sentinel Event Data 2022 Annual Review. https://www.jointcommission.org/-/media/tjc/documents/resources/patient-safety-topics/sentinel-event/03162023_

sentinel-event-_annual-review_final-(002).pdf. Accessed April 5, 2024.

18. Roy CG. Patient safety functions of State Medical Boards in the United States. *Yale J Biol Med.* 2021;94(1):165–173.

19. Federation of State Medical Boards. Continuing medical education. Board-by-board overview. https://www.fsmb.org/siteassets/advocacy/key-issues/continuing-medical-education-by-state.pdf. Accessed April 5, 2024.

20. CE Central. State CME Licensure Requirements. https://www.cecentral.com/licensure/cme/. Accessed April 5, 2024.

21. American Board of Medical Specialties. Standards for Continuing Certification. 2024. https://www.abms.org/wp-content/uploads/2021/11/ABMS-Standards-for-Continuing-Certification-20211029.pdf. Accessed April 5, 2024.

22. Bindon SL. Professional Development Strategies to Enhance Nurses' Knowledge and Maintain Safe Practice. *AORN J.* 2017;106(2):99–110

23. American Nurses Association. *Nursing: Scope and Standards of Practice.* 3rd ed. Silver Spring, MD: American Nurses Association. 2015.

24. Nurse.org. Nursing Continuing Education (CE) Requirements by State. https://nurse.org/resources/continuing-education/. Accessed April 5, 2024.

25. CE Central. State CPE Licensure Requirements. https://www.cecentral.com/licensure/cpe/.

26. National Commission on the Certification of Physicians Assistants. Continuing medical education. https://www.nccpa.net/maintain-certification/continuing-medical-education/. Accessed April 5, 2024.

27. Britnell M. Transforming health care takes continuity and consistency. *Harvard Business Review.* 2015, December 28.

https://hbr.org/2015/12/transforming-health-care-takes-continuity-and-consistency. Accessed April 5, 2024.

28. Schuetz B, Mann E, Everett W. Educating health professionals collaboratively for team-based primary care. *Health Aff.* 2010;29(8):1476–1480.

29. Frenk J, Chen L, Bhutta ZA, et al. Health professionals for a new century: Transforming education to strengthen health systems in an interdependent world. *The Lancet.* 2010;376(9756):1923–1958.

30. Lyndon A, Kennedy HP. Perinatal safety: from concept to nursing practice. *J Perinat Neonatal Nurs.* 2010;24(1):22–31

31. Lucey CR. Medical education: part of the problem and part of the solution. *JAMA Intern Med.* 2013;173(17):1639–1643.

32. Institute of Medicine of the National Academies. *Redesigning Continuing Education in the Health Professions.* Washington, DC: National Academies Press; 2010.

33. Barr H. Interprofessional Education: Today, Yesterday, and Tomorrow. A review. Commissioned by the Learning and Teaching Support Network for Health Sciences & Practice* from The UK Centre for the Advancement of Interprofessional Education (CAIPE). 2002.

34. Joint Accreditation for Interprofessional Continuing Education. 2021. Joint accreditation data report: embracing innovation in accredited continuing education for health care team—2020. https://jointaccreditation.org/wp-content/uploads/2023/02/904_20210623_2020-Joint-Accreditation-Data-Report_1.pdf Accessed April 5, 2024.

35. Newhouse RP, Spring B. Interdisciplinary evidence-based practice: moving from silos to synergy. *Nurs Outlook.* 2010;58(6):309–317.

36. Interprofessional Education Collaborative. *Team-Based Competencies: Building a Shared Foundation for Education and*

Clinical Practice. 2011. Washington, DC: Interprofessional Education Collaborative;2011.

37. Regnier K, Travlos DV. The role and rise of interprofessional continuing education. *J Med Regul*. 2019;10(3):6–13
38. Regnier K, Travlos DV, Pace D, Powell S, Hunt A. Leading change together: supporting collaborative practice through joint accreditation for interprofessional continuing education. *J Eur CME*. 2022;11(1):2146372
39. King HB, Battles J, Baker DP, Alonso A, Salas E, et al. TeamSTEPPS™: Team Strategies and Tools to Enhance Performance and Patient Safety. In: Henriksen K, Battles JB, Keyes MA, et al., editors. *Advances in Patient Safety: New Directions and Alternative Approaches* (Vol. 3: Performance and Tools). Rockville (MD): Agency for health care Research and Quality (US); 2008 Aug.
40. Grover A, Howley LD. Competency-based medical education—a journey or a destination? *JAMA Netw Open*. 2023;6(4):e237395.
41. Lockyer J, Bursey F, Richardson D, Frank JR, Snell L, et al. Competency-based medical education and continuing professional development: a conceptualization for change. Med Teach 2017; 39(6): 617–622
42. Institute of Medicine (US) Committee on Quality of Health Care in America. *Crossing the Quality Chasm: A New Health System for the 21st Century*. Washington (DC): National Academies Press (US); 2001.
43. Institute of Medicine (US) Committee on the Health Professions Education Summit; Greiner AC, Knebel E, editors. *Health Professions Education: A Bridge to Quality*. Washington (DC): National Academies Press (US); 2003
44. Gruppen L., Mangrulkar RS, Kolars JC. The promise of competency-based education in the health professions for improving global health. *Hum Resour Health*. 2012;10(43).

45. McMahon GT. What do I need to learn today?—the evolution of CME. *New Eng J Med.* 2016;374(15):1403-1406.

46. Griebenow R, Campbell C, McMahon GT, Regnier K, Gordon J, Pozniak E, et al. Roles and responsibilities in the provision of accredited continuing medical education/continuing professional development. *J Eur CME* 2017;6(1):1314416

47. Peck C, McCall, McLaren B, et al. Continuing medical education and continuing professional development: international comparisons. *BMJ.* 2000;320:432–435.

48. Brandt B, Shedling J. Is the CME system obsolete? *Minn Medicine.* 2010;93(11):35–7

49. Van Hemelryck F. CME accreditation in Europe: a survey of the situation in 27 EU member states. 2009. Accreditation Council of Oncology in Europe.

50. Garattini L, Gritti S, De Compadri P, Casadei G. Continuing medical education in six European countries: a comparative analysis. *Health Policy.* 2010 Mar;94(3):246–54. Epub 2009.

51. Arsicault M, Schlimberger M, Tursz T. FMC en cancérologie. Le point de vie de l'EFEC. *Oncologie.* 2007;9:33–36.

52. Maisonneuve H, Matillon Y, Negri A, Pallarés L, Vigneri R, Young HL. Continuing medical education and professional revalidation in Europe: five case examples. *J Contin Educ Health Prof.* 2009 Winter;29(1):58–62.

53. Ghidinelli M, Pozniak E, Kolanko C, Wilson S. The ongoing challenges faced by providers of CME-CPD in Europe. *J CME.* 2023;12(1).

54. Marinopoulos SS, Dorman T, Ratanawongsa N, et al. Effectiveness of Continuing Medical Education. Evidence Report/Technology Assessment No. 149. Rockville, MD: Agency for Health Research and Quality 2007; 1–69.

55. Forsetlund L, Bjørndal A, Rashidian A, Jamtvedt G, O'Brien MA, Wolf F, Davis D, Odgaard-Jensen, Oxman AD Continuing

education meetings and workshops: effects on professional practice and health care outcomes. Cochrane Database *Syst Rev.* 2009; 2: CD003030.

56. Cervero RM, Gaines JK. The impact of CME on physician performance and patient health outcomes: an updated synthesis of systematic reviews. *J Contin Educ Health Prof.* 2015;35(2):131–138.

57. Sampath J, Dietze DT, Toth PP, Cannon CP, Breslan SA. Are continuing medical education activities effective in improving the competence and performance of clinicians? Evidence from activities for primary care clinicians who manage patients with acute coronary syndromes. *Crit Pathw Cardiol.* 2012;11(1):1–9.

58. Federal Register. Code of Federal Regulations. Prescription Drug Advertising. 21 CFR 202.1(e)(7)(viii).

59. du Potet E. Medical education in a medcomms agency. *Medical Writing.* 2016;25(4):18–22.

60. U.S. Department of Health and Human Services. Food and Drug Administration. Office of Policy. Guidance for Industry. https://www.fda.gov/media/70844/download. Access April 5. 2024.

61. Austin S. FDA withdraws 2004 disease awareness guidance. https://casetext.com/analysis/fda-withdraws-2004-disease-awareness-guidance. Access April 5. 2024.

62. Ananya M, Cickova P, Davies R, O'Connor H, Hawksworth C, Walker S. An introduction to medical affairs for medical writers. *Medical Writing.* 2019;28(4):39–43

63. Accreditation Council for Continuing Medical Education (ACCME®). ACCME Data Report. Renewal and Growth in Accredited Continuing Education—2022. https://www.accme.org/sites/default/files/2023-07/2022%20ACCME%20Annual%20Data%20Report%201003_20230713.pdf. Accessed April 5, 2024.

64. Brody, H. Pharmaceutical industry financial support for medical education: benefit, or undue influence? *Journal of Law, Medicine & Ethics.* 2009;37(3):451–60.

65. Institute of Medicine (US) Committee on Conflict of Interest in Medical Research, Education, and Practice; Lo B, Field MJ, editors. *Conflict of Interest in Medical Research, Education, and Practice.* Washington (DC): National Academies Press (US); 2009. 5, Conflicts of Interest in Medical Education.

66. Steinman MA, Baron RB. Is continuing medical education a drug-promotion tool? YES. *Can Fam Physician.* 2007;53(10):1650–1657.

67. Bowman MA, Pearle DL. Changes in Drug Prescribing Patterns Related to Commercial Company Funding of Continuing Medical Education. *J Cont Ed Health Prof.* 1988;8(1):13–20.

68. Accreditation Council for Continuing Medical Education (ACCME®). Standards for Commercial Support: Standards to Ensure the Independence of CME Activities.SM https://www.accme.org/sites/default/files/2020-12/174_20201210_ACCME_Standards_for_Commercial_Support_0.pdf. Accessed April 5, 2024.

69. Fugh-Berman A. Industry-funded medical education is always promotion. *BMJ.* 2021;373:n1273. doi:10.1136/bmj.n1273.

Chapter 2: Credit and Accreditation

1. ACCME. Accreditation Council for Continuing Medical Education (ACCME®). *CME as Bridge to Quality.* Chicago, Illinois: Accreditation Council for Continuing Medical Education, 2008. https://www.accme.org/sites/default/files/null/436_ACCME_Booklet_CME_as_a_Bridge_to_Quality_0.pdf.

2. McMahon GT. Advancing Continuing Medical Education. JAMA. 2015;314(6):561–562.

3. United States Committee on Finance United States Senate. *Committee Staff Report to the Chairman and Ranking Member. Use of Educational Grants by Pharmaceutical Manufacturers.* 2007. https://www.finance.senate.gov/imo/media/doc/prb042507a.pdf.
4. Mack J. Trends in commercial support of CME. *Pharma Marketing News.* 2006. https://www.pharma-mkting.com/wp-content/uploads/PDF//pmn56-article01.pdf.
5. U.S. Senate Committee on Finance. *Baucus, Grassley continue work for independence of medical education.* May 1, 2007. https://www.finance.senate.gov/chairmans-news/baucus-grassley-continue-work-for-independence-of-continuing-medical-education
6. Accreditation Council for Continuing Medical Education (ACCME®). *Standards for Integrity and Independence in Accredited Continuing Education.* 2020. https://accme.org/sites/default/files/2022-06/884_20220623_Standards%20for%20Integrity%20and%20Independence%20in%20Accredited%20Continuing%20Education.pdf.
7. https://jointaccreditation.org/.
8. Pelletier S. The evolution of CME—and what's next? *MeetingsNet.* Feb 16, 2017. https://www.meetingsnet.com/continuing-medical-education/evolution-cme-and-what-s-next.
9. Accreditation Council for Continuing Medical Education (ACCME®). *CME Content: Definitions and Examples.* https://www.accme.org/accreditation-rules/policies/cme-content-definition-and-examples.
10. Aparicio A. Continuing Professional Development for doctors, certification, licensure and quality improvement. A model to follow? *Educación Médica.* 2015:16(1):50–56.
11. American Medical Association (AMA).*The AMA PHysician's Recgonition Award and Credit System.* 2017. https://www.ama-assn.org/system/files/pra-booklet.pdf.

12. Aparicio A, Chaudhry HJ, Staz M, Cain F, Mayo WS, et al. Supporting physician lifelong learning through effective continuing medical education and professional development. *Journal Med Regul.* 2016;102(1):7–15.

13. McMahon GT, Skochelak SE. Evolution of Continuing Medical Education: Promoting Innovation Through Regulatory Alignment. *JAMA.* 2018;319(6):545–546.

Chapter 3: Compliance and Ethics

1. Thomas J. Self-regulation and the relationship of physicians with the pharmaceutical industry. *Virtual Mentor.* 2005;7(4):288–293.

2. Mauss M. *The Gift: Forms and Functions of Exchange in Archaic Societies.* 2011, Martino Fine Books.

3. DeJong C, Aquilar T, Tseng CW, et al. Pharmaceutical industry-sponsored meals and physician prescribing patterns for Medicare beneficiaries. *JAMA Int Med.* 2016;176:1114–1122.

4. Department of Justice. TAP Pharmaceutical Products Inc. https://www.justice.gov/archive/opa/pr/2001/October/513civ.htm. Accessed April 5, 2024.

5. Peterson M. 2 drugmakers to pay $875 billion to settle fraud case. *New York Times.* Oct 4, 2001. https://www.nytimes.com/2001/10/04/business/2-drug-makers-to-pay-875-million-to-settle-fraud-case.html. Accessed April 5, 2024.

6. FDA Guidance for Industry. Industry Supported Scientific and Educational Activities (Nov. 1997), 62 Fed. Reg. 64093, 64097 https://www.fda.gov/media/75334/download. Accessed April 5, 2024.

7. Office of the Inspector General, Compliance Policy Guidance (CPG) for Pharmaceutical Manufacturers, 68 Fed. Reg. 23731, 23738 (May 5, 2003), available at http://oig.hhs.gov/authorities/docs/03/050503FRCPGPharmac.pdf. Accessed April 5, 2024.

8. Pharmaceutical Research and Manufacturers of America (PhRMA). Code on Interactions with Health Professionals. https://www.phrma.org/-/media/Project/PhRMA/PhRMA-Org/PhRMA-Org/PDF/A-C/Code-of-Interaction_FINAL21.pdf. Accessed April 5, 2024.

9. Accreditation Council for Continuing medical Education (ACCME®). Standards for Integrity and Independence in Accredited Continuing Education. 2020. https://www.accme.org/accreditation-rules/standards-for-integrity-independence-accredited-ce. Accessed April 5, 2024.

10. US Department of Health and Human Services. Office of the Inspector General. Fraud and Abuse Laws. https://oig.hhs.gov/compliance/physician-education/fraud-abuse-laws/. Accessed April 5, 2024.

11. Barber H, Nexsen M. New Stark Law and Anti-Kickback Statue Physician Wellness Program Exemption. https://www.jdsupra.com/legalnews/new-stark-law-and-anti-kickback-statute-5871470/.

12. Pfizer. *The Orange Guide.* 2022. https://cdn.pfizer.com/pfizercom/2022_Orange_Guide.pdf. Accessed April 5. 2024.

13. Van Norman GA. Off-Label Use vs Off-Label Marketing of Drugs: Part 1: Off-Label Use-Patient Harms and Prescriber Responsibilities. *JACC Basic Transl Sci.* 2023;8(2):224–233.

14. Van Norman GA. Off-Label Use vs Off-Label Marketing: Part 2: Off-Label Marketing-Consequences for Patients, Clinicians, and Researchers. *JACC Basic Transl Sci.* 2023;8(3):359–370.

15. Sullivan T. The National Taskforce—Get the Facts Campaign: On-label and off-label usage of prescription medicines and devices, and the relationship to CME. *Policy and Medicine.* May 4, 2018. https://www.policymed.com/2010/04/ama-taskforce-get-the-facts-campaign-on-label-and-off-label-usage-of-prescription-medicines-and-devices-and-the-relatio.html. Accessed April 5. 2024.

16. U.S. Food and Drug Administration. FDA Label: Full-text search of drug product labeling. https://www.fda.gov/science-research/bioinformatics-tools/fdalabel-full-text-search-drug-product-labeling. Accessed April 5. 2024.
17. U.S. Food and Drug Administration. Drug approvals and databases. https://www.fda.gov/drugs/development-approval-process-drugs/drug-approvals-and-databases. Accessed April 5. 2024.
18. National Library of Medicine. *DailyMed.* https://dailymed.nlm.nih.gov/dailymed/. Accessed April 5. 2024.
19. United States ex rel. Penelow v. *Janssen Prods.* https://casetext.com/case/united-states-ex-rel-penelow-v-janssen-prods. Accessed April 5. 2024.
20. Physician Payment Sunshine Act. U.S. Food and Drug Administration, 2021. https://www.physicianleaders.org/articles/the-sunshine-act-what-every-physician-needs-to-know. Accessed April 5. 2024.
21. CME Coalition. Independent Medical Education Compliance Guide. May 2022.
22. Centers for Medicare & Medicaid Services. Open Payments. https://www.cms.gov/openpayments. Accessed April 5. 2024.
23. American Medical Association/Accreditation Council for Continuing Medical Education. Accreditation Council for Continuing Medical Education (ACCME®) and American Medical Association (AMA) Glossary of Terms and Definitions. https://www.accme.org/sites/default/files/2018-04/011_20170421_Glossary_of_Terms.pdf. Accessed April 5. 2024.
24. Accreditation Council for Continuing Medical Education (ACCME®). Key steps for identification, mitigation, and disclosure of relevant financial relationships. https://accme.org/sites/default/files/2020-12/885_20201210_Tools%20

for%20Identifying%20Mitigating%20and%20Disclosing%20 Relevant%20Financial%20Relationships.PDF. Accessed April 5. 2024.

25. Prasad V, Rajkumar SV. Conflict of interest in academic oncology: moving beyond the blame game and forging a path forward. *Blood Cancer J.* 2016;6(11):e489.
26. Coverstone JS. Ethics in CEHP, Part 2: We have a code of ethics now. Almanac. March 8, 2023.
27. Korenstein D, Chimonas S. Deadly conflict: physicians, the medical profession, and the opioid epidemic. *Am J Med Qual.* 2021;36:197–9.
28. Lo B, Field MJ, eds. *Conflict of Interest in Medical Research. Education, and Practice.* 2009.
29. Chimonas S, Mamoor M, Zimbalist SA, Barrow B, Bach PB, Korenstein D. Mapping conflict of interests: scoping review. *BMJ.* 2021;375:e066576.

Chapter 4: The Context of Health Care

1. *Classifying health workers: Mapping occupations to the international standard classification.* Geneva: World Health Organization; 2019.
2. McGlynn EA, Asch SM, Adams J, et al. The quality of health care delivered to adults in the United States. *N Eng J Med.* 2003;348:2635–2645.
3. Institute of Medicine (US) Committee on Quality of Health Care in America, Kohn LT, Corrigan JM, Donaldson MS, eds. *To Err Is Human: Building a Safer Health System.* Washington (DC): National Academies Press (US); 2000.
4. Institute of Medicine (US) Committee on Understanding and Eliminating Racial and Ethnic Disparities in Health Care; Smedley BD, Stith AY, Nelson AR, editors. *Unequal Treatment: Confronting Racial and Ethnic Disparities in Health Care.* Washington (DC): National Academies Press (US); 2003.

5. Institute of Medicine (US) Committee on Quality of Health Care in America. *Crossing the Quality Chasm: A New Health System for the 21st Century.* Washington (DC): National Academies Press (US); 2001.

6. Lucey CR. Medical education: part of the problem and part of the solution. *JAMA Intern Med.* 2013;173(17):1639–1643.

7. Centers for Medicare & Medicaid Services (CMS). Proposed Rule, Medicare Program; CY 2018 Updates to the Quality Payment Program. https://www.federalregister.gov/documents/2017/06/30/2017-13010/medicare-program-cy-2018-updates-to-the-quality-payment-program. 2017. Accessed April 5, 2024.

8. Agency for Healthcare Research and Quality. Working for Quality. Report to Congress: National Strategy for Quality Improvement in Health Care. 2011. https://www.ahrq.gov/sites/default/files/wysiwyg/research/findings/nhqrdr/nhqr11/nhqr11.pdf. Accessed April 5, 2024.

9. National Council of State Boards of Nursing. NCSBN research projects significant nursing workforce shortages and crisis. https://www.ncsbn.org/news/ncsbn-research-projects-significant-nursing-workforce-shortages-and-crisis. Accessed April 5, 2024.

10. Definitive Healthcare. *Addressing the health care staffing shortage.* 2023. https://www.definitivehc.com/sites/default/files/resources/pdfs/Addressing-the-health care-staffing-shortage-2023.pdf. Accessed April 5, 2024.

11. Greaney TL, Schleffler RM. The proposed vertical merger guidelines and health care: little guidance and dubious economics. *Health Affairs.* April 17, 2020.

12. Zhu JM, Hua LM, Polsky D. Private Equity Acquisitions of Physician Medical Groups Across Specialties, 2013–2016. *JAMA.* 2020;323(7):663–665.

13. Gondi S, Song Z. Potential implications of private equity investments in health care delivery. *JAMA.* 2019;321(11):1047–1048.

14. Dov Bruch J, Roy V, Grogan CM. The financialization of health in the United States. *New Engl J Med.* 2024;390:178–182.

15. Appelbaum E, Batt R. *Financialization in Health Care: The Transformation of US Hospital Systems.* https://cepr.net/wp-content/uploads/2021/10/AB-Financialization-In-health care-Spitzer-Rept-09-09-21.pdf. Accessed April 5, 2024.

16. Hunter BM, Murray SF. Deconstructing the financialization of health care. Dev Change 2019;50:1263–1287

17. Sackett DL, Rosenberg WM, Gray JA, Haynes RB, Richardson WS. Evidence based medicine: what it is and what it isn't. *BMJ.* 1996;312(7023):71.

18. Zimerman AL. Evidence-based medicine: A short history of a modern medical movement. *AMA J Ethics. Virtual Mentor.* 2013;15(1):71–76

19. Thoma A, Eaves FF, A brief history of evidence-based medicine (EBM) and the contributions of Dr David Sackett, *Aesthetic Surgery Journal.* 2015; 35(8): 261–263

20. Sur RL, Dahm P. History of evidence-based medicine. *Indian J Urol.* 2011;27(4):487–489.

21. Ratnani I, Fatima S, Abid MM, Surani Z, Surani S. Evidence-Based Medicine: History, Review, Criticisms, and Pitfalls. *Cureus.* 2023;15(2):e35266

22. Straus SE, McAlister FA. Evidence-based medicine: a commentary on common criticisms. *CMAJ.* 2000;163(7):837–841.

23. Sepulveda LJF. Clinical judgment in the era of evidence-based medicine. 2017. https://kclpure.kcl.ac.uk/portal/en/studentTheses/clinical-judgement-in-the-era-of-evidence-based-medicine. Accessed April 5, 2024.

24. Charles C, Gafni A, Whelan T. Shared decision-making in the medical encounter: what does it mean? (or it takes at least two to tango). *Soc Sci Med.* 1997;44(5):681–692.

25. Légaré F, Adekpedjou R, Stacey D, Turcotte S, Kryworuchko J, Graham ID, et al. Interventions for increasing the use of shared decision making by health care professionals. *Cochrane Database of Systematic Reviews.* 2018;7.

26. Kane HL, Halpern MT, Squiers LB, Treiman KA, McCormack LA. Implementing and evaluating shared decision-making in oncology practice. *CA Cancer J Clin.* 2014;64(6):377–388.

27. Shared decision making in cardiology: a systematic review and meta-analysis P. Mitropoulou, N. Grüner-Hegge, J. Reinhold and C. Papadopoulou. *Heart.* 2023;109(1):34–39.

28. National Quality Forum. *NQP Shared Decision Making Brief.* 2017. https://www.qualityforum.org/Publications/2017/10/NQP_Shared_Decision_Making_Action_Brief.aspx. Accessed April 5, 2024.

29. Henry TA. American Medical Association. *Why you need to be a systems thinker in health care.* https://www.ama-assn.org/education/changemeded-initiative/why-you-need-be-systems-thinker-health-care. Accessed April 5, 2024.

30. Berwick DM, Nolan TW, Whittington J. The triple aim: care, health, and cost. *Health Aff (Millwood).* 2008;27(3):759–769

31. Agency for Healthcare Research and Quality. *Talking quality: Reporting to Consumers on Health Care Quality.* Accessed April 5, 2024. https://www.ahrq.gov/talkingquality/index.html.

32. Agency for Healthcare Research and Quality. 2019 National Healthcare Quality and Disparities Report. Content last reviewed July 2023. Agency for Healthcare Research and Quality, Rockville, MD. https://www.ahrq.gov/research/findings/nhqrdr/nhqdr19/index.html. Accessed April 5, 2024

33. American Boards of Internal Medicine. *Choosing Wisely. An Initiative of the ABIM Foundation.* https://www.choosingwisely.org/. Accessed April 5, 2024.

34. Busse R, Panteli D, Quentin W. An introduction to healthcare quality: defining and explaining its role in health systems. In: Busse R, Klazinga N, Panteli D, et al., editors. *Improving healthcare quality in Europe: Characteristics, effectiveness and implementation of different strategies* [Internet]. Copenhagen (Denmark): European Observatory on Health Systems and Policies; 2019. (Health Policy Series, No. 53.) 1.

35. Agency for Healthcare Research and Quality. *About learning health systems.* https://www.ahrq.gov/learning-health-systems/about.html. Accessed April 5, 2024.

36. Centers for Medicare and Medicaid. *Patient-Reported Outcomes Measures.* https://mmshub.cms.gov/sites/default/files/Patient-Reported-Outcome-Measures.pdf. Accessed April 5, 2024.

37. Backhouse A, Ogunlayi F. Quality improvement into practice. *BMJ.* 2020;368, m865.

Chapter 5: Planning Education

1. Taylor MJ, McNicholas C, Nicolay C, Darzi A, Bell D, Reed JE. Systematic review of the application of the plan-do-study-act method to improve quality in healthcare. *BMJ Qual Saf.* 2014;23(4):290–298.

2. Harting D, Vakil R. Best practices for writing CME needs assessments. *AMWA Blog.* 2020. https://blog.amwa.org/best-practices-for-writing-cme-needs-assessments. Accessed April 5, 2024.

3. National Institutes of Health. The use of generative artificial intelligence technologies is prohibited for the NIH peer review process. https://grants.nih.gov/grants/guide/notice-files/NOT-OD-23-149.html. Accessed April 5, 2024.

4. Norman GR, Shannon SI, Marrin ML. The need for needs assessment in continuing medical education. *BMJ.* 2004;328(7446):999. 13.

5. Pilcher J. Learning needs assessment: Not only for continuing education. *J Nurses Prof Dev.* 2016;32(4):122–129.

6. Society for Academic Continuing Medical Education/ Accreditation Council for Continuing Medical Education. *CE Educator's Toolkit.* https://accme.org/sites/default/files/2022-04/CE%20Educator%27s%20Toolkit.pdf. Accessed April 5, 2024.

7. Parry NMA. The needs assessment in continuing medical education. *Medical Writing.* 2014;23(2):125–128

8. Accreditation Council for Continuing Medical Education. *FAQ Search. In the Educational Needs Criterion, what is meant by a "professional practice gap?"* https://www.accme.org/faq/educational-needs-criterion-what-meant-professional-practice-gap. Accessed April 5, 2024.

9. Dirksen J. *Design for How People Learn.* 2nd ed. New Riders. 2016.

10. Diamond L KJ, Sulkes D. *The Quality Improvement Education (QIE) Roadmap: A Pathway to Our Future.* Chicago: Alliance for Continuing Education in the Health Professions. 2015.

11. Ruggiero JE, Robinson CO, Paynter NL. *Coordinated learning to improve evidence-based care: a model for continuing education in the new healthcare environment.* https://www.gene.com/assets/frontend/pdf/content/good/grants/Genentech_WhitePaper_TELMS_Coordinated_Learning_to_Improve_Evidence-based_Care_September-2015.pdf. Accessed April 5, 2024.

12. Backhouse A, Ogunlayi F. Quality improvement into practice. 2020. *BMJ.* 368, m865.

13. Howson, A. Multidisciplinary acute lymphocytic leukemia care: models of quality improvement. *Oncology Issues.* 2021;36(2):62–72.

14. Howson, A. Multidisciplinary multiple myeloma care: models of quality improvement. *Oncology Issues.* 2021;36(2);50–61.

15. Nathan S, Howson A, McCrea AD. Enacting Process Changes to Improve Outcomes in Idiopathic Pulmonary Fibrosis: A 2 Quality Improvement Education Initiative. https://www.annenberg.net/publications/IPF_QI_Manuscript1.pdf.

16. Howson A, Mutschler B, McCrea A. Designing and evaluating a gender-affirming educational initiative for optimal HIV care: an intrinsic case study. *Transgend Health.* 2021;6(5):296–301.

17. American Medical Association. *Performance improvement continuing medical education (PI CME).* https://www.ama-assn.org/education/ama-pra-credit-system/performance-improvement-continuing-medical-education-pi-cme. Accessed April 5, 2024.

18. Price DW, Davis DA, Filerman GL. "Systems-Integrated CME": The Implementation and Outcomes Imperative for Continuing Medical Education in the Learning Health Care Enterprise. *NAM Perspectives* 2021. Discussion, National Academy of Medicine, Washington DC.

19. Olson C. Twenty predictions for the future of CPD: implications of the shift from the update model to improving clinical practice. *J Contin Educ Health Prof.* 2012;32(3):151–152.

20. Ratnapalan S, Lang D. Health Care Organizations as Complex Adaptive Systems. *Health Care Manag.* 2020;39(1):18–23

21. Eccles M, Mittman BS. Welcome to implementation science. *Implement Sci* 2006;1:1.

Chapter 6: Adult Learning Principles

1. Ambrose SA, Bridges MW, Lovett MC. *How Learning Works. 7 research-based principles for smart teaching.* San Francisco: Jossey-Bass. 2010.

2. Merriam SB, Baumgartner L. *Learning in Adulthood. A Comprehensive Guide.* 2020. Hoboken, NJ: Jossey-Bass. Fourth Edition.

3. Gooding HC, Mann K, Armstrong E. Twelve tips for applying the science of learning to health professions education. *Med Teach.* 2017;39(1):26–31

4. Wlodarczyk S, Dhaliwal G. The learning sciences meet the learning health system. *JAMA Netw Open.* 2022;5(7):e2223113

5. Knowles MS. Introduction. In: Knowles MS & Associates, editors. *Andragogy in action: applying modern principles of adult learning.* San Francisco: Jossey-Bass Publishers; 1984. pp. 1–21

6. Mann K. Theoretical perspectives in medical education: past experience and future possibilities. *Med Educ.* 2011;45(1):60–68.

7. Dong H, Lio J, Sherer R, Jiang I. Some learning theories for medical educators. *Med Sci Educ.* 2021;31(3):1157–1172.

8. Blondy LC. Evaluation and Application of Andragogical Assumptions. *JIOL.* 2007;6(2): 116-130

9. Urhahne D, Wijnia L. Theories of motivation in education: an integrative framework. *Educ Psychol Rev.* 2023;35,45.

10. Dweck CS. *Mindset: The new psychology of success.* New York: Ballantine. 2006.

11. Han S, Stieha V, Poitevin E, Starnes TL. Growth Mindset in Adult Learning: Systematic Literature Review. Adult Education Research Conference. 2018: https://newprairiepress.org/aerc/2018/papers/3

12. Liu, TH., Sullivan, A.M. A story half told: a qualitative study of medical students' self-directed learning in the clinical setting. *BMC Med Educ.* 2021; 21, 494.

13. Van Merrienboer J, Sweller J. Cognitive load theory in health professional education: design principles and strategies. *Med Educ.* 2010;44:85–93.

14. Brown PC, Roediger HL III, McDaniel MA. *Make It Stick: The Science of Successful Learning.* Belknap; 2014.

15. Loerch AG. Learning Curves. In: Gass, S.I., Fu, M.C. (eds) *Encyclopedia of Operations Research and Management Science*. 2013. Springer, Boston, MA.

16. Murre JMJ, Dros J. Replication and analysis of Ebbinghaus' forgetting curve. *PLoS ONE*. 2015;10(7):e0120644.

17. Vygotsky L. Interaction between learning and development. In: Cole M J-SV, Scribner S, Souberman E, ed. *Mind in Society: The Development of Higher Psychological Processes*. Cambridge, MA: Harvard University Press; 1978:79–91.

18. Kolb DA. *Experiential learning: experience as the source of learning and development*. NJ: Prentice-Hall; 1984.

19. Freeman S, Eddy SL, McDonough M, et al. Active learning increases student performance in science, engineering, and mathematics. *Proc Natl Acad Sci U S A*. 2014;111(23):8410–8415.

20. Project ECHO® https://projectecho.unm.edu.

21. Mezirow J. Transformative learning: theory to practice. *New Direc Adult Cont Educ*. 1997;1997:5–12.

22. Schön DA. *Educating the Reflective Practitioner: Toward a New Design for Teaching and Learning in the Professions*. Jossey-Bass; 1987.

23. Sandars J. The use of reflection in medical education: AMEE guide no. 44. *Med Teach*. 2009;31:685–695.

24. Ng SL, Forsey J, Boyd VA. et al. Combining adaptive expertise and (critically) reflective practice to support the development of knowledge, skill, and society. *Adv in Health Sci Educ*. 2022;27:1265–1281.

25. Ajzen I. The theory of planned behavior. *Organizational Behavior and Human Decision Processes*. 1991;50(2):179–211.

26. Price DW, Wagner DP, Krane NK, et al. What are the implications of implementation science for medical education? *Medical Education Online*. 2015;20:270.

27. Prochaska JO, DiClemente CC. Stages of change in the modification of problem behaviors. *Prog Behav Modif.* 1992;28:183–218.

28. Johnson SS, Castle PH, Van Marter D, Roc A, Neubauer D. The effect of physician continuing medical education on patient-reported outcomes for identifying and optimally managing obstructive sleep apnea. *J Clin Sleep Med.* 2015;11(3):197–204.

29. Deci EL, Ryan RM. Self-determination theory: A macrotheory of human motivation, development, and health. *Canadian Psychology.* 2008;49(3):182–185.

30. Thi Nguyen VA, Konings KD, Scherpbier A, van Merrienboer, JJG. Attracting and retaining physicians in less attractive specialties: the role of continuing medical education. *Hum Resour Health.* 2021;19(1):69.

31. Thaler RH, Sunstein CR. Nudge: Improving Decisions about Health, Wealth, and Happiness. Yale University Press. 2008.

32. Kozlowski D, Hutchinson M, Hurley J, Rowley J, Sutherland J. The role of emotion in clinical decision making: an integrative literature review. *BMC Med Educ.* 2017;17(1):255.

33. Schunk DH, DiBenedetto MK. Self-efficacy and human motivation. In: *Advances in Motivation Science*, edited by A. J. Elliot. Chapter Four. Elsevier Academic Press. 2021:153–179.

34. Bandura A. Human agency in social cognitive theory. Am Psych. 1989;44(9):1175–1184.

35. Lave J, Wenger E. *Situated Learning: Legitimate Peripheral Participation.* Cambridge: CUP, 1990

36. Barab S, Barnett M, Squire K. Developing an empirical account of a community of practice: characterizing the essential tensions. *J Learn Sci.* 2002;11(4):489–542.

37. Barker M, Lecce J, Ivanova A, Zawertailo L, Dragonetti R, Selby P. Interprofessional Communities of Practice in Continuing Medical Education for Promoting and Sustaining Practice

Change: A Prospective Cohort Study. *J Contin Educ Health Prof.* 2018;38(2):86–93.

38. Dong H, Lio J, Sherer R, Jiang I. Some Learning Theories for Medical Educators. *Med Sci Educ.* 2021;31(3):1157–1172.
39. Cervero RM, Gaines JK. The impact of CME on physician performance and patient health outcomes: an updated synthesis of systematic reviews. *J Contin Educ Health Prof.* 2015;35(2):131–138.
40. Bucklin BA, Asdigian NL, Hawkins JL. et al. Making it stick: use of active learning strategies in continuing medical education. *BMC Med Educ.* 2021; 21:44.
41. Graffam B. Active learning in medical education: strategies for beginning implementation. *Med Teach.* 2007;29(1):38–42.
42. Shail MS. Using micro-learning on mobile applications to increase knowledge retention and work performance: a review of the literature. *Cureus.* 2019;11(8):e5307.
43. De Gagne J, Park H, Hall K, Woodward A, Yamane S, Kim S. Microlearning in Health Professions Education: Scoping Review, *JMIR Med Educ* 2019;5(2):e13997
44. Dirksen J. *Design for How People Learn.* 2nd ed. New Riders; 2016.
45. Ericsson KA. Acquisition and maintenance of medical expertise: a perspective from the expert-performance approach with deliberate practice. *Acad Med.* 2015;90(11):1471–1486.
46. Richards PS, Inglehart MR. An interdisciplinary approach to case-based teaching: does it create patient-centered and culturally sensitive providers? *J Dent Educ.* 2006;70(3):284–291.
47. Cioni, F. (2023). The background of The Shrew: Texts and intertexts. *Cahiers Élisabéthains*, 112(1), 77–90.
48. Tyng CM, Amin HU, Saad MNM, Malik AS. The influences of emotion on learning and memory. *Front Psychol.* 2017;8:1454.

49. Schaik EV, Howson A, Sabin J. Healthcare disparities. *MedEdPORTAL* 2014;10:9675.

Chapter 7: Assessment and Evaluation

1. Lucero KS, Moore DE. Continuing medical education outcomes are much more than statistical significance. *J CME*. 2023;12(1):2236893.
2. McMahon GT. What Do I Need to Learn Today? The Evolution of CME. *New Eng J Med*. 2016;374(15):1403–1406.
3. Marx J. CME: Dead or Alive? A Decade's Perspective. *AMWA J*. 2012;27(4):167–168.
4. Marinopoulos SS, Dorman T, Ratanawongsa N, et al. Effectiveness of Continuing Medical Education. Rockville, MD: Agency for Healthcare Research and Quality; 2007. Evidence Report/Technology Assessment 149. AHRQ Publication No. 07-E006.
5. Accreditation Council for CME (ACCME). Requirements for Accreditation. ACCME Website. http://www.accme.org/requirements. Accessed April 5, 2024.
6. Moore DE Jr, Green JS, Gallis HA. Achieving desired results and improved outcomes: integrating planning and assessment throughout learning activities. *J Contin Educ Health Prof.* 2009;29(1):1–15. doi:10.1002/chp.20001.
7. Bannister J, Neve M, Kolanko C. Increased educational reach through a microlearning approach: can higher participation translate to improved outcomes? *J Eur CME*. 2020;9(1):1834761.
8. Accreditation Council for Continuing Medical Education (ACCME®). The Value of Accredited Continuing Medical Education. 2015. https://www.accme.org/sites/default/files/705_20150708_The_Value_of_Accredited_CME.pdf.

9. Brady E. How to write sound educational outcomes questions: a focus on knowledge and competence assessments. *Alliance Almanac.* 2015;37(5):4–9

10. Myers L, Karl S. Sources of data in CE. *Alliance Almanac.* 2015;37(2):4–6.

11. Cahapay MB. Kirkpatrick Model: Its limitations as used in higher education. *Int J Assess Tools Ed.* 2021;8(1):135–144.

12. Haji F, Morin MP, Parker K. Rethinking programme evaluation in health professions education: beyond "did it work?". *Medical Education.* 2013;47: 342–351.

13. Walker R, Bennett, C, Kumar A, Adamski M, Blumfield M, et al. Evaluating online continuing professional development regarding weight management for pregnancy using the New World Kirkpatrick Model. *J Cont Ed Health Prof.* 2019;39(3):210–217.

14. Eukel H, Steig J, Frenzel O, Skoy E, Werremeyer A, Strand M. Opioid misuse and overdose: changes in pharmacist practices and outcomes. *J Contin Educ Health Prof.* 2020;40(4):242–247.

15. van Tuijl AA, Calsbeek H, Wollersheim HC, Laan RFJM, Fluit C, van Gurp PJ. Does a long-term quality and safety curriculum for health care professionals improve clinical practice? An evaluation of quality improvement projects. *J Contin Educ Health Prof.* 2020;40(1):3–10

16. Wilbur K, Elmubar A, Shabana S. Systematic review of standardized patient use in continuing medical education. *J Contin Educ Health Prof.* 2018; 38(1):3–10

17. Williams BW, Kessler HA, Williams MV. Relationship among knowledge acquisition, motivation to change, and self-efficacy in CME participants. *J Contin Educ Health Prof.* 2015;35: S13–S21.

18. Williams BW, Kessler HA, Williams MV. Relationship among practice change, motivation, and self-efficacy. *J Contin Educ Health Prof.* 2014;34 Suppl 1:S5–S10.

19. Lucero KS, Chen P. What do reinforcement and confidence have to do with it? A systematic pathway analysis of knowledge, competence, confidence, and intention to change. *J Eur CME.* 2020;9(1):1834759.

20. Lucero KS, Williams B, Moore DE Jr. The emerging role of reinforcement in the clinician's path from continuing education to practice. *J Contin Educ Health Prof.* Published online November 14, 2023.

21. Jolly B. Written assessment. In: T. Swanwick (Ed). *Understanding Medical Education: Evidence, Theory and Practice.* 2nd Ed. London: Wiley Blackwell. 2014.

22. Howson A, Turell W. Qualitative outcomes in CME/CPD: exploring nonlinear contexts and lived experiences in patient-directed interventions. *J Eur CME.* 2020;9(1):1834760.

23. Belcher E, Cerenzia W. Outcomes measurement in CME: Current trends, challenges and considerations. *Alliance Almanac.* Oct. 25, 2023.

24. McGowan BS, Mandarakas A, McGuinness S, et al. Outcomes Standardisation Project (OSP) for continuing medical education (CE/CME) professionals: background, methods, and initial terms and definitions. *J Eur CME.* 2020;9(1):1717187.

25. Légaré F, Borduas F, Jacques A, Laprise R, Voyer G, et al. Developing a theory-based instrument to assess the impact of continuing professional development activities on clinical practice: A study protocol. *Implementation Science.* 2011;6(1),1–6.

26. McMahon GT. Advancing continuing medical education. *JAMA* 2015;314(6): 561–562.

27. Cervero RM, Gaines JK. Effectiveness of continuing medical education: updated synthesis of systematic reviews. Chicago, IL: Accreditation Council for Continuing Medical Education, 2015.

28. Sampath J, Dietze DT, Toth PP, Cannon CP, Breslan SA. Are continuing medical education activities effective in improving

the competence and performance of clinicians? Evidence from activities for primary care clinicians who manage patients with acute coronary syndromes. *Crit Pathw Cardiol.* 2012;11(1):1–9.

29. Herrmann T, Peters P, Williamson C, Rhodes E. Educational outcomes in the era of the Affordable Care Act: impact of personalized education about non-small cell lung cancer. *J Contin Educ Health Prof.* 2015;35 Suppl 1:S5–12.
30. Monroe KS. The relationship between assessment methods and self-directed learning readiness in medical education. *Intern J Med Ed.* 2016;7:75–80.
31. Salinas G. Comparative effectiveness in CME: evaluation of personalized and self-directed learning models. *J Contin Educ Health Prof.* 2015;35 Suppl 1:S24–26.

Chapter 8: Key Formats and Outputs

1. Cervero RM, Gaines JK. The impact of CME on physician performance and patient health outcomes: an updated synthesis of systematic reviews. *J Contin Educ Health Prof.* 2015;35(2):131–138.
2. Moro C, Smith J, Stromberga Z. Multimodal Learning in Health Sciences and Medicine: Merging Technologies to Enhance Student Learning and Communication. *Adv Exp Med Biol.* 2019;1205:71–78.
3. Cook DA, Levinson AJ, Garside S, Dupras DM, Erwin PJ, Montori VM. Internet-based learning in the health professions: a meta-analysis. *JAMA.* 2008;300(10):1181–1196.
4. Salinas GD. CME effectiveness: utilizing outcomes assessments of 600+ CME programs to evaluate the association between format and effectiveness. *J Contin Educ Health Prof.* 2015;35 Suppl 1:S38–39.

5. Salter SM, Karia A, Sanfilippo FM, Clifford RM. Effectiveness of E-learning in pharmacy education. *Am J Pharm Educ.* 2014;78(4):83.
6. Fordis M KJ, Ballantyne CM, Jones PH, Schneider KH, Spann SJ, Greenberg SB, Greisinger AJ. Comparison of the instructional efficacy of internet-based CME with live interactive CME workshops: A randomized controlled trial. *JAMA.* 2005;294(9):1043–1051.
7. Curran VR FL, Kirby F. A comparative evaluation of the effect of internet-based CME delivery format on satisfaction, knowledge and confidence. *BMC Med Educ.* 2010;10(10).
8. Bloom BS. Effects of continuing medical education on improving physician clinical care and patient health: a review of systematic reviews. International journal of technology assessment in health care. 2005;21(3):380–385.
9. Cerenzia W, Salinas G. Tracking Shifts in Medical Information–Seeking Patterns Amidst the COVID-19 Pandemic. Poster, 2020, https://www.ceoutcomes.com/posters?lightbox=dataItem-lfjzeo5r9.
10. Harris JM, Jr., Sklar BM, Amend RW, Novalis-Marine C. The growth, characteristics, and future of online CME. *J Contin Educ Health Prof.* 2010;30(1):3–10.
11. Casebeer L, Brown J, Roepke N, et al. Evidence-based choices of physicians: a comparative analysis of physicians participating in internet CME and non-participants. *BMC Med Educ.* 2010;10:42.
12. Accreditation Council for Continuing Medical Education. 2019. ACCME Data Report: Growth and Advancement in Accredited Continuing Medical Education—2018. http://www.accme.org/2018datareport.
13. Accreditation Council for Continuing Medical Education (ACCME®). Learn Well: ACCME Data Report. Growth and

Evolution in Continuing Medical Education, 2016. Chicago: ACCME;2017.

14. Chaker R, Hajj-Hassan M, Ozanne S. The effects of online continuing education for healthcare professionals: a systematic scoping review. *Open Education Studies.* 2024; 6(1):20220226.

15. Sibley JB. Meeting the future: how CME portfolios must change in the post-COVID era. *J Eur CME.* 2022;11(1):2058452.

16. Stephenson CR, Yudkowsky R, Wittich CM, Cook DA. Learner engagement and teaching effectiveness in livestreamed versus in-person CME. *Med Educ.* 2023;57(4):349–358.

17. Gentry SV, Gauthier A, L'Estrade Ehrstrom B, et al. Serious gaming and gamification education in health professions: systematic review. *J Med Internet Res.* 2019;21(3):e12994.

18. Deterding S, Dixon D, Khaled R, Nacke L. Gamification: toward a definition. The ACM CHI Conference on Human Factors in Computing; May 7–12; Vancouver, Canada. 2011.

19. Akl EA, Kairouz VF, Sackett KM, Erdley WS, Mustafa RA, Fiander M, Gabriel C, Schünemann H. Educational games for health professionals. *Cochrane Database Syst Rev.* 2013 Mar 28;(3):CD006411.

20. Nelson T, Robinson K. Beyond engagement: harnessing gamification to achieve more meaningful outcomes in continuing medical education. *Alliance Almanac,* June 28, 2021.

21. McGaghie WC, Siddall VJ, Mazmanian PE, Myers J. American College of Chest Physicians Health and Science Policy Committee. Lessons for continuing medical education from simulation research in undergraduate and graduate medical education: effectiveness of continuing medical education. *CHEST.* 2009;135(3 Suppl):62S–68SS.

22. Khanduja PK, Bould MD, Naik VN, Hladkowicz E, Boet S. The role of simulation in continuing medical education

for acute care physicians: a systematic review. *Crit Care Med.* 2015;43(1):186–193.

23. Saleem M, Khan Z. Healthcare simulation: An effective way of learning in healthcare. *Pak J Med Sci.* 2023;39(4):1185–1190.

24. Warters M, Vigil K, Peters P. 2018 Innovation in CPD for the CE/CPD professional and/or enterprise award: a unique and innovative virtual patient simulation to meet the ongoing needs of CPD for health care providers. *Alliance Almanac*, March 1, 2018.

25. Kaul V, Morris A, Chae JM, Town JA, Kelly WF. Delivering a novel medical education "escape room" at a national scientific conference: first live, then pivoting to remote learning because of COVID-19. *CHEST.* 2021;160(4):1424–1432.

26. Fan CW. Using escape rooms to promote active learning & intraprofessional collaboration: a pilot study. *Am J Occup Ther.* 2023; 77(Supplement_2).

27. Salinas GD, Abdolrasulnia M. Effectiveness of INROADS into pain management, a nursing educational intervention. *J Contin Educ Nurs.* 2011;42(7):328–336.

28. Richards PS, Inglehart MR. An interdisciplinary approach to case-based teaching: does it create patient-centered and culturally sensitive providers?. *J Dent Educ.* 2006;70(3):284–291.

29. Kelly JM, Perseghin A, Dow AW, Trivedi SP, Rodman A, Berk J. Learning through listening: a scoping review of podcast use in medical education. *Acad Med.* 2022;97(7):1079–1085.

30. Newman J, Liew A, Bowles J, Soady K, Inglis S. Podcasts for the delivery of medical education and remote learning. *J Med Internet Res.* 2021;23(8):e29168.

31. Berk J, Trivedi SP, Watto M, Williams P, Centor R. Medical education podcasts: where we are and questions unanswered. *J Gen Intern Med.* 2020;35:2176–2178.

32. Belcher E, Cerenzia W. Outcomes measurement in CME: trends, challenges, and future considerations. *Alliance Almanac.* October 25, 2023.

33. Accreditation Council for Continuing Medical Education (ACCME ®). *Criterion 24: Patient/public representatives are engaged in the planning and delivery of CME.* https://www.accme.org/resources/video-resources/accreditation-commendation/criterion-24-patientpublic-representatives-are-engaged-planning-and-delivery-cme.

34. Howson A, Turell W, Roc A. Perceived self-efficacy in B-cell non-Hodgkin lymphomas: Qualitative outcomes in patient-directed education. *Health Education Journal.* 2018;77(4);430–443.

35. Ackbarali T. Improving health equity through tethered education. *Alliance Almanac.* March 14, 2023.

36. Drexel C, del Nido E, Newsome SD, Halter J. The influence of tethered and joint HCP and patient education on clinical practice behavior, patient activation, and empowerment. Poster presented at the Consortium of Multiple Sclerosis Centers Annual Meeting 2021. https://2021abstracts.cmscscholar.org/2021/10/25/the-influence-of-tethered-and-joint-hcp-and-patient-education-on-clinical-practice-behavior-patient-activation-and-empowerment/.

37. National Center for Education Statistics. Data Point: Adult literacy in the United States. 2019. https://nces.ed.gov/pubs2019/2019179/index.asp.

38. Sutherland S, Jalali A. Social media as an open-learning resource in medical education: current perspectives. *Adv Med Educ Pract.* 2017;8:369–375.

39. Wang AT, Sandhu NP, Wittich CM, Mandrekar JN, Beckman TJ. Using social media to improve continuing medical education: a survey of course participants. *Mayo Clin Proc.* 2012;87(12):1162–1170.

40. Frese M, Guerriero, McKinney J, Welch L. Social media in education: From program awareness to outcomes. *Alliance Almanac.* April 26, 2023.

41. Thamman R, Gulati M, Narang A, Utengen A, Mamas MA, Bhatt DL. Twitter-based learning for continuing medical education? *Eur Heart J.* 2020;41(46):4376–4379.

42. Kickel A, Vinther A. Leveraging social media to expedite education and foster communication among treaters. *Alliance Almanac.* Nov 28, 2023.

43. Van Ravenswaay L, Parnes A, Nisly SA. Clicks for credit: an analysis of healthcare professionals' social media use and potential for continuing professional development activities. *Medical Education Online.* 2024;29:1

44. CME Coalition. *Social Media Compliance Guide.* 2023. https://www.cmecoalition.org/uploads/1/2/9/0/12902828/cme_coalition_use_of_social_media.pdf.

45. Andrews RJ. How Florence Nightingale changed data visualization forever. Scientific American. August 1, 2022. https://scientificamerican.com/article/how-florence-nightingale-changed-data-visualization-forever/

Chapter 9: Competency and Craft

1. Lingard L. What we see and don't see when we look at 'competence': notes on a god term. *Adv in Health Sci Educ.* 2009;14:625–628.

2. Helmer-Hirschberg O. Analysis of the Future: The Delphi Method. Santa Monica, CA: RAND Corporation, 1967. https://www.rand.org/pubs/papers/P3558.html.

3. Alliance for Continuing Education in the Health Professions. Educating the Educator: Curriculum Structure. https://www.acehp.org/portals/0/docs/about/Educate_the_educator_curriculum_Final_020619.pdf.

4. Accreditation Council for Continuing Medical Education (ACCME®). *Standards for Integrity and Independence in Accredited Continuing Education*. 2020. https://accme.org/sites/default/files/2022-06/884_20220623_Standards%20for%20Integrity%20and%20Independence%20in%20Accredited%20Continuing%20Education.pdf.

5. Accreditation Council for Continuing Medical Education (ACCME®). *Accreditation Criteria*. https://www.accme.org/accreditation-rules/accreditation-criteria.

6. Rosenberg A, Walker J, Griffiths S, Jenkins R. Plain language summaries: Enabling increased diversity, equity, inclusion and accessibility in scholarly publishing. *Learned Publishing*. 2023;36:109–118.

7. Menear RA, Hernandez KN, Handley L, Lora AA. Nisly SA. Healthcare disparities: encouraging change through continuing professional development. *Journal of CME*. 2023;12(1).

8. The Commonwealth Fund. *Cultural Competence in Health Care: Emerging Frameworks and Practical Approaches*. Field Report. 2022. https://www.commonwealthfund.org/sites/default/files/documents/___media_files_publications_fund_report_2002_oct_cultural_competence_in_health_care__emerging_frameworks_and_practical_approaches_betancourt_culturalcompetence_576_pdf.pdf.

9. National Center on Disability and Journalism. Publishing accessible content. https://ncdj.org/resources/publishing-accessible-content/.

10. Gohil S, Vuik S, Darzi A. Sentiment analysis of health care tweets: review of the methods used. *JMIR Public Health Surveill*. 2018;4(2):e43.

11. Gooding HC, Mann K, Armstrong E. Twelve tips for applying the science of learning to health professions education. *Med Teach*. 2017;39(1):26–31.

12. Guevara K, Fattah L, Ritt-Olson A, et al. Busting myths in online education: Faculty examples from the field. *J Clin Transl Sci.* 2021;5(1):e149.
13. Center for Applied Special Technology (CAST). *The UDL Guidelines.* https://udlguidelines.cast.org/?utm_source=castsite&lutm_medium=web&utm_campaign=none&utm_content=aboutudl.
14. Deci EL, Ryan RM. Self-determination theory: A macrotheory of human motivation, development, and health. *Canadian Psychology.* 2008;49(3), 182–185.
15. Garwood CL, Salinitri F, Levine DL. Delivering interprofessional patient safety education using storytelling, a real-life medication error, and synchronous online platform. *Med Teach.* 2022;44(6):643–649.
16. Howson A. Proceed with caution: ChatGPT, content integrity, and the power of magical thinking in outcomes evaluation. *Alliance Almanac.* July 24, 2023.
17. van de Ridder JMM, Shoja MM, Rajput V. Finding the place of ChatGPT in medical education. *Acad Med.* 2023;98(8):867.
18. Cox K, Crim A, McGowan BS. Crafting effective AI prompts: Unleashing the power of language models. *Alliance Almanac.* Jan 11, 2024.
19. Victor RG, Lynch K, Li N, et al. A cluster-randomized trial of blood-pressure reduction in Black barbershops. *N Engl J Med.* 2018;378(14):1291–1301.
20. Wilson E. Can industry-funded CE/CME be unbiased? *AMWA J.* 2023;38(4):7–9.

Chapter 10: Building a CME/CE Writing Business

1. Upwork. *Freelance Forward 2023.* https://www.upwork.com/research/freelance-forward-2023-research-report.

2. Granovetter M. The strength of weak ties. *Am J Sociol.* 1973;78(6):1360–1380.

3. De Witte M. 50 years on, Mark Granovetter's "The Strength of Weak Ties" is stronger than ever. https://news.stanford.edu/2023/07/24/strength-weak-ties/.

4. Spector J. X/Twitter. https://twitter.com/jspector/status/1716689137682776469?s=46&t=hxqo0CUDOh4mlJkRlR3eHA.

5. Church A. *Free Money: Nine Counter-intuitive Moves For Life-Changing Freelance Income.* Tilt Publishing. 2024.

6. Ilise Benun. *The Creative Professional's Guide to Money.* HOW Books. 2011.

7. Harting D, Bowser AD. *Best Practices for Writing CME Needs Assessments: 2019 Survey Results.* Poster presented at the Annual Conference of the Alliance for Continuing Education for Health Professionals, 2020.

8. Bowser AD, Hach S, Harting D, et al. *Best Practices for Writing CME Needs Assessments: 5-Year Trend Analysis.* Poster presented at the Annual Conference of the Alliance for Continuing Education for Helath Professionals, 2020.

9. Laurie Lewis. *What to Charge. Pricing Strategies for Freelancers and Consultants.* 2011. Outskirts Press.

10. Grand View research. Medical writing market size, share and trends analysis report by type (clinical, regulatory), by application (medical juornalis, medico marketing), by end use, by region, and segment forecasts, 2023–2030. https://www.grandviewresearch.com/industry-analysis/medical-writing-market.

11. Blaising A, Kotturi Y, Kulkarni C, Dabbish L. Making it work, or not. *Proceedings of the ACM on Human-Computer Interaction.* 2021;4(CSCW3):1–29.

12. Gawande A. Personal Best. *The New Yorker.* Sept 26, 2011.

Chapter 11: Personal and Professional Well-Being

1. Jeffray J. Go freelance and beat burnout, Fiverr research shows. https://www.israel21c.org/go-freelance-and-beat-burnout-fiverr-research-shows/.
2. Leapers Annual Report. Mental Health of Freelancers and the Self-Employed in 2022. https://www.leapers.co/research/2022/report.
3. World Health Organization. Burnout an "occupational phenomenon": International Classification of Diseases. https://www.who.int/news/item/28-05-2019-burn-out-an-occupational-phenomenon-international-classification-of-diseases.
4. American Psychological Association. 2023 *Work in America Survey*. https://www.apa.org/pubs/reports/work-in-america/2023-workplace-health-well-being.
5. U.S. Department of Health and Human Services. Office of the U.S. Surgeon General. *Workplace well-being*. https://www.hhs.gov/surgeongeneral/priorities/workplace-well-being/index.html.
6. https://www.heartmath.com/.
7. Dore M. *I Didn't Do the Thing Today. Letting Go of Productivity Guilt*. Avery. 2022.
8. Hersey T. *Rest Is Resistance: A Manifesto*. Little, Brown. 2022.
9. Keng SL, Smoski MJ, Robins CJ. Effects of mindfulness on psychological health: a review of empirical studies. *Clin Psychol Rev*. 2011;31(6):1041–1056.
10. McKay S. *The Women's Brain Book: The Neuroscience of Health, Hormones, and Happiness*. Hatchette. 2019.
11. Jamieson L. Why everyone feels like they're faking it. *The New Yorker*. Feb 6, 2023. https://www.newyorker.com/magazine/2023/02/13/the-dubious-rise-of-impostor-syndrome.

12. Huecker MR, Shreffler J, McKeny PT, et al. Imposter Phenomenon. In: *StatPearls* [Internet]. Treasure Island (FL): StatPearls Publishing; Jan 2024. Available from: https://www.ncbi.nlm.nih.gov/books/NBK585058/.

13. Bravata DM, Watts SA, Keefer AL, Madhusudhan DK, Taylor KT, et al. Prevalence, predictors, and treatment of impostor syndrome: a systematic review. *J Gen Intern Med*. 2020 Apr;35(4):1252–1275.

14. Tulshyan R, Burey J-A. Stop telling women they have imposter syndrome. *Harvard Business Review*. Feb 11, 2021. https://hbr.org/2021/02/stop-telling-women-they-have-imposter-syndrome.

15. Saujani R. Smith College Commencement Speech. https://www.youtube.com/watch?v=7vFnM8JhkNc.

16. U.S. Department of Health and Human Services. Centers for Disease Control and Prevention. National Center for Health Statistics. Repetitive strain injuries in adults in the past 3 months: United States, 2021. https://www.cdc.gov/nchs/data/nhsr/nhsr189.pdf.

Appendix

Common Abbreviations In CME/CE

AAFP: American Academy of Family Physicians

AAMC: Association of American Medical Colleges

ABMS: American Board of Medical Specialties

ACCME: Accreditation Council for Continuing Medical Education

ACEHP: Alliance for Continuing Education in the Health Professions

ACP: American College of Physicians

AHME: Association of Hospital Medical Educators

AHRQ: Agency for Healthcare Research and Quality

AMA: American Medical Association

AMA PRA: American Medical Association Physician's Recognition Award

AOA: American Osteopathic Association

APA: American Psychiatric Association and American Psychological Association

CME: Continuing Medical Education

CMS: Centers for Medicare and Medicaid Services

CMSS: Council of Medical Specialty Societies

CPD: Continuing Professional Development

FDA: Federal Food and Drug Administration

FSMB: Federation of State Medical Boards

HEDIS: Health Care Effectiveness Data and Information Set

HHS: Department of Health and Human Services

IOM: Institute of Medicine

JCEHP: Journal of Continuing Education in the Health Professions

MAP: Medical Affairs Professional

MEC: Medical Education Company

NCQA: National Committee for Quality Assurance

OIG: Office of the Inspector General

PhRMA: Pharmaceutical Research and Manufacturers of America

PI: Performance/Practice Improvement

POC: Point-of-Care

RFP: Request for Proposals

SACME: Society for Academic CME

Regulatory Agencies

LCME: Liaison Committee on Medical Education (accredits allopathic medical schools)

NBME: National Board of Medical Examinations

ECFMG: Educational Commission for Foreign Medical Graduates

ACGME: Accreditation Council for Graduate Medical Education (residency and fellowship program accreditation)

ABMS: American Board of Medical Specialties (board certification for physicians)

ACCME: Accreditation Council for Continuing Medical Education providers

EACCME: European Accreditation Council for Continuing Medical Education

Glossary

Accreditation: The process by which an organization is officially recognized as meeting established standards for providing CME activities.

Accreditation Council for Continuing Medical Education (ACCME): The main accrediting body for CME providers in the United States.

Accredited CME Provider: An organization that has been approved by an accrediting body to plan, implement, and evaluate CME activities.

Certificate of Completion: A document issued to learners who have completed a CME activity, indicating the number of credit hours earned.

Commercial Bias: The presence of any influence from an ineligible company that may affect the content, presentation, or evaluation of a CME activity.

Conflict of Interest: A situation in which an individual has an opportunity to affect CME content with products or services from an ineligible company with which they have a financial relationship.

Continuing Medical Education: Educational activities that maintain, develop, or increase the knowledge, skills, and professional performance and relationships that a physician uses to provide services for patients, the public, or the profession.

Enduring Material: A nonlive CME activity that endures over time such as print materials, audio/video recordings, or online courses.

Faculty: Subject matter experts who prepare and deliver CME content.

Gap Analysis: The process of identifying the difference between current and desired knowledge, skills, or performance in a specific area of health care.

Interprofessional Continuing Education (IPCE): CME activities designed to address the professional practice gaps of the health care team.

Joint Accreditation: Accreditation awarded to CME providers that offer interprofessional continuing education by the ACCME, the Accreditation Council for Pharmacy Education (ACPE), and the American Nurses Credentialing Center (ANCC).

Ineligible Entity: Marketing, medical communications agencies, pharmaceutical companies, and education providers that are owned, in whole or in part, or otherwise influenced or controlled by manufacturers or other ineligible companies. ACCME also defines an entity as ineligible if it has begun a governmental regulatory approval process.

Learning Objectives: Statements that clearly describe what the learner will be able to do upon completion of a CME activity.

Maintenance of Certification (MOC): A process through which physicians demonstrate their commitment to lifelong learning and ongoing professional development.

Medical Writer: A professional who specializes in creating clear, accurate, and engaging medical content for various audiences, including CME materials.

Needs Assessment: The process of identifying the educational needs of the target audience to inform the development of CME activities.

Outcomes Measurement: The assessment of the impact of a CME activity on learners' knowledge, skills, performance, or patient outcomes.

Peer Review: The process by which CME content is evaluated by independent subject matter experts to ensure accuracy, balance, and freedom from commercial bias.

Performance Improvement CME (PI-CME): A type of CME activity that involves a structured, three-stage process designed to improve patient outcomes through practice-based learning and quality improvement.

Professional Practice Gap: The difference between actual and ideal performance or patient outcomes, which can be addressed through CME activities.

Writing Guides

Becker H. *Writing for Social Scientists: How to Start and Finish Your Thesis, Book, or Article.* 3rd edition. Chicago: University of Chicago Press. 2020.

Chen P. (ed). *The Best American Medical Writing 2009.* Kaplan. 2009

Franklin J. *Writing for Story: Craft Secrets of Dramatic Nonfiction.* Plume. 1994.

Kramer M, Call W. T*elling True Stories: A Nonfiction Writers' Guide from the Nieman Foundation at Harvard University*. Plume. 2007.

Lamott A. *Bird by Bird: Some Instructions on Writing and Life*. Vintage. 1995.

Pipher M. *Writing to Change the World: An Inspiring Guide for Transforming the World with Words*. New York: Riverhead Books. 2007.

Strunk W Jr, White E. *The Elements of Style.* 4th edition. New York: Longman. 2000.

Williams J. Style: *Ten Lessons in Clarity and Grace*. 8th edition. New York: Longman. 2005.

Zinsser W. On *Writing Well. The Classic Guide to Writing Nonfiction.* New York: Harper Perennial. 2016.

Zinsser W. *Writing to Learn*. New York: Harper Perennial. 1993.

Visual Communication Resources

Grandin T. Visual Thinking. *The Hidden Gifts of People Who Think in Pictures, Patterns, and Abstractions*. 2022. London: Rider.

McCandless D. *Information is Beautiful*. 2000. Collins.

Andy Kirk's website *Visualizing Data*. https://visualisingdata.com/

Instructional Design Resources

Brown PC, Rosediger HL III, McDaniel MA. *Make It Stick: The Science of Successful Learning.* The Belknap Press of Harvard University Press. 2014.

Dirksen J. *Design for How People Learn.* 2nd edition. New Riders. 2016.

Dirksen J. *Talk to the Elephant.* New Riders. 2023.

Medical Terminology Resources

Jones BD. *Comprehensive Medical Terminology*. 2016

Ehrlich A. *Introduction to Medical Terminology*. Cengage, 2014.

Kryder CL, Bass B. *Nude Mice: And Other Medical Writing Terms You Need to Know*. Booklocker. 2009.

Equity and Bias

Barrett NJ, Boehmer L, Schrag J, et al. An assessment of the feasibility and utility of an ACCC-ASCO implicit bias training program to enhance racial and ethnic diversity in cancer clinical trials. *JCO Oncol Pract.* 2023;19(4):e570–e580.

BMJ Opinion. *Ten steps to gender equity: The BMJ's resolutions.* https://blogs.bmj.com/bmj/2021/03/08/ten-steps-to-gender-equity-the-bmjs-resolutions/.

Guerra C, Pressman A, Garrett-Mayer E, et al. Increasing racial and ethnic equity, diversity, and inclusion in cancer treatment trials: evaluation of an ASCO-Association of Community Cancer Centers site self-assessment. *JCO Oncol Pract.* 2023;19:e581–e588.

Menear, R. A. et al. Healthcare disparities: encouraging change through continuing professional development. *Journal of CME.* 2023;12(1).

Smith K. Women's health research lacks funding—in a series of charts. *Nature.* 2023;617(7959):28–29.

Lopez L, Hart LH, Katz MH. Racial and ethnic health disparities related to COVID-19. *JAMA.* 2021;325(8):719–720

Plain Language Resources

PlainLanguage.Gov. *Federal Plain Language Guidelines*. 2011. https://www.plainlanguage.gov/media/FederalPLGuidelines.pdf

University of Maryland. *Plain Language Medical Dictionary*. https://apps.lib.umich.edu/medical-dictionary/

United States Centers for Disease Control and Prevention. *Plain Language Thesaurus for Health Communications*. 2007.

www.cdc.gov/other/pdf/everydaywordsforpublichealthcommunication.pdf

Generative-AI Cheat Sheet in CME/CE

https://bit.ly/genAIcheatsheet

www.ingramcontent.com/pod-product-compliance
Lightning Source LLC
Chambersburg PA
CBHW022101210326
41518CB00039B/350